"If you think your shoelace is a banana peel, I won't tell you that you are wrong." Those were the words from a young University student that I tried to witness to. If you think that he is a fluke, he is not. He is a post-modern who believes that all truth is valid truth. He, like millions just like him, claim that two people can have two opposing worldviews and still be correct. At least Pontius Pilate asked Jesus what truth is. Today, truth is whatever you want it to be.

Karl Marx declared, *"The first battlefield is the re-writing of history."*

Friedrich Nietzsche proclaimed, *"I am afraid we are not rid of God because we still have faith in grammar."* The Bible asks, "And if the foundations are destroyed, what can the righteous do?" Know what you believe. Know what is true. Read this book by Brannon Howse.

Todd Friel
Host of "The Way of the Master Radio"

By conducting the research and writing this book, Brannon has done a real service on behalf of Christians. This book is an instant classic, a resource that should be on the shelf of every Christian. This is the kind of book you reach for many times in a given year to assist you in answering the questions you are asked by your children, friends and co-workers.

Tim Wildmon
American Family Association and Radio Network
President

TABLE OF CONTENTS

1.1 — If God does not exist, all things are permissible.
  (Test question #1 pg. 23)

1.2 — One of the Ten Commandments is, "Thou shalt not kill"; thus it stands to reason that God is opposed to war and nations going to war. **(Test question #2 pg. 24)**
  — The Bible states that the government does not bear the sword in vain. Numerous verses throughout the Bible make it clear that capital punishment administered by the government, for those that have committed capital crimes, is Biblically acceptable. **(Test question #3 pg. 24)**

1.3 — The Ten Commandments originally provided a basis for our legal and political system, creating justice and peace.
  (Test question #4 pg. 26)

1.4 — Since God is not the author of law, the author of law must be man. In other words, law is law simply because the highest human authority—the state—has said it is law and is able to back it up by force. Since man and society evolve, law must as well. **(Test question #5 pg. 30)**
  — There are no specific, God-given principles related to law, or if there are, they should not be the foundation of today's legal systems. **(Test question #6 pg. 30)**
  — Our judicial system should allow judges, through their decisions and rulings, to guide and shape the foundational basis of law. **(Test question #7 pg. 30)**

contrary to reason, science and history.
(**Test question #19 pg. 54**)
— God used the process of biological evolution to create the world as we know it today. (**Test question #20 pg. 54**)

2.3 — The more we discover about the universe, the more we discover design. (**Test question #21 pg. 58**)

2.4 — There is evidence for a worldwide flood.
(**Test question #22 pg. 62**)

2.5 — Life begins at conception. (**Test question #23 pg. 64**)

2. Follow-up—For Further Thought about Science

3.1 — The most Biblically based tax system would be one built on a flat tax where everyone pays the same percentage of their income in taxes. (**Test question #24 pg. 67**)

3.2 — It is the responsibility of the federal government to create wealth. (**Test question #25 pg. 71**)
— The Biblical purpose for wealth is to provide for one's family, proclaim the Gospel, be a blessing to others, and test a person's stewardship and loyalty to God. (**Test question #26 pg. 71**)
— When you study the Bible as a whole, it becomes clear that God is very supportive of an economic system based on private property, the work ethic, and personal responsibility.
(**Test question #27 pg. 71**)
— Making the incomes of its citizens as equal as possible should be one of the top priorities of any legitimate government.
(**Test question #28 pg. 72**)
— Making as much money as you can is more important than whether you have a good reputation. (**Test question #29 pg. 72**)

3.3 — All forms of government-sponsored socialism to some degree stifle economic growth and prosperity. (**Test question #30 pg. 75**)

3.4 — Physically and mentally healthy adults that do not work should

be allowed to suffer the consequences of their actions.
(**Test question #31 pg. 80**)

Contents

6.3 — The Bible, rightly divided, should be the foundation for all our beliefs, actions, and conduct. (**Test question #50 pg. 140**)
— Believers should not only base their philosophy in Christ, but they should know how to respond to critics and skeptics of Christianity with the reasoning and basis of our Biblical worldview. (**Test question #51 pg. 140**)
— A Christian can develop a Biblical worldview for every major area of life by studying the Bible from beginning to end in context. (**Test question #52 pg. 140**)
— The Bible is God's revealed Word and should be the basis of our worldview. (**Test question #53 pg. 140**)
— God had no beginning and has no end. (**Test question #54 pg. 141**)
— God is the Creator of the universe. (**Test question #55 pg. 141**)
— Your worldview is the foundation of your values, and your values are the foundation of your actions.
(**Test question #56 pg. 141**)

6.4 — Both Secular Humanism and Marxism are religious worldviews.
(**Test question #57 pg. 144**)

6.5 — All religions are equally true. (**Test question #58 pg. 146**)
— Jesus Christ lived a sinless life. (**Test question #59 pg. 146**)
— There is more than one way to God. (**Test question #60 pg. 146**)

6.6 — Good people can earn their way to heaven if their good deeds outweigh their bad deeds. (**Test question #61 pg. 148**)

6.7 — The Bible is a consistent revelation from beginning to end.
(**Test question #62 pg. 149**)
— The Bible is a reflection of God's character and nature.
(**Test question #63 pg. 150**)

6.8 — Christians should never speak publicly about what someone has said or written publicly before first talking to them in private. (**Test question #64 pg. 152**)

6.9 — Christians should present the Gospel in a seeker-friendly, non-offensive manner that avoids using terms such as hell, sin, the wrath of God and judgment day. (**Test question #65 pg. 152**)
— Repentance is necessary for salvation. (**Test question #66 pg. 153**)

6. Follow-up—For Further Thought about Religion

Contents

SECTION 7—SOCIAL ISSUES 161

Contents

FOREWORD

DAVID A. NOEBEL

In the early 1990s James Dobson and Gary Bauer wrote *Children At Risk*. They revealed how Secular Humanism had become the predominant way of thinking in most of the power centers of our society including the universities, news media and entertainment industry among others. Ten years later Princeton's Robert George approvingly quoted James Kurth who identified "The Real Clash" within Western Civilization as between the "Judeo-Christian worldview" and "those who have abandoned that worldview." Those who have abandoned that worldview included feminism, multiculturalism, gay liberation and lifestyle liberalism.

Ruth Tucker more than reinforces both Dobson and George when she wrote *Walking Away From Faith* in which she says that "Humanism is alive and well," and it is Secular Humanism that is the underlying reason why Christian teens are walking away from the Christian faith. It is this type of background that makes Brannon Howse's latest work so important.

Howse details the move away from our Christian worldview (that has sustained America's religious foundations) toward a naturalistic, sex-worshipping, God-denying, evolutionary-affirming Secular Humanism. This worldview is warring against Christianity in all areas, and Christians need to fully understand this threat to their moral and mental wellbeing if they plan to survive and thrive. In light of this ongoing battle of ideas, beliefs, and convictions for the minds and hearts of Christians everywhere Howse's work is must reading, and I cannot recommend it too highly.

David A. Noebel
Summit Ministries

FOREWORD

RAY COMFORT

There is no one like Brannon Howse. He is a walking encyclopedia of knowledge—a one-man Internet of information. He is clear proof of Intelligent Design. I thank God for him, not only because he is a personal friend, but because he is a bulldog for the truth.

The Bible is clear that we are to love the Lord our God with all our heart, soul, strength, and *mind*. We are to contend for the faith and expose every high and lofty thing that lifts itself against the knowledge of God. Brannon has used the Worldview Weekend conferences, his website, his radio program, and his guest appearance on many radio and television programs to reach multitudes with the truth and validity of a biblical worldview for all areas of life—law, science, economics, history, family, social issues, religion, and education.

Many former skeptics and critics have been so influenced by the case for Christ presented by Brannon Howse that they have surrendered their lives to Jesus Christ and even entered full-time ministry. He recently shared with me an e-mail one young man had sent to him. It speaks so clearly of the great need for Christians to lovingly present the truth of a biblical worldview that I want to share it with you:

> Brannon, I took your worldview test a few years ago and ranked as a secular humanist worldview thinker. At the time, I got mad at it and mad at your organization. I took the test again just a few weeks ago and ranked as a strong Biblical worldview thinker. I knew I'd changed vastly in recent times, but never how much. I've become a new man since those few years back, and I'm happy for it....
>
> I'd always been a strong believer in God's existence and the salvation found in Christ. However, I realize now that I never really understood it during all of those years. Even though I accepted the Bible as truth, looking back I realize how much I twisted meaning to find what I wanted to see instead of what was there. This "liberal theology" is due a lot, I believe, to the media

17

and societal structure in which we live. I have seen many, many others fall victim to it, as well as false doctrines such as theistic evolutionism. Thankfully, those misinterpretations are in my past and I now stand with the real truth in hand.

As I silently observe my college contemporaries, I see that they are like I once was—having a terribly skewed interpretation of God's Word, or in many cases, even worse—they deny the Lord outright. Watching this, along with an even greater passion for the lost, inspired me to begin studying for the ministry. I'd spent about 12 years of my life preparing for and gearing towards becoming an attorney. Now, all I want to do is spread the message of our Lord.

The rest of my life is now dedicated to telling people the truth about the universe's Creator, the fall, and our salvation through Jesus Christ the Lord.

I pray this man's story inspires in you a great zeal for contending, defending, and proclaiming a biblical worldview. Nothing can transform a life like a relationship with Jesus Christ.

In his book, Brannon has done a wonderful job of articulating the scriptural perspective. To know how you think (and how to fix your worldview if need be), all you have to do is take his worldview test and then read Put Your Beliefs to the Test.

It's my prayer that God uses this book to glorify His name and to reach the lost world with the everlasting Gospel.

Ray Comfort
September, 2006

Introduction—The Worldview Test

In 2002 I developed a test on Biblical perspectives that, in its first four years online, was taken by more than 50,000 people. My goal for the test was that it would be a service to thousands like you who want to know how their worldview rates according to Biblical standards and to make improvements if needed. The Bible tells us in Romans 12:2 not to be conformed to this world but to be transformed by the renewing of our minds. Unfortunately, many self-professing Christians think Biblically in some ways but like a liberal or Secular Humanist in others. Our Christian calling, though, is to bring *every* thought captive to the obedience of Jesus Christ.

Hundreds of those who have taken the test e-mailed me and asked if I would provide them with a detailed response for each question from a Biblical perspective. Thus this book was born.

If you haven't taken the test yet, I recommend that you do it before reading this book. You can find the test at www.worldview-weekend.com (click "Free Online Worldview Test"). Let me caution you, though, that many people have scored poorly and gotten rather angry and defensive. I often receive e-mails from individuals who charge that Worldview Weekend test does not so much evaluate whether you think like a Christian but like a Republican. My response is that if one political party is closer to a Biblical worldview than another, then that is fine, but our standard of right or wrong is the Bible and Biblical principles, not a political party or mere human opinion.

While the Bible does not mention abortion, the lottery, euthanasia, the federal minimum wage, inheritance tax, or many other such issues by name, it offers clear commands and principles for each of these issues. Whereas the Bible says "do not murder," this makes it clear that abortion is wrong. We are instructed not to take advantage of the poor, to be involved in get-rich-quick-schemes, or to covet. Hence, we can say the lottery is wrong. The Bible is a reflection of the character and nature of God, and we can have a decidedly Biblical worldview on the issues of our day by "studying to show ourselves approved." In 2 Timothy 2:15 this direction is affirmed: "Be diligent to present yourself approved to God, a worker who does not need to be ashamed, rightly dividing the word of truth. Having command of a Biblical worldview does not come easy. It requires work—and a worker who studies.

As you read this book and the Biblical principles it illuminates, please understand that what *I* think as the author of this book does not matter. What matters is what *God* has said as the author of *the* Book—the Bible. If my book steps on some people's liberal toes and they get upset, they need to take that up with the Lord, not me. I have endeavored to write about the issues of our day from the perspective of what God has written.

By the way, after you've taken the test, you will get an instant score. You'll know immediately how your worldview stacks up in the areas of law, economics, civil government, religion, social issues, sociology (family issues), education, and science. Your worldview will be rated for these eight areas as one of the following: Strong Biblical Worldview Thinker, Moderate Biblical Worldview Thinker, Secular Humanist Worldview Thinker, Socialist Worldview Thinker, or Communist/Marxist/Socialist/Secular Humanist Worldview Thinker. You will also receive an overall worldview rating. And you'll find out how your worldview compares with others in your age category and those with a similar background. I promise you'll find your personal report very interesting and informative, so please make sure you complete all of the pre-test background questions that are necessary to the final evaluation.

Finding out "what happened on your test and why" is where this book comes in. The Table of Contents lists every question on the test, the correct Biblical answer, and where in this book you'll find the explanation for the answer. Since many questions cover related topics, quite a few are grouped together and discussed in a single explanation. Where you answered Biblically, you'll find encouragement in the explanations and likely gain some confidence for defending your position. Where you answered toward the non-Biblical end of the spectrum, I hope you'll see clearly how God's Word speaks and then take joy in your new clarity in understanding and applying His Word in your life.

My hope is that, as you read, you'll hunger for ever more depth of conviction about the Biblical view of life. To that end, I've included at the end of each section additional questions to prompt further thinking about the answers revealed in the book. I also want to invite you to one or more Worldview Weekends. The schedule of cities, dates, and speakers is posted at www.worldviewweekend.com. In addition, the site features a wide range of worldview books, videos, and teaching material for elementary ages through adult that can be purchased at the online bookstore.

One more suggestion: For even greater encouragement on your faith journey, read this book, and then take the test again. Knowing the truth will set you free to enjoy more of God.

Thank you for putting your worldview to the test.

Sincerely,
BRANNON S. HOWSE
President & Founder
Worldview Weekend

SECTION 1—LAW

1.1— If God does not exist, all things are permissible.

True. (Test question #1)

More people have died prematurely during the past 100 years due to the idea that there is no God than from all diseases, natural disasters, and non-manmade causes combined. The no-God, humanistic worldview allowed Hitler, Stalin, and Mussolini to justify the murder of millions upon millions of people. More recently, you could add Pol Pot, Ho Chi Minh, and Mao Tse Tung, but even that would not exhaust the portfolio of unrestrained destroyers of humanity. If there is no God to which man is accountable, then the only standard is survival of the fittest or "might makes right."

Yale University history professor Donald Kagan acknowledges the consequences of a worldview that says God is dead. Often called Nihilism, this philosophy is based primarily on the writings of Friedrich Nietzsche. Such thinking leaves a society, culture, or country at the mercy of whomever has won the latest coup, revolution, or invasion. But as Kagan helps us see, the problem is that this sort of thinking is not just "over there." He warns:

> [A] vulgar form of Nihilism has a remarkable influence in our educational system through our universities. The consequences of the victory of such ideas would be enormous. If both religion and reason are removed, all that remains is will and power, where the only law is that of tooth and claw.[1]

If government is the highest authority—and all rights are given to people by the government—then what the government *gives,* the government also can take away. On the other hand, if our rights are given to us by a Creator, then they are "inalienable rights" for all people, all times, and all places as stated in the U.S. Declaration of Independence. Our God-given rights cannot justly be taken from us by government because they did not come from government. To be sure, rights can be infringed upon and violated but not taken away. Or, under the right circumstances, they can be protected and encouraged.

In his 1961 inaugural address, President John F. Kennedy proclaimed, "The rights of man come not from the generosity of the state but from the hand of God."

Similarly, President Harry Truman at an attorney general's conference in 1959 claimed, "If we don't have a proper fundamental moral background, we will finally end up with a totalitarian government which does not believe in rights for anybody except the State."

Bill Federer, historian and prolific author, connects an individual's belief to his or her religion because the actions of the government are influenced by the religion of those in charge:

> Thus it follows, that as long as a person is doing "actions," they have thoughts preceding those actions—and that collection of thoughts is that person's "system of belief" or "religion." As long as the government is doing "actions," the government has thoughts preceding those actions—and that collection of thought is the government's "system of belief" or "religion." So there can never really be a separation of "religion" and government—as long as the government is doing "actions" there are thoughts or beliefs underlying those actions. The ACLU is not trying to be "religion" neutral, but, in fact, it is promoting a religion—a "non-deity based" secular humanist system of belief.[2]

The twentieth century was the most murderous 100 years in history, and it is due largely to tyrants and dictators who did not acknowledge any authority higher than themselves. Hitler killed as many as 6 million Jews and 5 million non-Jews during his Holocaust. Stalin likewise destroyed some 20-50 million people. Mao destroyed 70 million Chinese. The false "isms" destroyed 170 million lives in the twentieth century.

Our Founding Fathers believed that as soon as Americans cease to believe in God, they will be laying the foundation for a tyrant to take control, stealing our God-given freedoms. The Founding Fathers also believed that religion is vital to law, order, the security of liberty, and even good manners. While not desiring to establish a state church, they wrote again and again about the importance of religion. They really understood there to be a God to whom they were accountable.

1.2— One of the Ten Commandments is, "Thou shalt not kill"; thus it stands to reason that God is opposed to war and nations going to war. *False.* (Test question #2)
  — The Bible states that the government does not bear the

sword in vain. Numerous verses throughout the Bible make it clear that capital punishment administered by the government, for those that have committed capital crimes, is Biblically acceptable. *True.* (Test question #3)

The death penalty and waging war are two different aspects of one moral issue on which Christians are divided. We tend to think of them separately—we execute an individual for a crime or we go to war against a hostile nation—but from a Biblical standpoint, the two issues are closely related.

A few well-meaning Christians are pacifists and do not believe God wants them in the military. In case of war, being in military service would inevitably involve directly or indirectly killing people. For that reason, the American government allows true pacifists to claim "conscientious objector" status and avoid military service. Likewise, some serious Christians object to the death penalty, no matter what crime has been committed.

While these sentiments may seem admirable, it is a Biblical fact that God gives authority to governments to administer justice by means of capital punishment for murder and other serious crimes. It is also true that God directs the fates of nations through the exercise of judgment and war on those who have committed national evils.

Genesis recounts that God used capital punishment to judge a wicked and apostate world. He killed most of the earth's population through a mega-flood, saving only Noah and his immediate family. Years later, in a precision strike, God blasted Sodom and Gomorrah for rampantly evil lifestyles.

In Exodus, God drowned Pharaoh's army in the Red Sea to protect the Hebrews. Yet, never one to play favorites, He later broke open the ground and swallowed some Israelites who had been worshiping an idol and engaging in orgies.

God allows for killing another human being only in the cases of self-defense and capital punishment. Exodus 22:2, for instance, reads: "If the thief is found breaking in, and he is struck so that he dies, there shall be no guilt for his bloodshed." And in Genesis 9:6 the responsibility for bringing justice to a victim of murder is given specifically to the assailant's fellow human beings: "Whoever sheds man's blood, by man his blood shall be shed; for in the image of God He made man."

Some would argue that Jesus changed the way these things should be handled, but to show that capital punishment is still appropriate today, let's look at the New Testament perspective. Romans 13:1-4 reads:

Let every soul be subject to the governing authorities. For there is no authority except from God, and the authorities that exist are appointed by God. Therefore whoever resists the authority resists the ordinance of God, and those who resist will bring judgment on themselves. For rulers are not a terror to good works, but to evil. Do you want to be unafraid of the authority? Do what is good, and you will have praise from the same. For he is God's minister to you for good. But if you do evil, be afraid; for he does not bear the sword in vain; for he is God's minister, an avenger to execute wrath on him who practices evil.

Paul is clear that the government has the God-given right to dispense justice, including capital punishment. In war, government will "carry the sword" to bring justice to those who have committed capital crimes. At times, it is also a form of national self-defense.

When President Bush sent troops into Afghanistan to capture or destroy terrorists who were involved in killing more than 3,000 Americans on September 11, 2001, the president was Biblically justified. The commander-in-chief of the United States has the Biblical and constitutional authority to use the country's military to defend America. He may kill those who seek to kill us and bring justice to those who have killed innocent people. When President Bush invoked the term "a just war" to describe the war on terror after 9/11, his thinking was consistent with a Biblical perspective. The president is given the power of the sword and with it the responsibility to use it Biblically.

Justice is part of a Christian worldview, and there are times when bringing justice requires violence against individuals or nations that deserve such wrath. Bringing the sword to bear is a Biblical duty.

1.3— The Ten Commandments originally provided a basis for our legal and political system, creating justice and peace. *True*. (Test question #4)

The deliberate use of the Ten Commandments by our Founding Fathers as the basis of America's legal system and constitutional republic is proof they never intended to create a secular nation or government. The Founders also did not intend for the First Amendment to be used as a tool to eradicate religious expression and practices from American government.

Speaking of the Ten Commandments, John Adams, Founding Father and second president of the United States, wrote:

> The moment the idea is admitted into society that property is not as sacred as the laws of God, and that there is not a force of law and public justice to protect it, anarchy and tyranny commence. If "Thou shalt not covet," and "Thou shalt not steal," were not commandments of Heaven, they must be made inviolable precepts in every society, before it can be civilized or made free.[3]

President John Quincy Adams similarly declared:

> The law given from Sinai was a civil and municipal as well as a moral and religious code...laws essential to the existence of men in society and most of which have been enacted by every nation which ever professed any code of laws.[4] Vain indeed would be the search among the writings of profane antiquity [secular history]...to find so broad, so complete and so solid a basis for morality as this Decalogue [Ten Commandments] lays down.[5]

Founder Noah Webster wrote that all governmental laws that support justice and morality stem from the Christian religion and the Ten Commandments:

> The opinion that human reason left without the constant control of Divine laws and commands will...give duration to a popular government is as chimerical [unlikely] as the most extravagant ideas that enter the head of a maniac...Where will you find any code of laws among civilized men in which the commands and prohibitions are not founded on Christian principles? I need not specify the prohibitions of murder, robbery, theft [and] trespass.[6]

There is no reason our courts should be squeamish about display of the Ten Commandments in public buildings, since it is a long-established practice in this nation. In his commentary, *The Ten Commandments in American Law and Government*, Matthew D. Staver notes:

When a governmental practice has been "deeply embedded in the history and tradition of the country," such a practice will not violate the Establishment Clause because the practice has become part of the "fabric of our society." (See March v. Chambers, 463 U.S. 783, 786 (1983).)

The Ten Commandments played a significant role in the development of American law. The incorporation of the Ten Commandments into law and policy, in fact, pre-dates the Constitution. This intermingling of the Ten Commandments in American law and government began even before the practice of legislative prayers. The writers of the First Amendment would never have dreamed that their words would one day be used to banish the Decalogue from public property and governmental principles.

Even the Supreme Court once honored the role the Ten Commandments has played in our system of law and government.[7] Matthew Staver recounts a number of federal cases from 1961, 1980, 1984 and 1987 that acknowledge the influence of the Ten Commandments on our nation:

- *McGowan v. Maryland*, 366 U.S. 420, 450 (1961) (Frankfurter, J., concurring) ("Innumerable civil regulations enforce conduct which harmonizes with religious canons. State prohibitions of murder, theft and adultery reinforce commands of the Decalogue.");

- *Stone v. Graham*, 449 U.S. 39, 45 (1980) (Rehnquist, J., dissenting) ("It is equally undeniable...that the Ten Commandments have had a significant impact on the development of secular legal codes of the Western World.");

- *Lynch v. Donnelly*, 465 U.S. 668, 677-78 (1984) (describing the depiction of Moses with the Ten Commandments on the wall of the Supreme Court chamber and stating that such acknowledgments of religion demonstrate that "our history is pervaded by expression of religious beliefs...");

- *Edwards v. Aguillard*, 482 U.S. 578, 593-94 (1987)

(acknowledges that the Ten Commandments did not play an exclusively religious role in the history of Western civilization.)[8]

These and many other cases reveal that the purpose of the Ten Commandments was not only for religious people and churches, but for all of society. Staver adds:

> Each of the Ten Commandments has played some significant role in the foundation of our system of law and government. Twelve of the thirteen original colonies adopted the entire Decalogue into their civil and criminal laws.[9]

States have held to similar conclusions. In 1950, the Florida Supreme Court declared:

> A people unschooled about the sovereignty of God, the Ten Commandments, and the ethics of Jesus could never have evolved the Bill of Rights, the Declaration of Independence, and the Constitution. There is not one solitary fundamental principle of our democratic policy that did not stem directly from the basic moral concepts as embodied in the Decalogue...[10]

In 1983 a United States district court in Virginia declared:

> Further, biblical influences pervade many specific areas of law. The "good Samaritan" laws use a phrase lifted directly out of one of Jesus' parables. The concept of the "fertile octogenarian," applicable to the law of wills and trusts, is in a large part derived from the book of Genesis where we are told that Sarah, the wife of the patriarch Abraham, gave birth to Isaac when she was "past age." In addition, the Ten Commandments have had immeasurable effect on Anglo-American legal development.[11]

In 1998, a Wisconsin appeals court quoted a 1974 Indiana Supreme Court opinion which stated: "Virtually all criminal laws are in one way or another the progeny of Judeo-Christian ethics. We have no intention to overrule the Ten Commandments."[12]

Presidents, too, have weighed in on the monumental importance of the Ten Commandments. In a February 15, 1950, address to the Attorney General's Conference on Law Enforcement Problems, President Harry S. Truman declared:

> The fundamental basis of this nation's laws was given to Moses on the Mount. The fundamental basis of our Bill of Rights comes from the teachings we get from Exodus and St. Matthew, from Isaiah and St. Paul. I don't think we emphasize that enough these days. If we don't have a proper fundamental moral background, we will finally end up with a totalitarian government, which does not believe in the rights for anybody except the State![13]

Even leaders of other countries have seen the role the Ten Commandments, God, and Christianity have played in American history. Former British Prime Minister Margaret Thatcher said of America:

> The Decalogue [Ten Commandments] are addressed to each and every person. This is the origin of our common humanity and of the sanctity of the individual. Each of us has a duty to try and carry out those commandments...If you accept freedom, you've got to have principles and the responsibility. You can't do this without a biblical foundation. Your Founding Fathers came over with that. They came over with the doctrines of the New Testament as well as the Old. They looked after one another, not only as a matter of necessity, but as a matter of duty to their God. There is not other country in the world which started that way.[14]

1.4— **Since God is not the author of law, the author of law must be man. Law is law simply because the highest human authority—the state—has said it is law and is able to back it up by force. Since man and society evolve, law must as well.** *False.* (Test question #5)
— **There are no specific, God-given principles related to law, or if there are, they should not be the foundation of today's legal systems.** *False.* (Test question #6)
— **Our judicial system should allow judges, through their**

decisions and rulings, to guide and shape the foundational basis of law. *False.* (Test question #7)

Secular humanism—and its core beliefs of moral relativism and Darwinian evolution—is the new, postmodern foundation on which America's courts and law schools are built:

> Twentieth-century jurisprudence is based on a Darwinian world view. Life evolves, men evolve, society evolves, and therefore laws and the constitution's meaning evolves and changes with time.[15]

It's not meant to be this way, but the name for this new legal philosophy is "legal positivism."

After reviewing the writings of the Critical Legal Studies movement—a group of radical lawyers, law professors, and law students—constitutional and legal scholar John Eidsmoe documents the implications of legal positivism:

> (1) There are no objective, God-given standards of law, or if there are, they are irrelevant to the modern legal system. (2) Since God is not the author of law, the author of law must be man; in other words, law is law simply because the highest human authority, the state, has said it is law and is able to back it up by force. (3) Since man and society evolve, therefore law must evolve as well. (4) Judges, through their decisions, guide the evolution of law (Note again: judges "make law"). (5) To study law, get at the original sources of law, the decisions of judges; hence most law schools today use the "case law" method of teaching law.[16]

Legal positivism is essentially the application of the philosophy of moral relativism to the law. Moral relativism is the belief that there is no such thing as moral absolutes, no standard that is right or wrong for all people, in all places, at all times. Moral relativism is also known as pragmatism. It gives rise to situational ethics, the belief that individuals are free to decide for themselves what is best for them and what gives them the most desirable outcome in any given situation.

"This philosophy of 'positivism' was introduced in the 1870s when Harvard Law School Dean Christopher Columbus Langdell (1826-

1906) applied Darwin's premise of evolution to jurisprudence."[17] It was further advanced by Dean Roscoe Pound and Supreme Court Justice Oliver Wendell Holmes, Jr. Holmes argued that there should be no fixed moral foundation for law:

> The felt necessities of the time, the prevalent moral and political theories...have a good deal more to do than the syllogism [legal reasoning process] in determining the rules by which men should be governed.[18]

That the "felt necessities of the time" and "prevalent moral and political theories" should be the basis of the rules by which men are governed is a shocking and dangerous premise. Such thinking has resulted in laws allowing countless abortions—including partial-birth abortions— in America. The late U.S. Senator Daniel Patrick Monahan called partial-birth abortion, "near infanticide." Using "felt necessities of the time" and "prevalent moral and political theories" could allow most anything to be justifiable depending on whose feelings, morals, and political theories are in force.

To give you an example of how serious this situation has become: before becoming a U.S. Supreme Court justice, Ruth Bader Ginsburg, while serving on a lower court, wrote of her belief that the sex age limit should be lowered to twelve. If that is something enough judges "feel is a necessity," based the perverted "moral and political theories" of Alfred Kinsey, for instance, it could become legal.

This kind of preference could become law under postmodern thinking. Consider one other example of how it is already happening: the 2003 U.S. Supreme Court ruling, *Lawrence v. Texas*. In this case, the court struck down the sodomy law of Texas—and by implication those of several other states—making homosexual sex legal. The justices not only ignored the Constitution and the Founders' original intent, but they went so far as to cite the law of another country in making their case! Legal positivism is clearly dangerous.

1.5— Under some circumstances Christians are called to disobey the laws of government. *True.* (Test question #8)
— Civil disobedience by Christians is always wrong and unbiblical. *False.* (Test question #9)

Although God set up the three distinct social institutions of family, church, and state with differing realms of responsibility and authority (we discuss this further in answer 5.3), many Christians mistakenly believe that civil government always trumps church and family government. This false understanding at times has caused Christians to offer more allegiance to civil government than to God by reallocating the rightful responsibility and authority of family and church governments to the state, and there is a serious danger in doing so.

To illustrate this peril, I'll tell you about my friend Mark Cahill, who is one of the most committed Christians I know. Mark regularly shares Jesus Christ with people because he knows that 60,000 people each day step into eternity. Mark says, "These people may leave this earth, but they are not dead. They are either alive and well or alive in hell."

Because of Mark's deep and kindly concern for eternal souls, he shares the Good News of salvation through Jesus Christ with as many as he can in any given day. In doing so, he has encountered some surprising obstacles. In 2004 alone, he was threatened with arrest nine times by *American* police officers for sharing his faith with people in airports, malls, and on public streets.

Amazingly, many police officers, through lack of understanding of the law and their acceptance of the ACLU's definition of the "separation of church and state," believe Mark is breaking some state or federal law. He is not, of course, but it may not be long before they are right, and Mark will be subject to arrest.

As America becomes increasingly secular, and the judiciary takes away more and more of our religious liberties, Christians need to become acquainted with the Biblical response to tyranny and to understand the proper time, place, and type of civil disobedience allowed by God. Unfortunately, many American pastors believe God condemns all civil disobedience, and others believe it is so rarely permissible as to be a non-option. I even know people who believe Corrie ten Boom sinned by hiding Jews in her home during the Nazi occupation of Europe!

This view is not uncommon among pastors who have convinced themselves that we can only disobey civil government when we are personally asked to disobey God and His laws. In other words, Corrie ten Boom was not personally asked to disobey the government of Hitler. She chose to disobey the government by safeguarding Jews.

What would you or I have done if we had lived in Europe during World War II and saw Jews being led off to ovens and concentration camps? If I am not personally asked to round them up or drive the truck that will carry them to their deaths, does that get me off the hook? Hardly. Those who think so are lazy, cowardly, unBiblical, or some combination of the three.

Brannon Howse

To bring my examples more to the present: I find it strange that some pastors will say, "Well, we may not like it, but Christians are called to obey the government even when we don't agree with its decisions, but the church is not called to get involved in politics." Then, as soon as the city council votes to allow a strip club to open down the street from the church, the pastor is not only unwilling to accept the decision of government officials but publicly encourages members of his church to run for city council in order stop the strip club from being built so close to the church. Is it just me, or is it not selfish for a church to be concerned about the strip club only if it is built in its neighborhood? Is it not selfish for the congregation to get involved in politics, opposing evil, and standing for righteousness only when it benefits personally? The church and its pastor should be involved in stopping the strip club from being built in their town no matter where the city council agrees to let it be built.

The unBiblical and self-serving views of civil disobedience and Christian activism come largely from an incorrect view of Romans 13. In *Moral Dilemmas*, Kerby Anderson does a great job of describing the most common misinterpretation of Romans 13:

> Some critics argue that civil disobedience is prohibited by the clear admonition in Romans 13:1, "Let every person be in subjection to the governing authorities. For there is not authority except from God, and those which exist are established by God" (NASB). Yet even this passage seems to provide a possible argument for disobeying a government that has exceeded its authority. The verses following these speak of the government's role and function. The ruler is to be a "servant of God," and government should reward good and punish evil. Government that fails to do so is outside God's mandated authority and function. Government is not autonomous; it has delegated authority from God. It is to restrain evil and punish wrongdoers. When it does violate God's delegated role and refuses to reward good and punish evil, it has not proper authority. The apostle Paul called for believers to "be subject" to government, but he did not instruct them to "obey" every command of government. When government issues an unjust or unbiblical injunction, Christians have a higher authority. One can be "subject" to the authority of the state but

still refuse to "obey" a specific law which is contrary to biblical standards.[19]

Similarly, Francis Schaeffer warned, "One either confesses that God is the final authority, or one confesses that Caesar is Lord." We will serve God or serve man, but we cannot serve both. We obey government officials except when those authorities support civil laws that violate the laws of God. First Peter 2:13-14 also makes it clear that God's plan for civil government is to punish evildoers and to protect and praise those who do right: "Therefore submit yourselves to every ordinance of man for the Lord's sake, whether to the king as supreme, or to governors, as to those who are sent by him for the punishment of evildoers and for the praise of those who do good."

Kerby Anderson describes the significance of "Lex Rex," a great historical piece written on the subject of civil authority:

> The best articulation of these biblical principles can be found in Samuel Rutherford's essay "Lex Rex." Arguing that governmental law was founded on the law of God, he rejected the seventeenth-century idea of the "divine right of kings." The king was not the ultimate authority, God's law was (hence the title Lex Rex, "The law is king"). If the king and the government disobeyed the law, then they were to be disobeyed. He argued that all men; including the king were under God's law and not above it. According to Rutherford the civil magistrate was a "fiduciary figure" who held his authority in trust for the people. If that trust was violated, the people had a political basis for resistance. Not surprisingly "Lex Rex" was banned in England and Scotland because it was seen as treasonous and fomenting political rebellion.[20]

While we can hope never to have to disobey the laws of our communities and country in order to walk in good conscience with God, there is no guarantee that we'll never be called to civil disobedience. Knowing where you stand from a Biblical viewpoint, though, is the first step in being prepared to do what God requires.

1.6— A God-given responsibility of government is to protect the righteous and punish the wicked.

True. (Test question #10)

— **As long as government is serving the purpose for which God created it, government is approved by God.**
True. (Test question #11)

When civil government steps outside of God's ordained purpose and persecutes righteous people, promotes evil, and does injustice to the innocent, the moral authority of the civil government has been lost, and Christians are free to disobey. As we just said, disobedience to government may be required in the process of opposing evil, promoting righteousness, defending the weak, and providing for the safety of one's family.

While God allows governments to come into being, that does not mean God approves of every government. To draw an analogy: God allowed the terrorist attacks on September 11, 2001, but God did not approve of them. If, for example, the people of Cuba are sick and tired of the killings, beatings, and imprisonments dispensed by the government of their country, they are Biblically justified in overthrowing Castro (who has clearly *not* fulfilled the God-given purpose of civil government).

Scripture calls rulers "ministers of God." The description "ministers" shows clearly how important the responsibility of a civic leader actually is. Since Scripture calls these people "ministers," it stands to reason that God would call Christians into this occupation just as He calls some people into the ministry of being a full-time pastor.

Christians in Germany should not have shown "honor" to Hitler. The Bible says we are to give honor to those who are due honor, and Hitler did not deserve any such thing. He was not a "minister of God" and was not a legitimate government official because he violated the God-ordained purpose for civil government.

While God allowed Hitler to come to power, He did not approve of him. I do not believe God would hold it against German pastor Dietrich Bonhoeffer for assisting in the assassination attempt on Hitler. Pastor Bonhoeffer understood Romans 13 correctly and understood the Biblical mandate to defend the defenseless and to oppose evil. He also understood the Biblical right of self-defense.

We live in a fallen world where man has a free will to do good or evil. While it is true that the church often flourishes during times of extreme persecution, this happens largely because of the civil disobedience of Christians who worship underground, smuggle Bibles, and distribute Scripture contrary to the laws governing them. Some governments are so evil, corrupt, and ungodly, Christians are obliged not to support them because to do so would be to participate in what they do.

According to Christ, the government should work in harmony with the church (Matthew 22:21), and when it does, God approves of the government in power. Understand, though, that church government is not inevitably superceded by civil government. Many people in the Bible took part in civil disobedience:

- When Pharaoh commanded the Hebrew midwives to kill all male Hebrew babies, Moses' mother lied to Pharaoh and did not carry out his command (Exodus. 1-2);

- When Nebuchadnezzar ordered Shadrach, Meshach, and Abednego to bow down to his golden image, they refused and were cast into a fiery furnace (Daniel 3);

- Daniel prayed to God in spite of the king's dictate to the contrary (Daniel 6);

- In Acts, when Peter and John were commanded not to preach the gospel, their response was, "We ought to obey God rather than men" (Acts 5:29).[21]

We must do the same.

1.7— Legislating morality is a violation of the separation of church and state. *False.* (Test question #12)

"You can't legislate morality!" is a favorite charge by those who oppose legislation but have a weak argument against its passage. Unfortunately, many Christians have bought this silly line without thinking it through. The reality is that liberals and humanists love to legislate *their* morality.

All laws support someone's morality. This means it is meaningless to pose the question in terms of "separation of church and state" because the morals of some group, organization, church, fellowship, association, or other assemblage will be involved. Those of us who desire to see partial birth abortion outlawed, for instance, are attempting to bring Biblical morality to bear on the issue. On the other hand, those who support legislation that allows the procedure want to maintain a morality based on a relativistic, humanist worldview. The question is not *if* morality can be legislated but *whose* morality will be legislated. Laws *always* reflect someone's view of right and wrong. Laws against murder, rape, stealing, child pornography, and kidnapping all reinforce the belief that murder, rape, stealing, child pornography, and kidnapping are immoral and shouldn't be allowed.

Sometimes people counter with arguments such as "Just because you legislate morality does not mean people will obey the law." That is true, of course, but just because not everyone obeys the laws against murder does not mean we should legalize homocide.

Nevertheless, statistics show that the overwhelming majority of Americans follow our laws even when they are not being watched. For example, most Americans voluntarily pay their taxes, obey traffic rules, and register for the Selective Service at age eighteen.

Another objection you'll hear is "You can't change the heart with legislation." Although that is not completely true (I'll explain why below), changing of the heart is not the foremost goal of legislation, so the argument is largely irrelevant. The primary goal of laws are to create a stable, secure society. That means setting up a system to help keep people's baser instincts—lust, greed, hatred—in check. If nothing else, laws need to discourage people from engaging in criminal acts simply because they're afraid of punishment.

There is evidence, however, that over time, laws *can* change the heart. Consider the issue of slavery, for instance. For more than half of the nineteenth century, many Americans thought they should be allowed to enslave some people based on the color of their skin. In twenty-first-century America, though, you will be hard pressed to find anyone who thinks slavery is morally acceptable. Over time, the law against slavery has caused people to change the way they think and feel about the issue.

This changing of the heart, though, can go against us as well. In 1960, few Americans would have agreed that abortion is morally acceptable. But because the highest court in the land ruled in 1973 that the killing of an unborn child is legal, many Americans have come to believe abortion is morally acceptable. The Supreme Court's position has had a powerful—and negative!—impact on the morals of countless Americans. That's because most people really do equate the law with what is right. They *assume* legislation is moral.

In his outstanding book, *Why We Can't Stay Silent,* Tom Minnery of Focus on the Family writes:

When people say, "You can't legislate morality," they probably mean there is a limit to how effective laws are in bringing people to act rightly....Admittedly, we can't force anyone to acknowledge God or willingly obey Him, but like it or not, they either have to accept God's ideas about what's right and wrong or pay the consequences. We've just said that biblical morality: No lying, cheating, stealing, murdering, et cetera, is good for society, and we should be pleased that our forefathers had enough sense to translate these godly principles into law.

Why did the founders decide America's laws were to be based on God's laws? Because they believed God's moral law was written on the hearts of all people. In his book, *Original Intent,* David Barton points out: "The Founders believed the Bible to be the perfect example of moral legislation and the source of what they called, 'the moral law'."

The Bible offers numerous verses that relate morality to government. Scripture calls all nations to promote righteousness—right living and justice:

• Righteousness exalts a nation, but sin is a reproach to any people (Proverbs 14:34).

• By the blessing of the upright the city is exalted, but it is overthrown by the mouth of the wicked (Proverbs 11:11).

• When the righteous are in authority, the people rejoice, but when a wicked man rules, the people groan (Proverbs 29:2).

• Blessed are those who hunger and thirst for righteousness, for they shall be filled (Matthew 5:6).

So legislating morality is not a violation of any standard, principle, or proper philosophy of government. Moral purpose is behind every law. Despite the beliefs of many misguided individuals, Christians must be involved in the legislative process if we hope to promote righteousness and be light in a dark world.

LAW

1.8— **The wording "separation of church and state" is found in the U.S. Constitution.** *False.* (Test question #13)

— **The separation of church and state must be enforced, prohibiting the acknowledgment of God in the public schools, governmental buildings, in public meetings, and on public property.** *False.* (Test question #14)

— **The American Civil Liberties Union is interested in defending the Constitutional rights of Americans and the original intent of the Founding Fathers.** *False.* (Test question #15)

Nineteenth-century U.S. Supreme Court Justice Joseph Story clearly explained the meaning of the First Amendment: "The whole power over the subject of religion is left exclusively to the State governments to be acted upon according to their own sense of justice and the State constitutions."[22]

The original draft of the First Amendment to the Constitution was introduced in the Senate on September 3, 1789, and stated, "Congress shall not make any law establishing any religious denomination." The second version stated, "Congress shall make no law establishing any particular denomination." The third version was similar declaring, "Congress shall make no law establishing any particular denomination in preference to another." But the final version passed later that same day became the First Amendment that is still part of our Constitution: "Congress shall make no law establishing religion or prohibiting the free exercise thereof."[23]

The intent of the Founders was not to restrict religion. To the contrary, the founders required any territory applying for statehood to show respect for religious sensibilities as directed by the Northwest Ordinance, which governed applications for states to join the Union. Article III of the Northwest Ordinance declares: "Religion, morality, and knowledge, being necessary to good government and the happiness of mankind, schools, and the means of education, shall forever be encouraged."[24]

Thomas Jefferson, when discussing the original intent of the First Amendment wrote: "Certainly, no power to prescribe any religious exercise or to assume authority in religious discipline has been delegated to the general [federal] government. It must rest with the States."[25]

The Founders were committed to the Bible and Christianity, and the First Amendment was not intended to separate the Christian religion from either the federal government or state governments.

Joseph Story, an associate justice of the United States Supreme Court, believed the First Amendment was not written to suppress Christianity but to keep Christian denominations from competing with one another to become the official national religion. The Founders did not want anyone—even if their beliefs were contrary to Christianity—to be persecuted for their religious beliefs or convictions:

> The real object of the First Amendment was not to countenance, much less to advance, Mahomedism, or Judaism, or infidelity, by prostrating Christianity; but to exclude all rivalry among Christian sects, and to prevent any national ecclesiastical establishment, which should give to a hierarchy the exclusive patronage of the national government. It thus cut off the means of religious persecution (the vice and pest of former ages), and of the subversion of the rights of conscience in matters of religion which had been trampled upon almost from the days of the Apostles to the present age....Probably at the time of the adoption of the Constitution, and of the first amendment to it...the general, if not the universal, sentiment in America was that Christianity ought to receive encouragement from the State, so far as was not incompatible with the previous rights of conscience and the freedom of religious worship. An attempt to level all religions and to make it a matter of state policy to hold all in utter indifference would have created universal disapprobation, if not universal indignation.[26]

You'll notice that the earlier quotation of the First Amendment says nothing whatsoever about the "separation of church and state." Although many Americans believe the phrase is found in the U.S. Constitution, it is not. The expression "separation of church and state" originated in a letter Thomas Jefferson wrote to the Danbury Association of Baptists. Jefferson used the phrase to assure the Baptists that the government would not interfere with their practice of religion. However, the U.S. Supreme Court corrupted the meaning of Jefferson's phrase in a 1947 ruling. *Everson v. Board of Education* debated whether or not it was constitutional for a state to use taxpayer dollars to pay for bus transportation of students to a Catholic school. In handing down their decision, the Supreme Court deliberately took the separation phrase from Jefferson's letter out of context, changed the meaning of his words, and began to propagate a lie to the American people.

In subsequent cases, the federal courts used the "separation of church and state" phrase, and in the 1962 case, *Engel v. Vitale*, the Supreme Court violated the Tenth Amendment of the U.S. Constitution by telling the state of New York it could not have students begin the school day with a nondenominational prayer. The Tenth Amendment states: "The powers not delegated to the United States by the Constitution, nor prohibited by it to the States, are reserved to the States respectively, or to the people."

This would suggest that if the State of New York wants students to begin the school day with a nondenominational prayer, the state has that right, because the U.S. Constitution does not give the federal government the power to control the education or religious activities of any state. The Court, however, arbitrarily decided otherwise.

No less a constitutional authority than Thomas Jefferson confirms this interpretation of the amendment:

> I consider government of the United States [the federal government] as interdicted by the Constitution from intermeddling with religious institutions, their doctrines, disciplines, or exercise. This results not only from the provision that no law shall be made representing the establishment or free exercise of religion [the First Amendment], but from that also which reserves to the States the powers not delegated to the United States [the Tenth Amendment]. Certainly, no power to prescribe any religious exercise or to assume authority in any religious discipline has been delegated to the General [federal] Government. It must then rest with the states.[27]

The U.S. Constitution left religion up to each state and its citizens. The original intent of the First Amendment was to make it completely acceptable for any state to establish a state religion if the people of that state wanted to do so. Attorney Ann Coulter correctly points out in a column entitled "Disestablish the Cult of Liberalism" that:

> ...It is a fact when the First Amendment was ratified, several states had established religions. Fortunately for the burgeoning minority religions in states, the estab-

lished religions were things like "Episcopalianism" and "Congregationalism" rather than "Liberalism." [28]

Worldview Weekend speaker and attorney David Limbaugh is concerned about the same problem that Ann Coulter, many other conservative Americans, and I find troubling. Modern-day liberalism is actually the religion of Secular Humanism, yet liberals don't scream "separation" when that religion is funded in America's schools by taxpayers:

> If our self-professed separationists are truly motivated by the separationist principle, why don't they object when the government endorses values that are hostile to Christianity? Could it be their true motivation is a bias against Christian values?[29]

David Barton offers another insight into why the *Engel v. Vitale* ruling was so dangerous for each state and every individual in America:

> In the 1962 case, the Court redefined the meaning and application of a single word: the word "church." For 170 years prior to that case, the word "church"—as used in the phrase "separation of church and state"—was defined to mean "a federally established denomination." However, in 1962 the Court explained that the word "church" would now mean "a religious activity in public." This was the turning point in the interpretation of the First Amendment."[30]

Not only did the Court give a new meaning to "church," but, as David Barton points out, there was no historical precedent whatsoever for such a radical action by the Court to strip the states of their right to freedom of religion:

> The 1962 case which removed school prayer was the first case in Court history to use zero precedents. The Court quoted "zero" previous legal cases. Without any historical or legal base, the Court simply made an announcement: "We'll not have prayers in schools anymore; that violates the Constitution." A brand new direction was taken in America.[31]

43

I hope that about now you are scratching your head trying to figure out how the U.S. Supreme Court not only redefined the meaning of the First Amendment but effectively nullified the Tenth Amendment in order to bring its liberal worldview to bear on the American people. Only 1 or 2 percent of Americans even know that the U.S. Supreme Court, for all practical purposes, held its own constitutional convention in the 1940s, eliminated the Tenth Amendment, and stripped every state in the Union of their constitutionally protected freedom of religion. In *Original Intent*, David Barton explains the consequences America suffers to this day from the *Everson* decision:

> In *Everson*, the Court took the Fourteenth Amendment (which dealt with specific State powers) and attached to it the First Amendment's federal provision that "Congress shall make no law respecting an establishment of religion."
>
> The result of merging of these two Amendments was twofold: first, the Court reversed the bedrock constitutional demand that the First Amendment pertain only to the federal government; second, the Court declared that federal courts were now empowered to restrict not only the religious activities of the federal government but also those of States and individuals as well. The expansion of the Court's jurisdiction in the *Everson* decision was accomplished only by direct violations of the purpose for which both the First and Fourteenth Amendments were enacted.[32]

U.S. Supreme Court Justice William Douglas, in *Walz v. Tax Commission* (1970), comments on what he saw as a "revolution" resulting from the unconstitutional linking of the First and Fourteenth Amendments:

> ...reversing the historic position that the foundations of those liberties rested largely in State law...[T]he revolution occasioned by the Fourteenth Amendment has progressed as Article after Article in the Bill of Rights has been [selectively] incorporated in it [the Fourteenth] and made applicable to the States.[33]

The Founding Fathers would be appalled that judges with

their liberal worldview have used the Constitution as a weapon to strip the states of their God-given rights. In a clarion summary statement, Governeur Morris, a Founder who wrote the first draft of the Constitution, declares that the sole purpose of the Constitution is to protect freedom and liberty, not to justify tyranny: "The Constitution is not an instrument for government to restrain people, it is an instrument for the people to restrain the government—lest it come to dominate our lives and interests."[34]

1.9— The original source of law as embodied in the U.S. Constitution is meant only as a guideline. Laws are meant to evolve based on the most recent decisions of our nation's judges. *False.* (Test question #16)

As discussed earlier, the case-law philosophy introduced by Harvard Law School dean Christopher Columbus Langdell calls for the consideration of prior judicial rulings rather than merely the Constitution as a basis for legal decisions. Of this practice, David Barton notes, "Under the case-law approach, history, precedent, and the views and beliefs of the Founders not only became irrelevant, they were even considered hindrances to the successful evolution of a society."[35]

Langdell was not alone in his desire to move us away from strict adherence to the U.S. Constitution. John Dewey, a signatory of the *Humanist Manifesto I*, honorary president of the National Education Association, a powerful influence in American education, and one of the founders of the American Civil Liberties Union, believed that strict adherence to the Constitution was an obstacle to the type of humanist, socialistic change he and many like him desired to accomplish:

> The belief in political fixity, of the sanctity of some form of state consecrated by the efforts of our fathers and hallowed by tradition, is one of the stumbling-blocks in the way of orderly and directed change.[36]

Contrast this thinking with that of William Blackstone. While liberal judges and legal scholars now refer to judicial action as "making law," Blackstone never believed judges should make laws but that they were to study the U.S. Constitution to learn how to *apply* the law. David Barton explains Blackstone's authoritative position:

Numerous early American lawyers, legal scholars, and politicians cited Blackstone's work as a key legal source. For example, Blackstone is invoked as an authority in the writings of James Kent, James Wilson, Fisher Ames, Joseph Story, John Adams, Henry Laurens, Thomas Jefferson, John Marshall, James Madison, James Otis and more.[37]

In fact, so strong was its influence in America that Thomas Jefferson once quipped that American lawyers used Blackstone's commentaries on law with "the same dedication and reverence that Muslims used the Koran."[38]

Ignoring the U.S. Constitution and looking to previous rulings—including even those of other countries—to justify what the U.S. Constitution does not allow is the motivation behind case-law philosophy. When Earl Warren became chief justice of the U.S. Supreme Court, legal positivism began to make dramatic headway. In the 1958 case *Trop v. Dulles*, Chief Justice Warren declared that the Eighth Amendment of the U.S. Constitution could not have the same meaning as it did at the time it was written. (The amendment reads: "Excessive bail shall not be required, nor excessive fines imposed, nor cruel and unusual punishment inflicted.")

The *Trop v. Dulles* case involved the U.S. State Department's attempt to strip a man of his U.S. citizenship because he deserted from the armed forces during World War II. Trop's attorneys argued that this constituted "cruel and unusual punishment." Sympathetic, Warren stated "the Amendment must draw its meaning from the evolving standards of decency that mark the progress of a maturing society." In other words, morals and standards change and evolve over time as does the meaning of the Constitution. It was a watershed moment in constitutional law. Since then, no ruling has been safe from the danger of the case-law use of precedents to justify whatever decisions the justices want to make.

1. Follow-up—For Further Thought about Law

1. List four things that are permissible if God does not exist.

2. What authority does Romans 13 give to civil government?

3. What is another word for the Decalogue?

4. What did President Truman say would happen to America if we reject a Biblical, moral foundation for our nation?

5. What is it called when Secular Humanists apply moral relativism to the law?

6. What are the five points of legal positivism?

7. Why do liberal judges prefer to look at case law and the laws of other nations rather than the U.S. Constitution, Bill of Rights and the Declaration of Independence?

8. Judges are not to make law but to discover or _____ the law.

9. What should be the original source of all laws?

10. According to Romans 13:3-4, who is to be afraid of the government?

11. Based on Romans 13:1-5, the main responsibility of civil government is to reward and protect the _____ and punish the _____.

12. Under what basis is it Biblically acceptable for Christians to be involved in civil disobedience?

13. Give four examples of laws that legislate morality.

14. What are some of the goals of the ACLU?

15. What is the most important thing you learned from this chapter, and how will it impact your thinking, actions and how you talk to others about the issues impacting our country?

SECTION 2—SCIENCE

2.1— **If the research and theory of a group of scientists contradicts the Word of God, the error is with the scientists, not the Bible.** *True.* (Test question #17)

— **Strictly speaking, evolution vs. creationism is not a scientific debate but a theological debate.**
True. (Test question #18)

In contrasting scientific studies of the last several centuries with those that have gone before, the term "modern science" is the common way to refer to what we do now. Adherents to modern processes rightly pride themselves on the "scientific method," which has brought about every technological revolution from airplanes to microchips. The bedrock of this science is observation and repeatable experimentation. Which means that, strictly speaking, no study of origins—naturalistic, theistic, evolutionary, or creationistic—is science in this way. Since none of us observed the creation of the world and we cannot repeat that event, the clash over the question of origins is not a scientific debate but a philosophical one.

Creationists, evolutionists, theologians, and humanists all have the same evidence, and the data is more like the puzzle pieces an archaeologist assembles from an excavation than like the observations in a chemistry lab. Another way to say it is that one view, naturalistic evolution, is just as scientific or not as the other, intelligent design. The central issue is the grid through which each interprets the information.

Since evolutionists have no evidence for macro-evolution, or vertical change, from one species into another, they have arbitrarily redefined evolution to mean horizontal change, an observable phenomenon correctly qualified as "micro-evolution." Micro-evolution happens, but it is not one species changing into another. It is the changing of characteristics within a given species. An everyday dog breeding program can change the size of a dog, but this is horizontal, not vertical, change. The breeder starts with a dog and ends up with a dog—a bigger, smarter, prettier, dog perhaps, but a dog, nonetheless, not a small horse.

Despite their claims to the contrary, evolutionists have no unassailable proof that any species any time in history, anywhere on the globe has ever changed into some other species. That's why they argue the case for macro-evolution from the observation of micro-evolution, minimizing the chasm that separates the two. But to offer an analogy: the gulf is less like a hop across the brook in a city park than it is like trying to step across the wide spot in the Grand Canyon. To say that macro-evolution happened because we've observed micro-evolution is like suggesting that matter transfer should be an everyday experience since we all have television sets in our living rooms.

An all-knowing Intelligent Designer created everything, or It did not. The implications of a supernatural being creating the world with order and design is diametrically opposed to the worldview of humanists who declare they are their only god and the captain of their own souls and destinies.

Evolution is a belief system requiring blind faith, not the approach that concludes that an Intelligent Designer has been at play in our universe. An evolutionist must believe—in the face of mathematical impossibility and contrary to several known laws of the universe—in billions upon billions of "good" mutations occurring at just the right time and in the right order. The intelligent design theorist (which includes, but is not limited to, creationists) must have faith in just one thing: an all powerful creator that stands outside of creation and who has the capacity to generate the evidently designed things all around us. This latter faith is based on the reasonable assumption that things which look as if they were designed were, in fact, designed by a power capable of creating it.

Evolutionists have excluded the possible answer—and it *is* a possible answer—that an Intelligent Designer made the world. Such a ridiculous ban is equal to a teacher telling a class of students there is no such thing as gravity and then asking them why an apple falls from a tree. The teacher has eliminated the very answer to the question proposed. As a result, whatever response the students come up with can only be an inaccurate interpretation of the falling-apple phenomenon. The presupposition guarantees students won't discover gravity and, worse, in the case of the evolution debate, that they won't find God anywhere they look.

This hope of keeping people away from God is a powerful toxin in the stream of rational thought. Evidence not supporting, evolutionists hold on to Darwin's theory even though it pre-dates the discovery of the cell's complexity and DNA, even though no fossils demonstrate transitional forms, and even though their own reckonings set an age of the universe that is only a nano-fraction of the length of time their process would take even using the most conservative mathematical models available. The antiquated theory of evolution seems to have the same appeal to its adherents as the flat-earth theory held centuries ago. Ironically, it is not the "religious" community these days who are the modern flat-earthers. Apparently, we're the ones who can draw the rational conclusions from what we see, even if the status quo tries to squash the evidence.

This evidence-squashing now enjoys an 80-year history of increasing success. In the famous Scopes trial of 1925, the American Civil Liberties Union defended the teaching of evolution in public schools. True educational freedom, attorney Clarence Darrow argued, requires the teaching of both theistic and naturalistic versions of origins. Any person with a well-rounded education should know the differing views on something as important as the most basic question in the universe.

Certainly the ACLU in 1925 was nearly so well-intentioned as to simply want academic freedom for all. But it is true that a well-educated person should understand the arguments for and against the major theories about how we got here. Building on the momentum started by Scopes, however, the ACLU has fought hard to keep creationism from being taught in America's public schools. With the aid of the National Education Association and other liberal groups, it has been stunningly successful in the censorship of facts and reality.

Since the ACLU and NEA have always been supported by prominent humanists, though, we should not be shocked by their contempt for the creationist worldview. Evolution, as outlined in the *Humanist Manifesto I, II* and *2000*, is a major doctrine of Secular Humanism. Instead of believing in God as the basis for their religion, humanists believe in nature or "natural science"—naturalism. The reason is supposedly to avoid resting an intellectual foundation built on what secularists call "blind faith." The Christian faith, however, is anything but blind from an intellectual standpoint. Arguments *for* the God of the Bible are well-founded. What liberal humanists have substituted for a reasonable faith in a Creator God is, I would contend, blind *science*. Dr. D.G. Lindsay agrees and describes the intellectual underpinnings of evolution this way:

> Evolution is a religion that attributes everything to "nature." It demands a faith that is totally blind. Since the evolutionist believes nature and its laws are the guiding force in the universe, he is totally at odds with the Christian faith and the essential miraculous aspect

of creation. The miraculous events of the Bible deviate from the known laws of nature, or at least from our understanding of them.

However, the evolutionist is blind to the fact that his religion, evolution, violates every known law for its own existence, making atheistic evolution more incredible (miraculous) than the Christian faith.[39]

In real life, logic applies. If we see a painting, we assume there was a painter. If an airplane flies overhead, there's a pilot. It doesn't matter that we don't see the painter or the pilot. Elementary logic guarantees in our minds that they exist. If something looks like it was designed—a building, a watch, an airplane, or a cosmos—we are safe to assume it was. Not so, however, in the world of blind science. Naturalistic humanists believe there is no God, not because that is the logical conclusion, but because that is their preference.

These people do not have the intellectual high ground. Rather, they abandoned the heights occupied by deeply committed Christian scientists like Galileo, Copernicus, Pasteur, and Newton long ago. The humanist has no choice but to reject God and believe in man and naturalistic evolution because the alternative is to say there is a Supernatural Creator and Intelligent Designer. Their problem is that if such a Creator exists, then He is the author of the laws of nature, and we are accountable to Him. But being accountable to anyone other than self is not acceptable to the humanist. As a result, humanists reject out of hand any and all evidence that challenges their desired reality. It is philosophy, not science.

Naturalists look only at theories that don't contradict their presupposition. Consider the *a priori* discounting of evidence advocated by the *Humanist Manifesto II*:

> We find insufficient evidence for belief in the existence
> of a supernatural; it is either meaningless or irrelevant
> to the question of the survival and fulfillment of the
> human race. As non-theists, we begin with humans not
> God, nature not deity.

Anything that calls into question the original humanist presupposition (that there is no God) is rejected, even if it means having faith in an idea, belief, or theory that is mathematically not possible and even it if it contradicts bedrock scientific facts or the laws of physics. Their version of science must blind itself to logical deductions in order to draw the conclusion they prefer.

Four years after the ACLU worked the Scopes trial, Professor D.M.S. Watson, one of the leading biologists and science writers of his day, explained that the real goal behind evolution is to reject the alternative—a belief in God. Watson notes, "Evolution [is] a theory universally accepted not because it can be proven by logically coherent evidence to be true, but because the only alternative, special creation, is clearly incredible."[40]

Professor Richard Lewontin, a geneticist and self-proclaimed Marxist, reveals why the dogmatic humanist continues to accept evolution despite its improbability and the unscientific propositions on which it is built:

> We take the side of science in spite of the patent absurdity of some of its constructs, in spite of its failure to fulfill many of its extravagant promises of health and life, in spite of the tolerance of the scientific community for unsubstantiated just-so-stories, because we have a prior commitment, a commitment to materialism. It is not that the methods and institutions of science somehow compel us to accept a material explanation of the phenomenal world, but, on the contrary, that we are forced by our a priori adherence to material causes to create an apparatus of investigation and a set of concepts that produce material explanations, no matter how counter-intuitive, no matter how mystifying to the uninitiated. Moreover, that materialism is an absolute, for we cannot allow a Divine Foot in the door.[41]

So why has materialism become the assumption behind science? Is it because it provides the most rational foundation? No. Professor Lewontin explained it quite clearly. It's because only materialism provides the liberal humanist's preferred philosophical base.

Humanists must perform—and the ACLU must defend—a monumental set of mental gymnastics to uphold the new version of educational freedom that allows only one view of origins to be taught in our public schools. Although the humanist typically mocks as unscientific those who believe in a creator God, when the science of their worldview is proven to be unscientific and mathematically impossible, they ignore the facts and create preposterous theories simply to side-step the logical belief in an Intelligent Designer.

Each new school year brings us again to the front lines of the evolution war in America's public schools, and each year the secular left can be heard screeching louder than a barrel of monkeys, ballyhooing that the teaching of creation or its close relative, intelligent design, has no place in America's schools because it is not scientific but religious. Liberals have redefined science to mean "evolution." Therefore, evolutionists say if you believe in something else—intelligent design or creationism, for example—you do not believe in science.

But let's be clear about this for a moment and return to an unmanipulated denotation of the term.

2.2— Biological evolution (life from non-life to human beings) runs contrary to reason, science and history. *True.* (Test question #19)

— God used the process of biological evolution to create the world as we know it today. *False.* (Test question #20)

To believe in naturalistic causes for the universe and life as we know it, the evolutionist has to reject known laws of science. The laws of thermodynamics—the most fundamental laws of the physical sciences—confirm that the universe had a beginning. Let me explain.

The First Law of Thermodynamics, also known as the Law of Energy Conservation, states that the total amount of energy in the universe remains constant. Although energy can change form, it cannot be created or destroyed. This being the case, we know that natural processes—of which energy conservation is one—cannot create energy, and therefore something outside of and independent of the universe had to create energy.

The Second Law of Thermodynamics is also referred to as the Law of Energy Decay or the Law of Entropy. It states that the amount of energy available for what scientists term "useful work" (simply speaking, it means "existence") is running down or being depleted. In other words, like a watch you wind up, the world is running down, and if it is known to be running down, that means there had to be a point at which it was wound up. Therefore the universe has not always been here, as some have tried to argue (although most recognize the impossibility of such a position these days). If the cosmos were infinitely old, like the watch, it would have already unwound—long, long ago. It had to have a beginning.

Another fact of the Second Law is that the universe, since its beginning, has been going from a state of orderliness to a state of disorder. Evolution contradicts this law by stating that the world has gone from disorder to more complex order. The fact that evolutionists believe a primordial soup fostered life that became more and more organized to the point of developing the human eye, ears, brain, and DNA is not consistent with the Second Law of Thermodynamics. Further, the evolutionist has to believe that order and precision came out of an explosion.

In the 1960s, when facing the challenge of the First and Second Laws of Thermodynamics, the Big Bang theory was born. This is a positive, in many ways, for those who believe in an Intelligent Designer because the theory acknowledges a beginning. It caused evolutionists to change their strategy away from saying the earth has always existed.

The Big Bang also opens another large can of worms for the evolutionist, because once the idea of a beginning is in place, the natural question to ask is: What or who caused it? And this isn't an unreasonable, metaphysical question. As with the Laws of Thermodynamics, cause and effect is an established scientific fact. Other questions also follow naturally from the first. If a "who" caused it, who is the "who"? If a "who" did not cause the Big Bang, then what did?

Most humanists, of course, try to answer the "what" question, ignoring (without any logical reason) the "who" possibility. Yet in the "what" direction, dead ends abound. Matter does not come from non-matter. The gases needed to create the Big Bang could not just magically appear by themselves. The law of cause and effect assures that matter does not come from non-matter. The order required for life to "emerge" has been shown to be mathematically impossible.

Another reasonable question to ask someone who believes in the Big Bang is: When has an explosion ever been shown to result in precision and order?

One good reason to probe the "who" side of the Big Bang Theory is explained by Walter Brown in his book *In the Beginning*:

> The big bang had to have exploded with just the right degree of vigor for our present universe to have formed. If it had occurred with too little velocity, the universe would have collapsed back in on itself shortly after the big bang because of gravitational forces; if it had occurred with too much velocity, the matter would have

streaked away so fast that it would have been impossible for galaxies and solar systems to subsequently form. To state it anther way, the force of gravity must be fine-tuned to allow the universe to expand at precisely the right rate (accurate to within 1 part in 10^{60}).[42]

In his book *God and the Astronomers*, Robert Jastrow, founder and former director of NASA's Goddard Institute for Space Studies, summarizes the most current evidence that the universe had a beginning:

Now three lines of evidence—the motions of the galaxies, the laws of thermodynamics, and the life story of the stars—pointed to one conclusion: all indicated that the Universe had a beginning.[43]

Norman Geisler makes a similar observation in *When Skeptics Ask*:

Now if we are speaking of a beginning of the universe— a movement from no matter to matter—then we are clearly in the realm of unrepeatable events covered by origin science.[44]

Christians have been mocked for believing in a God that created the world, yet now naturalistic evolutionists stumble all over, changing their positions, fearful of what other scientific discoveries will cause them to zig and zag to miss another fatal blow. The question really is how many fatal blows will it take? Like the cat that has nine lives, evolution is quickly coming to a point of total demise. Intellectual honesty is on the side of the theistic worldview.

Already few premier scientists believe strictly in Darwin's evolution. Henry Margenau noted, "If you take the top notch scientists, you find very few atheists among them."[45]

Only an evolutionist attempting to justify an atheistic worldview would be desperate enough to believe that mutations are a positive thing. When have you ever heard of a good mutation? Charles Colson and Nancy Pearcey point out the natural answer:

Since breeding does nothing more than shuffle existing genes, the only way to drive evolution to the new levels of complexity is to introduce new genetic material.

And the only natural source of new genetic materials in nature is mutations. In today's new neo-Darwinism, the central mechanism for evolution is random mutation and natural selection.[46]

The odds are spectacularly against the possibility that enough good mutations would outweigh the bad mutations to allow a species to transition from one into another. Not only are mutations *not* usually a good thing, they are often fatal.

Scientists have spent years in laboratories subjecting fruit flies and the like to mutations in an attempt to change one species into another. But after killing thousands of fruit flies and successfully changing eye color, wing size, and other characteristics, scientists find that the fruit flies always remain fruit flies. Consider this incredible statement by former chief science advisor with BBC Television:

> It is a striking, but not much mentioned fact that, though geneticists have been breeding fruit flies for sixty years or more in labs all round the world—flies which produce a new generation every eleven days—they have never yet seen the emergence of a new species or even a new enzyme.[47]

Biophysicist Dr. Lee Spetner, who taught information and communication at Johns Hopkins University, wrote in his book *Not by Chance*:

> In this chapter I'll bring several examples of evolution [i.e., instances alleged to be examples of evolution], particularly mutations, and show that information is not increased....But in all reading I've done in the life-sciences literature, I've never found a mutation that added information. All point mutations that have been studied on the molecular level turn out to reduce the genetic information and not to increase it. The NDT [neo-Darwinian theory] is supposed to explain how the information of life has built up by evolution. The essential biological differences between a human and a bacterium is in the information they contain. All other biological differences follow from that. The human genome has much more information than does the

bacterial genome. Information cannot be built up by mutations that lose it. A business can't make money by losing it a little at a time.[48]

But remember, according to Darwin himself, mutations are absolutely necessary for the evolutionary process to work. Further expert testimony reveals even more about the absolute lack of any possibility that mutations would do what Darwin claimed. While professor of genetics at the University of Wisconsin, James F. Crow noted:

> Even if we didn't have a great deal of data on this point, we could still be quite sure on theoretical grounds that mutants would usually be detrimental. For a mutation is a random change of a highly organized, reasonably smoothly functioning living body. A random change in the highly integrated system of chemical processes which constitute life is almost certain to impair it—just as a random interchange of connections in a television set is not likely to improve the picture.[49]

And geneticist Richard B. Goldschmidt summarizes: "If life really depends on each gene being as unique as it appears to be, then it is too unique to come into being by chance mutations."[50]

2.3— The more we discover about the universe, the more we discover design. *True.* (Test question #21)

When you look at a beautiful painting, you know it had a painter. When you look at a sculpture, you know it had a sculptor. When you look at a building, you know an architect designed it. However, when naturalists look at the world, they choose not to credit a designer with the feat. The mystifying order and complexity of the universe and its contents loudly proclaim a designer, and common sense dictates that the greater the design, the greater the designer. Historian and philosopher of science Stephen Meyer has said, "We have not yet encountered any good in principle reason to exclude design from science."[51]

William Paley went to Cambridge in 1759 to study mathematics. He later taught at Cambrige for nine years and was a great defender of Christianity. Paley argued that there must be only one Designer, since there is displayed in nature a uniformity of divine purpose in all parts of the world.[52]

Paley refined what is known as the teleological argument for the existence of God. The analysis begins by observing the design in the world and concludes that there is a designer beyond the world. William Paley characterized the argument this way:

(1) Every watch has a watchmaker;
(2) The world is more complex than a watch;
(3) Hence, the world must have had a world maker.[53]

In more contemporary times, George Gallup, the famed statistician, claimed:

> I could prove God statistically! Take the human body alone. The chance that all the functions of the individual would just happen is a statistical monstrosity![54]

With that in mind, let's look at just a few examples of how complex and orderly many things are that we take for granted:

• Your brain weighs just over three pounds but can do what tons of electrical equipment cannot. It contains up to 15 billion neurons, each a living unit within itself. These neurons boast more than 100,000 billion (10^{14}) electrical connections—more than all the connections in all the electrical appliances in the world.[55]

• The human heart is a ten-ounce pump that operates without maintenance or lubrication for about 75 years, making it an engineering marvel.[56]

• In the fraction of a second that it takes you to read one word on this page, the marrow in your bones produces over 100,000 red blood cells.[57]

• The human eye contains 130,000 light sensitive rods and cones which generate photochemical reactions that convert light into electrical impulses. *One billion* such impulses are transmitted to the brain *every second*. The eye can make over 100,000 separate motions and, when confronted with darkness, can increase its ability to see 100,000 times. It comes complete with automatic aiming, automatic focusing, and automatic maintenance during the owner's sleep. To think that thousands of chance mutations accidentally formed such a structure is ludicrous. Also, within the evolutionary framework, the eye would have needed to evolve several times in different species, such as squids and arthropods. The human eye is so sophisticated that even now scientists and doctors do not fully understand it.[58]

• The ear is as much an acoustic marvel as the eye is an optic one. The inner ear is like a piano with 15,000 keys—that's how many different tones it can detect. Not only does the ear perform the function of hearing, but it controls equilibrium as well.[59]

• Each one of us developed from a single fertilized cell. In the nucleus of that little organic dot was the genetic programming for every aspect of the yet-undeveloped adult—organs, nerves, hair, skin color, and even personality traits. These were programmed into the incredibly tiny specks of matter called chromosomes. According to Ashley Montague in his book *Human Heredity,* the space occupied by all this data is remarkably small. If the blueprints for every one of the five billion human beings on Earth were gathered together, they would fit into the space of an aspirin tablet.[60]

It is fair to say that a single cell is the most complex structure known to man.[61] Some cells are so small that a million of them could occupy a space no larger than the head of a pin. Yet the blueprint for our entire makeup was contained within the chromosomes of the nucleus of the first cell.

The cell is a micro-universe, comprised of trillions of molecules—the building blocks for countless complicated structures that perform chains of complex biochemical reactions with precision. One biologist declared the awe-inspiring constitution of a cell:

Even if we knew all there is to know about how a cell works, we would still be baffled. How nerve cells create emotions, thoughts, behavior, memory and other perceptions cannot yet, if indeed ever, be described in the language of molecular biology.[62]

D.G. Lindsay expands on the complexity of the cell:

A single cell exhibits the same degree of complexity as a city with all of its systems of operation, communication and government. Within each tiny cell are power plants that generate energy; factories that produce foods essential for life; complex transportation systems that guide specific chemicals from one location to another; barricades that control the import and export of materials across the cell. Every minute structure within a cell has a specific function. Without the full complement of all these systems, the cell cannot function. In fact, even the slightest malfunction within the cell can bring about the immediate termination of its existence. How unbelievable that such awesome complexity could have arisen by chance![63]

A single amoeba's DNA has enough information capacity to contain the data stored in a thousand sets of encyclopedias.[64] DNA is the equivalent of a computer program (and every program had to have a programmer). Microsoft founder Bill Gates even notes, "DNA is like a computer program, but far, far more advanced than any software we've ever created."[65]

Every human adult carries about 100 billion miles of DNA strands—a distance greater than the diameter of the solar system—and each cell has four to six feet of the DNA ladder. And every adult human has 100 trillion cells.[66]

In his remarkable book *Darwin's Black Box: The Biochemical Challenge to Evolution,* Michael Behe explains that many biological systems are "irreducibly complex." If any one part were missing—because the needed part had not yet evolved, for instance—the entire system would not work. Many such irreducibly complex systems support life, and if the missing part keeps the life support system from functioning, that is a fatal blow.

Behe argues forcefully that there are several cellular functions that could not possibly have formed gradually by any natural process, including "cilium, vision, blood clotting, or any complex biochemical process."[67] And if not formed by a natural process, the only alternative is a supernatural process by a supernatural designer.

Behe also notes: "Other examples of irreducible complexity abound, including aspects of DNA reduplication, electron transport, telomere synthesis, photosynthesis, transcription regulation, and more."[68] From these facts, Behe draws a bold but inescapable conclusion:

> The result of these cumulative efforts to investigate the cell—to investigate life at the molecular level—is a loud, clear, piercing cry of "design!" The result is so unambiguous and so significant that it must be ranked as one of the greatest achievements in the history of science.[69]

2.4— There is evidence for a worldwide flood.
True. (Test question #22)

In the summer of 2006, explorer, adventurer, and featured Worldview Weekend speaker Dr. Bob Cornuke led a fourteen-man crew to Iran and returned with stunning evidence that theirs is the long-anticipated, even coveted discovery of the remains of Noah's Ark. Bob's team consisted of a Who's Who of business, law, and ministry leaders, including Barry Rand (former CEO of Avis), the multiple best-selling author and Christian apologist Josh McDowell, Frank Turek (co-author with Norm Geisler of *I Don't Have Enough Faith To Be an Atheist*), Boone Powell (former CEO of Baylor Medical Systems), and Arch Bonnema (president of Joshua Financial). They examined what they believe are the remains of the ship Noah used to escape the ravages of a worldwide flood.

After studying the discovery site, Bonnema observed, "These beams not only look like petrified wood, they are so impressive that they look like real wood—this is an amazing discovery that may be the oldest shipwreck in recorded history."

Were it not for the reality of a cataclysmic flood, it would be inexplicable that the shipwreck is perched on a slope 13,120 feet above sea level. The discovery team returned to the U.S. from rugged mountains in Iran with astonishing video footage of a monstrous black formation which looks like rock but bears the amazing image of hundreds of massive, wooden, hand-hewn beams.

The arkish object is about 400 feet long and consists of rocks that look remarkably like blackened wood beams, while other rock in the area is distinctively brown. And many pieces are "cut" at 90-degree angles. Even more intriguing, some of the wood-like rocks actually proved to be petrified wood, and it is noteworthy that Scripture recounts that Noah sealed his ark with pitch—a black substance.

Scouring the mountains all around the object, team member Steve Crampton found thousands of fossilized sea shells blanketing the landscape. Cornuke brought back a one-inch-thick rock slab choked with fossilized clams.

High above the ark site—at 15,300 feet—the team also found wood splinters and broken pottery shards under snow and rock. It showed evidence that ancients had thought this an important worship site for hundreds—if not thousands—of years. The landing location would also have been an unusually hospitable place to live. The team notes that every ecosystem helpful to humans is reachable within a 25-mile radius of the ark's location.

Cornuke initially got involved in the search for the ark after meeting Apollo 15 moon-walking astronaut Jim Irwin. In the 1980s Cornuke participated with Irwin in several searches on Mount Ararat in Turkey but was disappointed with the results. After several years of frustrating expeditions, Cornuke started looking elsewhere for the ark.

Cornuke found clues in the Bible that the ark might be on a mountain other than the famed Mount Ararat of Turkey. His observation was based on the Genesis 11 account that says descendants of Noah came to the Mesopotamian valley *from the east*. According to Cornuke, that would put the Biblical mountains of Ararat somewhere in the northern reaches of Iran. He also cited ancient historians such as Nicholas of Damascus and Flavius Josephus who wrote just before and after Christ that timbers of the ark had survived in what would today be the higher mountains of Iran.

Although his research is by far the most definitive ever, Dr. Cornuke is not the first to suggest Noah's ark came to rest in Iran rather than Turkey. In 1943 an army observer named Ed Davis said he saw the ark on a high mountain in Iran. Sergeant Davis was a road construction engineer in Iran during World War II, building army highways from the Persian Gulf to the Caspian Sea. During his tour of duty there, some Iranian friends told Davis of the ark and led him to the site. After the war, Sgt. Davis passed a lie detector test affirming his testimony about actually seeing timbers from an ark-like object high in the mountains of Iran.

Before his death, Davis became acquainted with Bob Cornuke and gave him a map showing the way to the object. "It was right where Ed said it was in his map," Cornuke relayed. "After seeing it from a distance I thought it at first unimpressive, but once we stood on the object we were all amazed at how it looked just like a huge pile of black and brown stone beams."

Dr. Cornuke has used the Bible as his primary guidebook to one Biblical location and artifact after another. Some of America's leading businessmen, an attorney who has argued several cases before the U.S. Supreme Court, and two leading Christian apologists believed Dr. Cornuke's evidence for the ark was compelling enough to make a daring trip to the politically volatile state of Iran. Their triumphant expedition adds great credence to the Biblical story of a worldwide flood.

2.5— Life begins at conception. *True.* (Test question #23)

Liberals continue to argue that abortion is morally acceptable because the fetus in its early stages is not a live human being. But their contention is inestimably weaker now than it was when abortion was legalized in 1973 and is only getting more so. It becomes increasingly difficult to rationally justify full-term abortion when an ultrasound clearly shows the baby is human and not a dog or cat.

A four-year-old knows that dogs have dogs, cats have cats, birds have birds, and humans have humans. To claim the fetus is not human goes against common sense *and* science. Kerby Anderson describes the medical and scientific evidence that the fetus is a live human being:

> Death used to be defined by the cessation of heartbeat. A stopped heart was a clear sign of death. If the cessation of heartbeat could define death, could the onset of a heartbeat define life? The heart is formed by the eighteenth day in the womb. If heartbeat were used to define life, then nearly all abortions would be outlawed. Physicians now use a more rigorous criterion for death: brain-wave activity. A flat EEG (electroencephalograph) is one of the most important criteria used to determine death. If the cessation of brain-wave activity can define death, could the onset of brain-wave activity define life? Individual brain waves are detected in the fetus in about forty to forty-three days. Using brain-wave activity to define life would outlaw at least a majority of abortions.[70]

All along the way of fetal development, there is clear evidence of the humanity of the unborn baby:

• At three weeks the backbone, spinal column, and nervous system are forming. The kidneys, liver, and intestines are taking shape.

• At five weeks the neural tube enlarges into three parts, soon to become a very complex brain. The spine and spinal cord grow faster than the rest of the body and give the appearance of a tail.

• At seven weeks facial features are visible, including a mouth and tongue. The eyes have a retinas and lenses. The major muscle system is developed, and the unborn child practices moving. The child has its own blood type, distinct from the mother. These blood cells are now produced by the liver instead of the yolk sac.

• In week eight, brainwaves can be measured and the fingers can be seen, and in the ninth week the toes will develop.

• In the tenth week the heart is almost completely developed and very much resembles that of a newborn baby. An opening in the atrium of the heart and the presence of a bypass valve direct much of the blood away from the lungs, as the child's blood is oxygenated through the placenta. Twenty tiny baby teeth are forming in the gums.

• In the twelfth week the vocal cords are complete, and the child can and does sometimes cry silently. The brain is fully formed, and the child may even suck his or her thumb. The eyelids now cover the eyes, and will remain shut until the seventh month to protect the delicate optical nerve fibers.[71]

And this is the development of the baby in just its first 12 weeks of life—the first trimester!

2. FOLLOW-UP—FOR FURTHER THOUGHT ABOUT SCIENCE

1. Why don't humanistic liberals want to believe in God despite all the evidence for His existence?

2. Having the belief that either God is or God is not is a presupposition that impacts everything else you believe. Describe the beliefs that stem from each presupposition.

3. To be an evolutionist, in what do you have to have faith?

4. List three reasons why macro-evolution cannot be true and is not scientific?

5. After the laws of thermodynamics were discovered, what did evolutionists have to invent in order to describe how the world began?

6. What is the First Law of Thermodynamics?

7. What is the Second Law of Thermodynamics?

8. The greater the design the greater the _____.

9. Evolutionists don't believe in the supernatural, only in the _____ _____ world.

10. Define the term atheist.

11. What are the three points of the teleological argument?

12. List four things that point to an Intelligent Designer.

13. Why do humanists not want creation taught in America's public schools?

14. Explain briefly why is evolution versus creation not a scientific debate but a theological debate.

15. What did you learn from this chapter that will affect how you think and live?

SECTION 3—ECONOMICS

3.1— The most Biblically based tax system would be one built on a flat tax where everyone pays the same percentage of their income in taxes. *True.* (Test question #24)

The Humanist Manifestos call for punishing wealthy people by requiring them to pay a higher tax rate. Although the Bible teaches that we are not to covet, when the government takes from the rich through a punitive tax system, it is not only discouraging work but is coveting—and acquiring—money to which it has no ethically legitimate claim.

Humanists generally want to redistribute wealth through some form of socialism, but their goal is not even possible. While money can be redistributed, redistribution can never provide enough money to make everyone wealthy. When the government attempts to take from the rich to give to the "poor," they really are taking capital from businesspeople who then are unable to expand their companies, start new companies, and create additional jobs which energize the economy. They are also less able to consume products themselves.

When fewer goods and services are purchased, people at all income levels suffer. If new cars remain on the sales lot, for instance, jobs are lost from the factory assembly line down to the car dealer. When home sales slump, wages disappear for the builder, the mortgage banker, realtor, home inspector, carpenter, concrete company, bricklayers, roofing company, landscaper, carpet layer, and movers. It is a fallacy to think the government can take by force from those with wealth in order to benefit the economy.

Consider another angle on the taxation issue as well. The Lord only asks for a 10% tithe of what we earn. I submit that if God requests only 10% of our income for His work, the government has no need of 50% or more. The combination of federal taxes, state tax, sales taxes, tolls, airline tax, car tax, property tax, gasoline tax, et al, is far more than 50% if you earn an average income. However, most Americans do not realize how much they pay in taxes because many are "hidden taxes"—meaning people pay them without recognizing them as taxes (such as an amount figured into the purchase price of a product).

Notice, too, that God did not set up a progressive tithing system where the more you make, the larger the percentage you tithe. David Barton offers this observation from Scripture:

The current income tax structure in the United States mandates a higher tax rate or percentage the more a person makes. This tax system is contradicted by scripture, especially Exodus 30:11-15, which provided a "half a shekel" tax for everyone numbered. Verse 15 states: "The rich shall not give more and the poor shall not give less than half a shekel." In addition, the Biblical tithe is not applied progressively, rather it is applied equally to everyone ("And all the tithe of the land, whether of the seed of the land or of the fruit of the tree, is the Lord's. It is holy to the Lord....And concerning the tithe of the herd or the flock, of whatever passes under the rod, the tenth one shall be holy to the Lord." Lev. 27:30,32).[72]

Scripture commands *everyone* to tithe 10% of their income. So why should the government not follow this example? Since civil government was created by God, it makes sense that the tax system should reflect God's standards. That's far from what we see in our current system, of course. In 1960, the average taxpayer worked 36 days to pay all of his or her taxes, but by 2003, it took 189 days. That means American taxpayers now work half the year just to pay their taxes.[73]

Many Christians defend the government's unBiblical tax policies by citing Jesus' words that we should render unto Caesar what is Caesar's. The question arises, though, "what is Caesar's?" Is Caesar entitled to 50% of what you earn? That's certainly questionable. In addition, Jesus Christ was speaking of the Roman Empire. In America, we are Caesar in that we are a government of the people, by the people, and for the people.

Not only is a progressive income tax being unBiblical, so is the capital gains tax, as described by author, historian, and Worldview Weekend speaker, David Barton:

> The capital gains tax, which is a tax on profits, actually penalizes a person for success (i.e., the more profit a person makes, the higher the tax rate they pay; profit/windfall of an initial investment) the more profit you make, the more you have to pay. However, in the Bible, the more profit you make, the more you are rewarded. Both the parable of the talents (Matthew 25:14-30) and the parable of the minas (Luke 19:12-27) conflict with the notion of a tax on capital gains. "For to everyone

who has, more will be given, and he will have abun-
dance; but from him who does not have, even what
he has will be taken away." In other words, the Bible
implies that those who do well (invest) with what they
have will be given more.[74]

The Bible even speaks about how the hourly minimum wage
law is a violation of the Biblical principle of private contract. David
Barton explains:

> The parable of the landowner and laborers (Matt 20:1-
> 16) is applicable to the employer/employee relationship
> and the issue of wages. The landowner hires workers
> at different times of the day and yet pays each worker
> the same amount at the end of the day. When the work-
> ers hired first complain, the landowner replies, "Did
> you not agree with me for a denarius? Take what is
> yours and go your way. I wish to give to this last man
> the same as to you. Is it not lawful for me to do what
> I wish with my own things? ("things" is translated as
> "money" in some versions)" There is an implication
> that the landowner had a right to determine the wages
> his workers received, as well as an implication that the
> workers could accept or reject the landowner's offer
> of work. James 5:4 provides a balance in that the Lord
> hears the cries of the laborers who are cheated out of
> wages they are due.[75]

John Stossel, author and anchor of ABC News program *20/20*,
notes in his book *Myths, Lies and Downright Stupidity* how the minimum wage law actually hurts the low-income workers it purports to
help:

> Just as price controls discourage production, wage
> controls discourage hiring. The poorest workers are
> hurt most. When you fix wages above the market rate,
> the rate freely set by the give-and-take of supply and
> demand, you temporarily help experienced workers by
> giving them an artificial raise. But you also take away all
> incentive to hire an "entry-level" worker.[76]

Stossel goes on to point out how few Americans actually earn minimum wage:

> Russell Roberts, an economics professor at George Mason University, makes it a practice when he gives lectures to "educated" groups to ask them what proportion of the workforce earns the minimum wage. These are congressional staffers, law professors, and journalists. The typical answer is 20 percent of the workforce. The correct answer is less than 3 percent. "It's always a good reality check for people," he says. "People need to realize that competition for workers keeps wages up, not legislation.[77]

Another angle on Biblical taxation principles relates to inheritance. What parents do not want to leave both a spiritual inheritance and a financial inheritance to their children and grandchildren? However, thanks to our government and its unBiblical inheritance tax, also known as the "death tax," it is becoming increasingly difficult to leave a financial inheritance to children and grandchildren. Note well what the Bible says about leaving an inheritance and how our federal government is violating this Biblical principle:

> The Bible speaks to the issue of inheritance numerous times. Proverbs 13:22 states "A good man leaves an inheritance to his children's children" (something that is not likely with the current estate tax which can take up to 55% of an estate, leaving 45% to the children; when the children pass it on to the grandchildren, up to 55% of the remaining 45% can be taken, leaving only 27% of the original that would be passed on to the "children's children"). Ezekiel 46:18 states that "the prince shall not take any of the people's inheritance by evicting them from their property; he shall provide an inheritance for his sons from his own property, so that none of My people may be scattered from his property." Other scriptures that deal with inheritance are Proverbs 19:14, I Chronicles 28:8, and Ezra 9:12.[78]

Further, it is a myth that the wealthy do not pay their share. A 2003 study reveals that 80% of taxes were paid by just 20% of

Americans. In fact, here's how various income levels contribute to the tax collections in the United States:

- The top 5% pay 53% of all income taxes;

- The top 10% pay 65%;

- The top 25% pay 83%;

- The top 50% pay 96%;

- The bottom 50% pays a mere 4% of all income taxes.

That is to say that the top 1% pays more than *ten times* the federal income tax as the bottom 50%! But note this:

- The top 1% earns only 17.5% of all income;

- The top 5% earns 32%;

- The top 10% earns 43%;

- The top 25% earns 65%;

- The top 50% earns 86% of the income.[79]

If you compare the breakdowns of taxes and incomes, you'll see that the higher income brackets pay far more than their share of taxes—in some cases, three times as much. If the tax structure were "flattened," they would still pay more tax than lower income people, but the burden would be fairly distributed.

3.2— It is the responsibility of the federal government to create wealth. *False.* (Test question #25)
— The Biblical purpose for wealth is to provide for one's family, proclaim the Gospel, be a blessing to others, and test a person's stewardship and loyalty to God. *True.* (Test question #26)
— When you study the Bible as a whole, it becomes clear that God is very supportive of an economic system

based on private property, the work ethic, and personal responsibility. *True.* (Test question #27)
— **Making the incomes of its citizens as equal as possible should be one of the top priorities of any legitimate government.** *False.* (Test question #28)
— **Making as much money as you can is more important than whether you have a good reputation.** *False.* (Test question #29)

When the Biblical principles on which the free enterprise system is based are put into practice, capitalism produces success for all that choose to participate. However, those who do not adopt Biblical principles of conduct and character will not reap the rewards of this system, because it is based on personal responsibility.

When Biblical principles are ignored—or thwarted—the free enterprise system suffers and can even break down. Just as socialism will not function in the long run because of mankind's sin nature, the free enterprise system can be hindered if people do not check their sinful tendencies. Unlike socialism, however, the free enterprise system offers such great rewards that people are encouraged to apply the principles that make the system effective.

Free enterprise works best when people are honest, moral, hard-working, responsible, conscientious, and selfless. When selfishness and pride come into play, greed and dishonesty follow. But people do not want to do business with those they cannot trust, and therein lies the self-correcting nature of the system. People with whom others do not want to do business go out of business.

On the other hand, when people are honest and serve their customers, their honesty and quality of service establishe a reputation, and their business grows. The Bible teaches that a good name is to be preferred over great riches. A good reputation facilitates a person's ability to make more money because of the opportunities that come his or her way. Those who seek to get rich quickly often succumb to dishonesty and acquire a reputation which causes them to lose out on opportunities for business deals and projects that otherwise would have made them a good deal of money. Our system continues to work because more people are honest than dishonest in most of their financial and business relationships.

In addition to honesty, free enterprise is built on the Biblical principle of working hard. In 2 Thessalonians 3:6-12 Paul tells us to follow his example of working so as not to rely on others to provide for him. He admonishes those who are lazy to get to work or starve. Under socialism, where everyone is guaranteed an income, the government taxes citizens at exhorbitant rates to support lazy people as well as the lavish lifestyles of the elite ruling class. As a result, there is no incentive to work, to risk, to be an entrepreneur, to invest, save, serve others, or to start a business.

The free enterprise system rewards healthy self-interest. It is not only acceptable but Biblical to pursue what is in your best interest as long as you don't look after yourself at the expense or harm of someone else. For instance, it is in my best interest to have a job, to make money, to pay my bills, to save for the future, to purchase goods and services at the best possible price, and to sell goods and services at the highest, fair price the market allows. It is also in my best interest to read my Bible, to pray, to go to church, and to accept Jesus Christ as my Lord and Savior. These aspects of self-interest also have benefits to the others with whom I have relationships—my family, friends, co-workers, business acquaintances, and customers.

There are many things we do based on our best interests, and the free enterprise system rewards the individual that rejects laziness in deference to working hard at a job, serving customers, and providing for his or her family. Honesty, hard work, a good reputation, and the promise of material blessings for following God's commands are the basis of the free enterprise system. It is not by chance that America became the wealthiest nation in the world. Biblical principles work—for Christians and non-Christians alike.

Unfortunately, free enterprise is naturally offensive to most humanists. Humanists do not want to be accountable to God or God's laws and as a result always seek ways to thwart God's laws. If humanists want to benefit financially without following God's laws, they are left with no choice but to turn to the state and relativism. Socialistic control is always the consequence.

Some humanists believe that for now the free enterprise system has to be tolerated until a workable plan for socialism can be implemented. Humanist Sidney Hook, for example, laments that "until some way can be found to organize a society in which everyone's way of earning a living is at the same time a satisfactory way of living his or her life, there will always be a problem of incentive."[80]

While there are pitfalls in the free enterprise system, they are exaggerated when man's sinful nature or big government encroaches on or manipulates the free market. Kerby Anderson addresses some of the benefits of the free enterprise system as well as the arguments liberals make against it:

> Historically, capitalism has had a number of advantages. It has liberated economic potential. It has also provided the foundation for a great deal of political and economic freedom. When government is not controlling markets, then there is economic freedom to be involved in a whole array of entrepreneurial activities.
>
> Capitalism has led to a great deal of political freedom, because once you limit the role of government in economics, you limit the scope of government in other areas. It is no accident that most of the countries with the greatest political freedom usually have a great deal of economic freedom.
>
> The first economic criticism is that capitalism leads to monopolies. These develop for two reasons: too little government and too much government. Monopolies have occurred in the past because government has not been willing to exercise its God-given authority. Government finally stepped in and broke up the big trusts that were not allowing the free enterprise system to function correctly.
>
> But in recent decades, the reason for monopolies has often been too much government. Many of the largest monopolies today are government sanctioned or sponsored monopolies that prevent true competition from taking place. The solution is for government to allow a freer market where competition can take place.
>
> Let me add that many people often call markets with limited competition monopolies when the term is not appropriate. For example, the three major U.S. car companies may seem like a monopoly or oligopoly until you realize that in the market of consumer durables the true market is the entire western world.
>
> Capitalism is a system in which bad people can do the least harm, and good people have the freedom to do good works. Capitalism works well if you have completely moral individuals. But it also functions adequately when you have selfish and greedy people.[81]

The Bible offers more than 2,000 verses on the subject of money. It discusses private property, private contracts, caring for the poor, laziness, staying out of debt, not being greedy, working for your food and investing for the future, leaving an inheritance to children, bribery, extortion, profit and loss, serving your customer, and much more. Here is a summary of the basic lessons from the Bible about money:

- Do not set your heart on riches, and especially be on your guard against oppression and robbery (Ps. 62:10; James 5:1-6).

- God calls us to be contented with what we have rather than coveting what others have (Ex. 20:17; Heb. 13:5).

- If we place so much importance on money that we start loving it, we are liable to unleash all kinds of evil and sorrow (Ps. 52:1-7; Matt. 13:22; 1 Tim. 6:6-10; Rev. 3:17).

- Give God praise and thanks for any and all resources that you have, and honor Him by giving freely to others (Deut. 8:11, 17-18; Prov. 3:9-10; Matt. 10:8; Acts 20:35).

- Building your reputation around money is false; it can lead to dangerous and devastating results, as was the case for one couple in the early church (Acts 5:1-11).

- Wealth is a gift from God and should be received with thanksgiving, generosity, and stewardship (1 Tim. 6:17-18; 2 Cor. 8-9).[82]

3.3— All forms of government-sponsored socialism to some degree stifle economic growth and prosperity.
True. (Test question #30)

Socialism has been attempted many times in various ways and has always proven to be a complete failure. Whether it is an inheritance tax that punishes thrift by taxing the money saved during a lifetime, the progressive tax system that discourages work and investment, or restrictions and confiscation of private property through radical environmental policies, socialism does not work.

While some Christians believe the New Testament church endorsed socialism through the shared living of the early Christians, that is a serious misunderstanding of the history revealed in Acts. First century believers fostered a voluntary system of interdependence—not a compulsory system enforced by the power of a government.

The states of the former Soviet Union will spend decades—and perhaps longer— recovering from their seventy-year affair with socialism that kept them from modern levels of prosperity. Other societies have tried without any more success to make socialism a productive system by which to live and govern.

The underlying cause of socialism's failure is that it is based on a false belief about equality. It maintains that the outcome of everyone's work can and should be equal, but that is contrary to the nature of the people who make up any society. Whenever government forcibly tries to equalize salaries, the standard of living, education, and productivity take a nosedive.

Few people realize that socialism's proclivity for failure was first evidenced in America's colony established by the Pilgrims. When the Mayflower set sail on August 1, 1620, it carried 102 passengers, including 40 Pilgrims led by William Bradford. On the journey, Bradford set up an agreement that established laws for all members of their community, regardless of an individual's religious beliefs. The Pilgrims were steeped in the lessons of the Old and New Testaments and looked to the ancient Israelites for a model. Because of the precedents in Scripture, they never doubted that their experiment would work. During the first winter, however, half the Pilgrims—including Bradford's wife—died of starvation, sickness, or exposure. When spring finally came, Indians taught the settlers how to plant corn, how to fish for cod, and how to skin beavers for coats. Life improved for the Pilgrims, but still they did not yet prosper. The problem was that Bradford's master plan was constrained by the original contract into which the Pilgrims had entered with their merchant-sponsors in London. That contract required that everything the Pilgrims produced go into a common store to which each member of the community was entitled one common share. The land they cleared and the houses they built also belonged to the community.

Through the terrible first year, Bradford, who had become the governor of the colony, saw the fallacy in this form of collectivism and recognized it as the destructive force that had taken so many lives in the Pilgrim community. In a bold change, he assigned a plot of land to each family to work and manage, thus unleashing the power of the marketplace. His plan worked magnificently, turning around what had been dismal prospects for the small group.

Long before Karl Marx was born, then, the Pilgrims had experimented with socialism. As Rush Limbaugh points out, "What Bradford and his community found was that the most creative and industrious people had no incentive to work any harder than anyone else, unless they could utilize the power of personal motivation!"[83]

Writing about the experiences of the Pilgrims, Bradford himself observed:

> By taking away property, and bringing community into a common wealth...as if they were wiser than God.... For young men that were most able and fit for labor and service did repine that they should spend their time and strength to work for other men's wives and children without any recompense...that was thought injustice.[84]

The question becomes obvious: If socialism has proven to be a detriment to every society that has tried it, why do we permit this philosophy to be taught in America's schools? Socialism is consistent with the humanist worldview because humanists deny the sin nature of mankind and as a result believe socialism will work if people just try hard enough to implement its principles. In reality, people are sinful from birth, battling greed, selfishness, pride, anger, bitterness, envy, laziness, and dishonesty. All of these sinful human qualities prevent a system of economics based on equal work, equal income, and shared benefits from working.

In his book *The Battle for Truth,* Dr. David Noebel recognizes this central problem:

> If one denies the inherent fallen nature of man, socialism becomes the most attractive economic system for creating a heaven on earth. For the Humanist, there is no original sin to stand in the way of creating a helping, sharing, cooperative community on earth. Therefore, the economic system best suited to promote the ethics of Humanism and amend the evils of capitalism is socialism.[85]

John Dewey declared the imperative for socialism to succeed if liberalism and humanism (which I contend are one in the same) are to succeed. Dewey declared:

But the cause of liberalism will be lost for a considerable period if it is not prepared to go further and socialize the forces of production, now at hand, so that the liberty of individuals will be supported by the very structure of economics organization.[86]

John Dewey also proclaimed that "…social control of economic forces is…necessary if anything approaching economic equality and liberty is to be realized."[87]

John Kenneth Galbraith, a past Humanist of the Year, declared, "In an intelligently plural economy…a certain number of industries should be publicly owned."[88] Be clear that when Galbraith speaks of "publicly owned" he does not mean a public corporation that is traded on the stock market. He means owned by the government. Socialists want the government, not private industry, to own and control the means of production.

Whereas free enterprise gives the individual control of his or her own earthly future, destiny, and income, socialism puts a relatively few, powerful elite in control of whether or not a person has a job and how much income any given person will make for the benefit of the all-powerful state and its ruling class.

John Dewey (wrongly) believed that in a capitalistic system the supply and demand that fuels the free enterprise system are artificially manipulated. He maintained that the reason there are poor people is that supplies of food, clothes, and other necessities are deliberately limited so as to drive up prices. The exceptionally strange part of his believing so is that such centralized control is not even remotely possible in a capitalist economy, only in a socialist one. Nevertheless, Dewey claimed:

> There is an undoubted objective clash of interests between finance-capitalism that controls the means production and whose profit is served by maintaining relative scarcity, and idle workers and hungry consumers.[89]

The three different Humanist Manifestos have this to say concerning socialism and the redistribution of wealth and a guaranteed income:

- *Humanist Manifesto I*: "A socialized and cooperative economic order must be established to the end that the equitable distribution of the means of life be possible."

• *Humanist Manifesto II*: "We need to democratize the economy and judge it by its responsiveness to human needs, testing results in terms of the common good."… and… "World poverty must cease. Hence extreme disproportions in wealth, income, and economic growth should be reduced on a worldwide basis."

• *Humanist Manifesto 2000*: "We should strive to provide economic security and adequate income for everyone."

While socialism is the economic system of choice for most humanists, not all are convinced the free enterprise system should be scrapped entirely. Marvin Zimmerman contends "that the evidence supports the view that democratic capitalism is more productive of human good than democratic socialism."[90] Robert Sheaffer adds that "[N]o intellectually honest person today can deny that the history of socialism is a sorry tale of economic failure and crimes against humanity."[91]

Dr. Noebel reveals in his book that some socialists want to have an "American" form of socialism that is incremental in its approach but reaches the same completely socialistic end:

[Corliss] Lamont believes that the United States Constitution must still be honored, so he recommends that the American government purchase the means of production from their rightful owners. He does not specify whether the government or the capitalists will dictate the price, or where the government will get the money to pay for everything it buys. Once the intermediate steps toward socialism in the United States are taken, the socialistic Humanists are largely in agreement regarding the means of assuring a more "equal" society. Lamont, Dewey, Fromm, and Sellars all call for a redistribution of wealth in the form of a "guaranteed income" for every person in the country.[92]

No matter what they may wish for, though, if it is socialism, the system won't work.

3.4— Physically and mentally healthy adults that do not work should be allowed to suffer the consequences of their actions. *True.* (Test question #31)

Our Christian heritage has always taught that people are responsible for their actions and for their moral conduct, but these two pillars are now missing. As a result, much of America is succored by a welfare program out of control. Unwed mothers are rewarded monetarily for having more and more children out of wedlock, while couples who get married and have children are assessed a heavy tax simply for choosing to do the right thing.

The immoral and irresponsible lifestyles of untold numbers of welfare recipients are funded by a government that does not hold individuals to reasonable standards of personal responsibility and decency. Misguided psychologists and other such "professionals" worsen the problem by "discovering" new disorders or disabilities to excuse every human failing. While many have genuine disabilities, some of these real problems end up being ignored or not taken seriously because psychobabble and a victim mindset are rampant.

The result is that our nation is being destroyed from the inside. America needs to recommit itself to the heritage that made it great—a heritage based solidly on a Christian worldview, a strong faith in God, and a belief in His moral principles. This includes the standards of hard work, personal responsibility, right and wrong, good and evil, and true justice for all.

It is scandalous that support of current welfare programs is positioned as the only way to show compassion for the poor. Today's welfare programs are based not on compassion but on socialism and its constraining, motivation-numbing approach to economics. There are times when people need a little help to get back on their feet, but as one talk show host has said, "The safety net has turned into a hammock." There is a difference between showing compassion and rewarding irresponsibility, immorality, and laziness.

Americans have spent billions of dollars on welfare programs that subsidize laziness and irresponsibility. For families, individuals, and children in need of assistance, the burden should not be placed upon the government but on families and the church. Nothing in the U.S. Constitution gives the central government the right to take money from one group of Americans and give it to another. Unfortunately, now that the federal government has "grown teats" and become the cow upon which millions are dependent for their daily sustenance, we face the monumental problem of how to wean millions from government milk and into a life of work, responsibility, productivity, and self-determination.

In addition to the chronic problem of welfare-dependent people, we also must address the concern that some participants abuse the system. *Human Events* reported the particularly flagrant case of Linda Taylor, accused by Illinois authorities of fraudulently using aliases to receive welfare money. Known as the "Welfare Queen," Ronald Reagan mentioned her frequently, along with other welfare-abuse stories. She bilked the welfare system for at least $150,000, tax-free, and some estimates place the amount at $1 million. She used 127 aliases in 14 states, passing variously as a heart surgeon, a witch doctor, and a widow of eight husbands. Her defense attorney argued that she could not be convicted because it would create an unmanageable situation—if the state tried to prosecute all the people that took welfare money to which they weren't entitled, there would be nowhere to put them all.[93]

Although the welfare program is clearly out of hand, in 1996 when U.S. House Majority Leader Dick Armey proposed welfare reform, liberals went ballistic and predicted a national disaster. Here is a sampling of some of their great fears:

> • Patricia Ireland (National Organization for Women) warned that the bill "places 12.8 million people on welfare at risk of sinking further into poverty and homelessness."

> • The Urban Institute projected the bill would push 2.6 million people into poverty and cause 8 million families with children to lose income.

> • Peter Edelman (assistant secretary of the Department of Health and Human Services) resigned his post to protest President Clinton's signing the bill and claimed the bill would lead to "more malnutrition and more crime, increased infant mortality, and increased drug and alcohol abuse and abuse against children and women." [94]

So what has happened since the passage of the welfare reform bill? Here are a few statistics from Mr. Armey:

• There are 4.2 million fewer people living in poverty today.

• The poverty rate of single mothers is at its lowest point in U.S. history.

• Employment of single mothers has nearly doubled, and employment of mothers without a high school diploma has increased by 60 percent.

• The share of children living in single-mother families has fallen, with no corresponding increase in abuse against women and children.[95]

There is no Biblical justification for providing financial assistance to lazy people. When individuals are forced to accept responsibility by facing the consequences of wrong actions and decisions, they learn not to be irresponsible and lazy.

Government intervention also creates a disincentive for those who should be helping solve the problems of legitimately needy people. As more and more people have looked to the government instead of local churches for crisis assistance, churches have reduced or redirected their benevolent funds and programs.

Jesus tells us that the poor will always be with us. The reason is that people's sins often lead them into poverty. But it is important to understand that when the Bible speaks of "the poor" sometimes it is a reference to a person's spiritual, not financial, condition. Even when the Bible means the financially poor, however, it does not have in mind the American definition of poor. A Biblical definition is someone who does not have clothing, food, or shelter.

Dr. Theodore Dalrymple, author of the book *Life at the Bottom: The Worldview that Makes the Underclass,* has spent years as a psychiatrist treating the indigent in a slum hospital and a prison in England. Dr. Dalrymple believes we use the term "poor" to flippantly describe people that really are not poor in the sense that they have nothing and are on the verge of starvation. He explains the danger of our perspective on poverty:

A specter is haunting the Western world: the underclass. This underclass is not poor, at least by the standards that have prevailed throughout the great majority of human history. It exists, to a varying degree, in all Western societies. Like every other social class, it has benefited enormously from the vast general increase in wealth of the past hundred years. In certain respects, indeed, it enjoys amenities and comforts that would have made a Roman emperor or an absolute monarch gasp.[96]

So exactly why is the underclass in the condition they are? Dr. Dalrymple blames their worldview. Although his is not a Christian book, Dr. Dalrymple has come to this amazing conclusion through years of personal observation of the underclass. He explains:

I have, for example, interviewed some ten thousand people who have made an attempt (however feeble) at suicide, each of whom has told me of the lives of four or five other people around him. From this source alone, therefore, I have learned about the lives of some fifty thousand people: lives dominated, almost without exception, by violence, crime, and degradation....Moreover, having previously worked as a doctor in some of the poorest countries in Africa, as well as in very poor countries in the Pacific and Latin America...

....Patterns of behavior emerge, in the case of the underclass, almost entirely self-destructive ones. Day after day I hear of the same violence, the same neglect and abuse of children, the same broken relationships, the same victimization by crime, the same nihilism, the same dumb despair. If everyone is a unique individual, how do patterns such as this emerge?

Economic determinism, of the vicious cycle-of-poverty variety, seems hardly to answer the case. Not only is the underclass not poor, but ... If being poor really entailed a vicious cycle, man would still be living in the caves.[97]

Note well why Dr. Dalrymple believes we have the underclass:

Welfare states have existed for substantial periods of time without the development of a modern underclass: an added ingredient is obviously necessary. This ingredient is to be found in the realm of ideas. Human behavior cannot be explained without reference to the meaning and intentions people give their acts and omissions; and everyone has a Weltanschauung, a worldview, whether he knows it or not. It is the ideas my patients have that fascinate—and, to be honest, appall—me: for they are the source of their misery.[98]

The individuals, of course, bear much of the responsibility for their views, but they have been "helped" to assimilate this destructive approach to life. Dalrymple lays blame at the feet of liberal humanists and their if-it-feels-good-do-it worldview: "In fact, most of the social pathology exhibited by the underclass has its origin in ideas that have filtered down from the intelligentsia."[99]

"Intelligentsia" is another word for the liberal, humanistic, elitist educrats and social engineers. The liberals' morally relativistic worldview has been propagated among the underclass in many areas, but few are as obvious as the rampant sexual promiscuity. Recall what the Humanist Manifestos say about moral relativism, sex, and the pursuit of pleasure:

• *Humanist Manifesto II*:
"We affirm that moral values derive their source from human experience. Ethics is autonomous and situational."

"Ethics stems from human need and interest."

"We strive for the good life, here and now."

"...neither do we wish to prohibit, by law or social sanction, sexual behavior between consenting adults. The many varieties of sexual exploration should not in themselves be considered 'evil.'"

• *Humanist Manifesto I*:
"....the quest for the good life is still the central task for mankind."

While "ivory tower" liberals tout their perverse expressions of freedom, the underclass reaps the tragic consequences as described by Dr. Dalrymple:

Of nothing is this more true than the system of sexual relations that now prevails in the underclass, with the result that 70 percent of the births in my hospital are now illegitimate (a figure that would approach 100 percent if it were not for the presence in the area of a large number of immigrants from the Indian subcontinent)....

The intellectuals were about as sincere as Marie Antoinette when she played the shepherdess. While their own sexual mores no doubt became more relaxed and liberal, they nonetheless continued to recognize inescapable obligations with regard to children, for example. Whatever they said, they didn't want a complete breakdown of family relations any more than Marie Antoinette really wanted to earn her living by looking after sheep.

But their ideas were adopted both literally and wholesale in the lowest and most vulnerable social class. If anyone wants to see what sexual relations are like, freed of contractual and social obligations, let him look at the chaos of the personal lives of members of the underclass.

Here the whole gamut of human folly, wickedness, and misery may be perused at leisure—in conditions, be it remembered, of unprecedented prosperity. Here are abortions procured by abdominal kung fu; children who have children, in numbers unknown before the advent of chemical contraception and sex education; women abandoned by the father of their child a month before or a month after delivery; insensate jealousy, the reverse of the coin of general promiscuity, that results in the most hideous oppression and violence; serial stepfatherhood that leads to sexual and physical abuse of children on a mass scale; and every kind of loosening of the distinction between the sexually permissible and the impermissible.

The connection between this loosening and the misery of my patients is so obvious that it requires considerable intellectual sophistication (and dishonesty) to be able to deny it.

The climate of moral, cultural, and intellectual relativism—a relativism that began as a mere fashionable plaything for intellectuals—has been successfully communicated to those least able to resist its devastating practical effects.[100]

Christians must reach out to the underclass and seek to change their hearts and worldview by showing them their sinfulness and the need for a personal relationship with Jesus Christ. While not every poor person fits Dr. Dalrymple's characterization, a large proportion are clearly reaping what they have sown.

I know from first-hand experience that what Dr. Dalrymple writes is true. Weekly for five years while living in Minnesota, I volunteered at the Union Gospel Mission in St. Paul. I spoke and led music for the nightly service before the free meal. Except for a very few mentally ill people that had been left homeless after the death of a caregiving parent, I met people that chose to be homeless. Almost all had a home, had parents, or a wife and some even children, but chose to live a life of drugs, alcohol, and irresponsibility. Many of the men at the mission that showed up for the service (attendance at which was required if they wanted the mission's free meal) told me they choose to live as they do.

The chaplain explained numerous times that many of the men could return to their families if they would simply take responsibility for their actions, clean themselves up, get a job, and stop abusing drugs and alcohol. He explained that he had met men who at one time had been judges, doctors, attorneys, or businessmen who had destroyed their lives through drugs and alcohol.

Regardless of how the homeless come to be at the missions, the countless Union Gospel Missions around the nation are doing the work of the Lord in assisting those that want to get off drugs and alcohol and rebuild their lives. That's why I encourage all Christians to financially support and volunteer at the Christian mission in their area.

In spite of past bad decisions, many indigent people have come to Christ, and their lives have been transformed as only a personal relationship with Jesus can do. Such people need our support, encouragement, mercy, and grace as they try to become productive citizens.

3.5— The Bible states that money is the root of all evil.
False. (Test question #32)

Just to make quick work of question #32, here's the real quote: "For the love of money is a root of all kinds of evil, for which some have strayed from the faith in their greediness, and pierced themselves through with many sorrows" (1 Timothy 6:10). It is the *love* of money and *greed* that destroy people.

3. Follow-up—For Further Thought about Economics

1. The free enterprise system is not perfect because man is basically what?

2. Socialists want to redistribute what?

3. What have the Secular Humanists promoted in our nation's school's that has greatly harmed the underclass?

4. Despite the primary reason for poverty, how should Christians respond to the poor and underclass?

5. Name four Biblical principles upon which the free enterprise system is based.

6. Capitalism is a system in which bad people can do the least harm and good people can have the freedom to do the most what?

7. Why is a progressive tax system unBiblical?

8. Too often welfare programs have rewarded what qualitites?

9. Look up in the topical Bible verse appendix at the end of this book two verses on laziness and write them down.

10. Look up in the topical Bible verse appendix at the end of this book two verses on work and labor and write them down.

11. What happen when the Pilgrims tried socialism?

12. List four reasons why gambling and a state-sponsored lottery are unBiblical.

13. What did you learn from this chapter that will affect how you think and live?

SECTION 4—EDUCATION

4.1— Science, history, literature and other academic studies can be taught without a religious or philosophical foundation. *False.* (Test question #33)

— Biblically-minded Christians should look at issues as falling into one of two categories: the secular and the sacred. *False.* (Test question #34)

Random House Unabridged Dictionary of the English Language defines *religion* as "a set of beliefs." *Webster's New World Dictionary* defines *religion* as "a system of belief." The word *belief* is defined as opinions and "thoughts upon which people base their actions." Since an individual's worldview is the foundation of his or her values, and these values form the basis for behavior, it is clear that if you are alive and have a collection of beliefs, then you have a religion, and therefore *all* issues and *all* subjects are in some way religious, or sacred.

A few years ago I had a phone conversation with a man who was the acting president of a well-known religious organization. This man told me that he believed abortion is a moral and political issue but not a spiritual one. I was so amazed at his comment that I repeated what he said and asked if I had heard him correctly. This acting president of a Christian organization confirmed that I had heard him correctly. Fortunately, due to other comments made publicly that were in the same vein as his remarks to me, this gentleman was not confirmed by his peers as the official president of this religious association.

This gentleman's belief that abortion is not a spiritual issue but a moral and political position is sadly typical of what many in today's evangelical churches think. By contrast, I respect the honesty and intellectual integrity of many self-professing liberals and humanists who openly admit that they hold to certain ideas, beliefs, values, and ethics based upon a religious worldview. Too often, though, humanists deny a religious worldview as the foundation of their science, ethics, morals, values, economics, and law—while advocating a religion-free school system, government, and culture. The reality is that they simply want to replace America's founding religious belief system—which has given us the longest running constitutional republic in the history of the world—with a religious system that has been the failed foundation of the former Soviet Union, China, Cuba, and North Korea.

Many who once called themselves "religious humanists" are

adamant that their readers, followers, peers, and colleagues stop calling it *religious* humanism." Why? Because they fear that such an admission will cause the courts to reject their religion, which currently not only receives a free pass in America's schools but also receives federal funding. The complete understanding of this issue by Americans is the only way our nation will remain free and not become subject to a tyrant or dictator who believes that the "religion of force" makes right the survival of the fittest.

As conservatives seek to reclaim America, to defend and protect the freedoms given to us by God, it is imperative that we understand we are fighting a religious and spiritual worldview battle, regardless of what others may claim. In the courts, the schools, the state houses and the U.S. Congress, every issue is a religious issue.

When people teach history, law, science, economics, sociology, civil government, and social issues, they teach in light of their worldview. Whether specified or not, there are a number of issues at the core of any viewpoint on any subject. In all cases, a teacher will maintain a perspective that communicates *something* about every one of the following ideas:

- There is absolute truth, or there is not;

- Mankind has a free will, or he does not;

- The end justifies the means, or it does not;

- People will be held accountable for their actions, or they will not;

- God is, or God is not;

- Mankind can save himself, or he cannot;

- Individuals are autonomous and not bound by any higher authority or moral law, or they are not;

- Law evolves and changes, or laws should be based on the Ten Commandments that do not change;

- Marriage is between one man and one woman, or it can be between two men or between two women;

• All roads lead to God, or there is only one way;

• The Bible is the authoritative Word of God and is a reflection of God's character and nature, or it is just a historical work that holds no more authority than any other book;

• Life begins at conception and is sacred and to be protected, or active euthanasia and abortion are acceptable means of dealing with population control and ending an inconvenience;

• Parents are responsible to raise their children and inculcate them with their values and worldview, or "it takes a village" to raise a child;

• Christianity is truth, or Christianity is intolerant;

• Life has no eternal meaning, or all will be judged according to how they have lived;

• Mankind is here by chance, or God created us with a distinct purpose;

• People are created in the image of God, or they simply evolved from animals;

• We are to judge that which is right and wrong, or we should never pass judgment on anyone and accept all ideas and beliefs as equal.

EDUCATION

No matter what someone is debating, teaching, or discussing about any topic, beliefs, values, ideas, or ethics, that person's worldview will color the discussion and be communicated to the listener or reader—whether they know it or not or whether the person intends to convey a worldview or not.

4.2— The federal government should require students to pass a national test before graduating from high school.
False. (Test question #35)

Conservatives and liberals have argued for years over the need and constitutionality of a national student proficiency test that would be administered by the federal government. Some conservatives have even argued in favor of national testing. Throughout the debate, I have maintained that a mandated national test is unconstitutional because the Tenth Amendment to the U.S. Constitution makes it clear that the federal government has the right to be involved only in certain areas of our lives, and education is not one of them. A national test would lay the groundwork for the infringment of student rights, parental authority, and religious and political freedoms.

John Dewey, Karl Marx, Aldous Huxley, B.F. Skinner, and Benjamin Bloom cared about a student's academic achievement only if it would in some way benefit the state. They believed that before a student's academic knowledge could be used for the benefit of the state, his or her attitudes, values, feelings, and beliefs must be conformed to what the state wants. In his book, *My Pedagogic Creed*, John Dewey proclaimed:

> I believe the true center of correlation on the school subjects is not science, nor literature, nor history, nor geography, but the child's social activities.... I believe that the school is primarily a social institution....The teacher's business is simply to determine, on the basis of the larger experience and riper wisdom, how the discipline of life shall come to the child.... All these questions of the grading of the child and his promotion should be determined by reference to the same standard. Examinations are of use only so far as they test the child's fitness for social life.[101]

Dewey and his comrades wanted only to determine where to place students in the social and economic hierarchy.

Today's Outcome-Based Education test is used to determine a child's areas of weakness. Once these weaknesses are discerned—the attitudes, values, feelings, and emotions that do not fit with the state's preferred worldview, the curriculum—Bloom notes:

> The careful observer of the classroom can see that the wise teacher as well as the psychological theorists use cognitive behavior and the achievement of cognitive goals to attain affective goals...[A] large part of what

we call "good teaching" is the teacher's ability to attain affective objectives through challenging the student's fixed beliefs.[102]

In 1997, Governor Roy Romer of Colorado, while serving as a board member of the Goals 2000 panel, was asked how the panel was going to enforce national standards. Romer replied:

> I believe if you were to get all employers of this country saying that we would not hire anybody unless we see a high school graduate certificate that has on it the results of this potential employee's record....Then I think this nation will come to the realization that there is no job for them, there is no life for them....There is the motivation.[103]

The governor was blatantly committed to coercing Americans to line up for state inspection!

Chester Finn, former assistant secretary of education under Bill Bennett and one of the authors of Goals 2000, has recommended a system of rewards for those who conform to the federal government's standards and punishments for those who do not. Understand, though, that these are not so much academic standards as they are promotion of a humanistic worldview:

> Perhaps the best way to enforce this standard is to confer valuable benefits and privileges on people who meet it, and to withhold them from those who do not. Work permits, good jobs and college admission are the most obvious, but there is ample scope here for imagination in devising carrots and sticks. Drivers licenses could be deferred, so could eligibility for professional athletic teams. The minimum wage paid to those who earn their certificates [of mastery] might be a dollar higher.[104]

This certificate of mastery is really nothing more than an Outcome-Based Education diploma. In a truly scary adaptation of the plan, Nevada and Ohio are already moving to a smart-card version of the certificate, and many other states are looking to follow their lead. On May 23, 1996, *The Cincinnati Post* reported:

EDUCATION

Adults have credit cards and money cards. But soon, students in Cincinnati public schools will have a special card of their own, and what it could buy them is their future in the world of work. The "smart card," proposed by Procter & Gamble Chairman John Pepper, is expected to be in the hands of ninth-graders, and possibly seventh-graders, by the start of the next school year. Equipped with a computer chip, the card will contain a cumulative record of the student's grades, attendance, proficiency, test scores, extra-curricular activities, athletics and other accomplishments. By the time the student graduates, the card should contain all the pertinent information a prospective employer needs about the applicant. All employers would ask to see the Smart Card, and preference would be given to those with good performance.[105]

If the "Big Brother" implications of that idea don't alarm you, they should! Consider the possible requirements to be credited "with good performance": The standards could well be tied to politically correct thinking. Overwhelming evidence suggests that the Goals 2000, Outcome-Based Education standards are based on attitudes, values, and feelings, and who decides which conglomeration of ideas and attitudes are acceptable? I can guarantee you it won't be parents.

If you happened to see a report in the March 16, 1992, *New York Times International*, the idea of a scholastic smart card may sound familiar. The *Times* explained a sinister-sounding plan in China, the world's role-model for denial of personal liberties:

[A] file is opened on each urban citizen when he or she enters elementary school, and it shadows the person throughout life, moving on to high school, college, employer....The dangan contains political evaluations that affect career prospects....The file is kept by one's employer. The dangan affects promotions and job opportunities....Any prospective employer is supposed to examine an applicant's dangan before making hiring decisions.[106]

China confers a noble-sounding name on their education process, calling it life-long learning. What it means is life-long monitoring and the accompanying oppression by the state. Unfortunately, people don't recognize the same sinister potential in our state and federal education plans here in the United States. Legislation is brimming with references to "life-long learning." In 1977, U.S. Assistant Secretary of Education Mary Francis Barry said America was embarking on an education reform movement based on the four pillars of the Chinese model of life-long learning:

(1) Eliminate tests and grades;

(2) Make truth a relative concept;

(3) Educate to serve the masses;

(4) Merge education with labor.

We're basing our education on the Chinese model? When did following the lead of Communist China become a good idea? Yet the results are already beginning to show. In Las Vegas (you'll recall that Nevada is a smart card state), Rene Tucker's daughter Darcy was pulled out of a geography class without parental consent to be given a computerized assessment of career possibilities. Although Darcy aspires to become a veterinarian, the computer said she ought to be a bartender or waitress, and it spat out a list of courses she should take to that end. Mrs. Tucker said, "We're Christians, and the school stepped on my toes as a parent. It is my job to direct my child's career path, and it would not be in her best interest to be a bartender."[107] It might be in Nevada's best interests—given the insatiable hospitality needs of the gambling and entertainment industry—but not in Darcy's.

In his classic story of government oppression, *Brave New World*, Aldous Huxley explained this motivation for government control:

> To bring about the revolution we require....enabling government managers to assign any given individual to his or her proper place in the social and economic hierarchy. Round pegs in square holes tend to have dangerous thoughts about the social system and to infect others with their discontents.[108]

In other words, those who do not agree with the state's worldview or "standards" will not be allowed to pursue positions of power or influence either socially or economically.

Among 100 true or false questions included in a career exploration test used in six states are these:

- I have taught a Sunday school class or otherwise take an active part in my church;

- I believe in a God who answers prayers;

- I believe that tithing is one's duty to God;

- I pray to God about my problems;

- It is important that grace be said before meals;

- I read the Bible or other religious writings regularly;

- I believe in life after death;

- I believe that God created man in his own image;

- If I ask God for forgiveness, my sins are forgiven.

While it could be argued that such questions help determine a student's fitness for a career in Christian ministry, it does not take much imagination to see how they could be equally well used to screen someone out of certain occupations in the name of finding the "proper place" to assign each student.

Mark Tucker is president of the National Center on Education and the Economy, an organization that has led the charge in passing school-to-work legislation at the state and federal levels. Among his board members was Hillary Clinton, prior to becoming First Lady. In the February 4, 1998, issue of *Education Week*, Mark Tucker was quoted in an article written by Millicent Lawton as encouraging government control of individual destinies:

> State higher education systems would deny admission to those who didn't have the certificate [of mastery], and state leaders would prod employers to express a

preference for hiring job applicants who had the certificate. Both conditions would serve as powerful incentives for students.[109]

The goals of those who signed the Humanist Manifestos are being accomplished even now as we see the merging of education with labor policy or what many refer to as "corporate fascism." The *American Heritage Dictionary* defines corporate fascism as "a philosophy or system of government that advocates or exercises dictatorship through the merging of state and business leadership."

This sort of thinking has troubling roots. Karl Marx in the tenth plank of the *Communist Manifesto* calls for the merging of education with industrial production. Whether socialist, communist, or Marxist, the foundation of all these philosophies is the humanist worldview. In his book *Character and Destiny*, Dr. D. James Kennedy explains:

> Humanists are socialists by nature. Like Karl Marx, they see private property as primitive and selfish, nationalism and pride of country as dangerous, and allegiance to any power other than the socialist state should be illegal. Ideas, ethics, and the means of production belong to the state. For supporters such as Paul Kurtz, B.F. Skinner, John Dewey, Francis Crick, Isaac Asimov, and the other signers of the manifesto, communism and state socialism were the only logical solutions to mankind's problems. In the first edition of that thin volume, they wrote, "A socialized and cooperative economic order must be established to the end that the equitable distribution of the means of life be possible.... Humanists demand a shared life in a shared world."[110]

Whether Outcome-Based Education, certificates of mastery, the UN Convention on the Rights of the Child, the robbing of religious freedoms, the strengthening of federally controlled schools, or attacking the traditional family and its associated private property rights, private schools, and home schools, humanists have one ultimate goal: the creation of a humanistic, socialistic nation where everything is shared, everyone is the same, and the ruling class controls life in whatever ways they choose—all to benefit their own financial and political well-being.

EDUCATION

4.3— **The federal government should be directly involved in determining which students go to college, which go directly into the work force after high school, and what jobs they hold.** *False.* (Test question #36)

— **The federal government should allow only a federally licensed teacher to instruct a child, and in an educational setting.** *False.* (Test question #37)

America's schools are being turned into vocational centers where students are trained instead of educated. T.G. Stict, who served under Secretary of Labor Robert Reich, observed:

> Many companies have moved operations to places with cheap, relatively poorly educated labor. What may be crucial, they say, is the dependability of a labor force and how well it can be managed and trained, not its general education level.[111]

Through school-to-work the state decides which children will go on to college and which go straight to work following "training certification." After reviewing a student's educational history or portfolio, the government determines the career track or job the individual will hold. The state's determination takes precedence over the wishes of the individual and his or her parents. Those who have conformed to the federal and state standards are rewarded with further education and good jobs. Those who do not meet the outcome-based standards do not fare so well.

The California state Parent Teacher Organization has voiced the concern that "school-to-work is based on the premise that government control can do a better job of training individuals, satisfying occupational demands and managing the development of economic activities than can the effort and initiative of millions of individuals."[112] Similarly, Lynn Cheney, former chairperson of the National Endowment for the Humanities, warned of the dangers of school-to-work:

> A central thesis of school-to-work plans, for example, is that eighth-graders should choose careers. To help them along, schools administer interest and personality assessments that direct students toward specific occupations, often ones that have little to do with their ambitions. Kristine Jensen, a Nevada mother, told me

that her daughter, an honor student who wants to work for NASA, had been advised to consider a career in sanitation or interior design. Eunice Evans, a parental-rights advocate in Pennsylvania, described a boy in her neighborhood that wanted to be a doctor but was told it would be more appropriate for him to be a gas station attendant or a truck-driver.[113]

Ms. Cheney also noted the ominous goal of workforce development boards—liberally funded with federal money—that now exist in almost every state:

> To consider future market needs and decide which career choices schools should encourage. But predicting work-force needs is an iffy business. In 1989, for example, a prestigious study declared that by 1997, there would be a substantial shortage of humanities Ph.D's, when, in fact, there is now a glut.[114]

What we need is more public servants like Craig Hagen who will take a stand for what is right. In her congressional testimony, Lynn Cheney cited his courageous stand:

> Concern that schools in his state would get in the business of enforcing politically correct thinking led Craig Hagen, North Dakota's Commissioner of Labor, to resign from his state's school-to-work management team earlier this year. "I couldn't remain in that position with my principles," he said.[115]

Many conservatives have yet to understand the worldview war that has been raging within the educational establishment for years and how liberals have patiently worked to pass one piece of legislation after another that allows the federal government to take more and more control over both education and our economy. Some have ignorantly assisted in passing legislation that is now creating an educational and economic system that John Dewey, Benjamin Bloom, Aldous Huxley, Karl Marx, and B.F. Skinner would be proud of.

Sadly, President George W. Bush and Senator Ted Kennedy worked together to pass the re-authorization of the Elementary and Secondary Education Act they named "No Child Left Behind." We would be better off if President Bush would not have followed in his father's footsteps to further the federal takeover of education. Included in this federal legislation was the funding of "Small Learning Communities (SLCs)." Some cities that have already experimented with Small Learning Communities include Minneapolis, Houston, Boston, Chicago, Denver, Lancaster County, PA, and Prince George's County, MD.

To show you how this works: In Minneapolis, eighth-grade students were forced to make a career choice before they could go on to high school. Students had to fill out an application requesting approval for their first and second career choice. There was no guarantee their first or second career choice would be accepted. Not only that, students who missed the application deadline would have a career chosen for them by the school district.

It is becoming educationally in vogue to replace the term "school-to-work" with "Small Learning Communities." Parents generally are not aware nor are they informed that the choice their children make will determine their curriculum and work-based learning, resulting in seriously narrowed choices for the remainder of their high school years and beyond. Students who change their career choice—if allowed—require a teacher's sign-off and must go before a committee to request approval. If approval is granted, the student's new choice may require him to transfer to a different school and re-start the process of earning credits toward job certification in the newly chosen career path. Many students will be shocked to discover that their junior high career choice led them down a path to a diploma that keeps them from being accepted into college because of a lack of necessary credits.

I have been writing and researching on this topic since 1990, and I wonder how much more of what I and other education researchers have been warning will come to pass before Americans begin to elect officials who will stop the implementation of a planned economy that robs us of our freedoms and punishes Americans that profess a Biblical worldview. Mark my word: The attempt will be made to force students into career tracks consistent with what the state and federal governments predict will be job slots open in the coming years and not necessarily what the student desires to pursue.

Federal legislation such as Goals 2000 (which Bill Clinton signed into law in April 1994), the Elementary and Secondary Education Act of 1994, The Federal School-To-Work Opportunities Act of 1994, The Straight A's Act of 2000, The Workforce Investment Act,

The Reauthorization of the Elementary and Secondary Education Act of 2002, No Child Left Behind, and other pieces of legislation have all resulted in the federal government's increasing control of education and the economy in ways that are intrusive, unconstitutional, and destructive to academic achievement, parental authority, and America's free enterprise system.

4.4— Values clarification courses—situational ethics—should be taught to students in our educational system.
False. (Test question #38)

William Bennett, U.S. Secretary of Education under Ronald Reagan, has spoken out strongly against values clarification courses. Bennett reveals the dangers and consequences of the relativistic philosophies on which such curricula are based:

> People are bundles of wants; the world is a battlefield of conflicting wants; and no one has room for goodness, decency, or the capacity for a positive exercise of will. Moral maturity is certainly not to be found in the clarification of values, which is cast solely in the language of narrow self-gratification and is devoid of any considerations of decency whatsoever. Finally and ironically, Simon's [the author's] approach emphatically indoctrinates—by encouraging and even exhorting the student to narcissistic self-gratification.[116]

Situational ethics and values clarification courses come with many titles: *Quest, Pumsey's Program,* and *Finding My Way*, to name a few. Whatever the name, though, all share a common goal. Each derives from the intentions of humanists as outlined in the Humanist Manifestos. Consider these selections from the *Humanist Manifesto II*:

> • "We affirm that moral values derive their source from human experiences. Ethics is autonomous and situational, needing no theological or ideological sanction. Ethics stems from human need and interest. To deny this distorts the whole basis of life. Human life has meaning because we create and develop our futures."

• "Happiness and the creative realization of human needs and desires, individually and in shared enjoyment, are continuous themes of humanism. We strive for the good life, here and now."

• "While there is much that we do not know, humans are responsible for what we are or will become. No deity will save us; we must save ourselves."

• "Individuals should be encouraged to realize their own creative talents and desires. We reject all religious, ideological, or moral codes that denigrate the individual, suppress freedom...."

• "The many varieties of sexual exploration should not in themselves be considered evil." [117]

In step with such philosophy, Sidney Simon and Louis E. Raths, clarify the goal of their book, *Values Clarification:*

> To involve students in practical experiences making them aware of their own feelings, their own ideas, their own beliefs, so that the choices and decisions they make are conscious and deliberate, based on their own value system.[118]

And how does this thinking affect parent-child relationships? Richard A. Baer, Jr., in a *Wall Street Journal* article entitled "Parents, Schools, and Values Clarification," explains:

> The originators of values clarification simply assume that their own subjective theory of values is correct....If parents object to their children using pot or engaging in premarital sex, the theory behind values clarification makes it appropriate for the child to respond, "But that's just your value judgment. Don't force it on me."[119]

As long ago as 1988, the U.S. Department of Education, under Ronald Reagan, released a warning about values clarification courses:

> Curricula that emphasizes open-ended decision mak-

ing about using dangerous substances should likewise be rejected. Many curricula marketed are based on the controversial "values clarification" approach to teaching students decision-making skills and ethical standards. Values Clarification is a strategy that avoids leading the students to any particular conclusion, relying instead upon the child's inner feelings and logic to develop a set of values that are consistent with those embraced by the culture at large.[120]

Studies have shown that values clarification courses masquerade as drug and alcohol prevention programs while actually enticing kids to drink and experiment with drugs. After weeks and months of discussing how to use drugs, how they make you feel, and how to get them, a student's natural curiosity is raised dramatically. And since the studies draw no conclusion about what is right or wrong, there is no incentive for kids not to experiment with drugs and alcohol.

Professor William R. Coulson, a one-time promoter of values clarification courses, spent many years warning parents about the dangers of the courses he once helped develop. Professor Coulson reports:

> When I visited the Skills for Adolescence classroom in San Diego, there was a lot of talk about "I feel" statements. There is no way to explain but to say that students were practicing turning morality into reports of feelings. Although Skills for Adolescence is sold explicitly as drug education, there was not talk of drugs in the session I observed, and I was told that, by design, there would be none until the last three weeks of the course. Even then the focus would be on subjectivity and "decision making.[121]

Unfortunately, American parents have been intimated by liberal educational elitists who portray themselves as the "experts." As a result, they often remain silent and leave educational policy up to these specialists who argue that they have the training and experience to know what children really need.

The shocking attitude of a former Arizona superintendent of public instruction, Carolyn Warner, characterizes the position of liberal educational leaders:

Those who educate are more to be honored than those who bear the children. The latter gave them only life, the former teach them the art of living.[122]

"The art of living," according to the humanistic, liberal educrat, is to reject God and to embrace the worldview of Secular Humanism. The undermining of parental authority is all too common among humanist educators who see conservative parents, traditional values, and the Christian worldview as an obstacle to the successful brainwashing of America's children.

Dr. Raymond English, vice president of the Ethics and Public Policy Center, in a speech to the National Advisory Council on Education, Research and Improvement, revealed the dark side of the education establishment:

> Critical thinking means not only learning how to think for oneself, but it also means learning how to subvert the traditional values in your society. You're not thinking critically if you're accepting the values that mommy and daddy taught you. That's not critical.[123]

For years, every Gallup survey has shown that the overwhelming majority of Americans believe in God. Why then do we allow a small minority to determine an educational policy for us that not only denies God, but teaches moral relativism and a philosophy and worldview that contradicts the character and nature of God? Obviously, we shouldn't.

4.5— If it "works" for you then it must be true.
False. (Test question #39)
— **Truth is either nonexistent or unknowable.**
False. (Test question #40)
— **Truth is discovered by mankind, not created by mankind.** *True.* (Test question #41)

Many people today assault the idea of absolute truth by proclaiming that all truth is relative and situational, so individuals must decide what is right or wrong based on each situation they encounter, without reference to any overarching standard. The predominant form of this way of thinking is postmodernism, the belief that truth (and the consequent reality) is not discovered but is created by mankind.

People create truth when they survey a situation and choose a course of action that will give them the most self-serving results. This approach derives from the humanist worldview that proclaims "man is the measure of all things." Therefore people are always guided by doing what is in their own best interests.

If people are the highest measure, then we can decide what is and what is not truth. This is why so many people repeat the catch phrase, "That may be true for you, but it's not true for me."

A postmodern worldview allows that two opposing truth claims can be equal—unless one of the views is based on a fixed moral standard. An "absolute" view is not seen by the postmodernist as being equal but as being unacceptable because it is "intolerant." Christians, on the other hand, believe God created truth for people to discover and that God's truth is for all times, all places, and all people and, further, that all people will be held accountable by God at the end of their lives for what they did with that truth. To the postmodern humanist, Christianity is the enemy, the reason for all problems in our world, the worldview that slows progress, that prohibits equality, and sabotages world peace. Postmodern humanism allows no tolerance for Christianity.

To understand why this is so, consider the source for basic humanist beliefs. *The Humanist Manifesto* states:

> We believe that intolerant attitudes by orthodox religions and puritanical cultures, unduly repress sexual conduct...the many varieties of sexual exploration should not be considered evil...A civilized society should be a tolerant one...

French philosopher Michel Foucault is considered one of the founders of postmodern thinking. Among his ideas, Foucault believed that homosexuality is a species, not an action. Speaking of Foucault in his book, *The Idea of Decline in Western History,* Arthur Herman explains that to Foucault "even the notion of truth itself was a ruse of power."[124] He also reveals Michel Foucault's disturbing life:

> During his visits to the United States in the late seventies, Foucault became fascinated by San Francisco's gay scene with its bathhouses, leather bars, chains, whips, "glory holes," and sadomasochistic rituals.... When Foucault learned that he had contracted AIDS

EDUCATION

105

as the result of his pursuit of sexual transgression, that too became in his mind just another limit-experience: sex as a form of death, as well as the power to give death to others through sex. For at least two years after he contracted AIDS (from 1982 to 1984), Michel Foucault continued to visit his various gay orgy sites, knowingly passing the disease on to his anonymous partners. "We are inventing new pleasures beyond sex," Foucault told an interviewer—in this particular case, sex as murder.[125]

Postmodern thinking allowed Michel Foucault to justify murder in satisfying his deviant pleasures.

Postmodernists claim that each culture or community is free to determine for itself what is right or wrong. Stanley J. Grenz points out in *A Primer on Postmodernism*, "truth is relative to the community in which a person participates. And since there are many communities, there are necessarily many different truths."[126] This postmodern thinking is now frighteningly well accepted by young and old in America.

In a *U.S. News & World Report* article Professor Robert Simon shares his fears about the impact of postmodernism. The example he gives is unnerving. The professor notes that he has never met a student who denies that the Nazi Holocaust took place, but:

What he sees quite often, though, is worse: students who acknowledge the fact of the Holocaust but who can't bring themselves to say that killing millions of people is wrong... "Of course, I dislike the Nazis," one student told Simon, "but who is to say they are morally wrong?" Overdosing on non-judgmentalism is a growing problem in the schools. Two disturbing articles in the *Chronicle of Higher Education* say that some students are unwilling to oppose large moral horrors, including human sacrifice, ethnic cleansing and slavery, because they think that no one has the right to criticize the moral views of another group or culture.[127]

Now why would students say they do not agree with Hitler but cannot say what he did was wrong? It is because humanists have been alarmingly successful in infiltrating America's educational system with the moral relativism and situational ethics of the postmodern worldview. The assault on truth is essential to the successful proliferation of a humanistic worldview in law, science, economics, education, sociology, government, and religion. Humanists must deny fundamental truth in order to be free from the laws of nature and of nature's God. Only then can people genuinely write laws that change to fit whatever evil desires may be chic at a given time, and only then can they assert that morality and the law evolve.

The notion of absolute truth must also be undermined if naturalistic evolution is to successfully replace God as Creator—both of nature and nature's laws—in the minds of millions of Americans. The denying of an all-powerful, all-knowing God that rewards the righteous and punishes the wicked is the ultimate goal of humanism, and promoting evolution is a central strategy for accomplishing that goal. Only if you deny truth can you believe in evolution—which is both unscientific and mathematically impossible.

Humanists must attack truth in order to call evil America's Biblically based economic system of free enterprise that rewards hard work, responsibility, serving customers, and that honors private contracts and private property rights. This is because Secular Humanists' economy of choice is socialism with its unjust and non-Biblical concepts of redistribution of wealth, confiscation of private property, rewarding laziness, and disregard for private contracts and property. Socialism empowers a government to steal what honest, hard-working people have acquired.

In addition, liberals have to attack truth if their humanist organizations are to receive religious, tax-exempt status by the Internal Revenue Service while at the same time telling the courts and the American people their beliefs are secular so they can be the federally funded religion of America's educational system.

They must attack truth to convert Americans to the humanistic definition of marriage and sex. Only through a humanistic worldview can marriage be defined to include same-sex couples, and only through a humanist worldview can sexual promiscuity, experimentation, and an "if it feels good, do it" philosophy be justified.

Humanists attack truth in order to proclaim that human rights are not given by God but rather that rights are granted, secured, and protected by the highest authority that exists, the government. In his book *When Religion Becomes Evil*, Charles Kimball, a college professor at a well-known university, suggests that the hallmark of a religion "becoming evil" is when the religion makes absolute truth claims: "When zealous and devout adherents elevate teachings and belief of

EDUCATION

their tradition to the level of absolute truth, they open the door to the possibility that their religion will become evil." Today's postmodernists believe that any time someone upholds convictions based on absolute moral truth, it reflects intolerance and evil. (Prof. Kimball, by the way, fails to explain how someone with no benchmarks for judgment decides that something is evil.)

America's students are indoctrinated with such anti-Christian propaganda, and the process begins with teachers. One humanist, liberal educator that has brainwashed thousands upon thousands of teachers is Dr. Bill Spady. Spady was one the biggest promoters of outcome-based education in the 1980s and 90s. He encouraged teachers to prepare students to deal with the intolerance of Christian conservatives when he declared:

> Despite the historical trend toward intellectual enlightenment and cultural pluralism, there has been a major rise in religious and political orthodoxy, intolerance, fundamentalism, and conservatism with which young people will have to be prepared to deal.[128]

In September of 2004, former Vice President Al Gore revealed just how dangerous radical, humanist liberals can be when he went after President George W. Bush. President Bush not only called terrorists evil, but he also sought to bring capital punishment upon them through the use of the military. (President Bush also has stated in several interviews that he cannot separate his Christian faith from his job as president.) The worldview of President Bush is offensive to postmodernist Gore, who sees Bush and his Christian faith as evil because the president acknowledges absolute truth and uses his power as commander-in-chief to track down, arrest, and punish the terrorists that attacked America on 9/11.

In a 12,000-word profile on his "life and times" in *The New Yorker* magazine, Gore also revealed how liberals preach tolerance but are generally the most intolerant folks around. Here's how Al Gore characterized the faith of President George W. Bush:

> It's a particular kind of religiosity. It's the American version of the same fundamentalist impulse that we see in Saudi Arabia, in Kashmir, in religions around the world: Hindu, Jewish, Christian, Muslim.[129]

Al Gore equates the president's evangelical Christian faith with Wahhabi Islam, which has led to beheadings, massacres, the September 11th attacks, the killing of children, and countless others.

History is filled with individuals committed to a Secular Humanist worldview, who deny the God of the Bible, and who adhere to pagan philosophies. These beliefs laid the groundwork for justifying abuse, imprisonment, and murder of countless innocent people.

When was the last time a truly evangelical Christian beheaded someone, blew up a building filled with innocent people, flew a plane into an office tower, or slaughtered school children in the name of God? To the contrary, it was Christians and their accompanying worldview that led to the American Red Cross, the Salvation Army, the first American hospitals, the first rescue missions for the homeless, and the pro-life clinics that offer healthcare and adoption services to save thousands of babies from destruction each year.

As politically incorrect as it may be to say this, the worldview of people like Al Gore, John Kerry, and Ted Kennedy is what makes *them* dangerous as they approve and work for the taking of innocent life through abortion—even late-term abortion. The same worldview that has allowed Al Gore and his ilk to vote in favor of legislation and policies that fund the killing of unborn babies is the same worldview that allowed Hitler, Stalin, and Mussolini to justify the murder of millions. Such a comment may seem extreme to some Americans, but the roots of the worldview are the same. They are not built on a genuine compassion for anyone.

Founding Father Dr. John Witherspoon would doubtless agree that most of today's radical, Secular Humanists are enemies of America:

> [H]e is the best friend to American liberty who is most sincere and active in promoting true and undefiled religion and who sets himself with the greatest firmness to bear down on profanity and immorality of every kind. Whoever is an avowed enemy of God, I scruple not [do not hesitate] to call him an enemy to his country.[130]

Indeed, religion can be evil. Islam is an evil and violent religion. However, I contend that Al Gore and Professor Kimball are wrong when they decry the moral absolutes of Christianity as evil. History reveals that the twentieth century was the bloodiest of all centuries, and Secular Humanism was the foundational worldview (the religion) of those who committed every one of the atrocities.

Today's postmodern adults and students are so consumed with being tolerant and nonjudgmental that there are those who say we should not even call wrong or evil the terrorists that attacked America on September 11, 2001. In a *Time* magazine essay entitled "God Is Not on My side. Or Yours," Roger Rosenblatt declares:

> One would like to think that God is on our side against the terrorists, because the terrorists are wrong and we are in the right, and any deity worth his salt would be able to discern that objective truth. But this is simply good-hearted arrogance cloaked in morality—the same kind of thinking that makes people decide that God created humans in his own image. The God worth worshipping is the one who pays us the compliment of self-regulation, and we might return it by minding our own business.[131]

In a more palatable vein, Yale University student Alison Hornstein wrote in the December 17, 2001, issue of *Newsweek* an article entitled "The Question That We Should Be Asking—Is Terrorism Wrong?". "My generation may be culturally sensitive," she notes, "but we hesitate to make moral judgments." After that dramatic understatement, she continues:

> Student reactions expressed in the daily newspaper and in class pointed to the differences between our life circumstances and those of the perpetrators, suggesting that these differences had caused the previous day's events. Noticeably absent was a general outcry of indignation at what had been the most successful terrorist attack of our lifetime. These reactions and similar ones on other campuses have made it apparent that my generation is uncomfortable assessing, or even asking whether a moral wrong has taken place.[132]

In her article, Alison describes how on September 12, one day after the murder of more than 3,000 people at the hands of Islamic terrorists:

> A professor said he did not see much difference between Hamas suicide bombers and American soldiers who died fighting in World War II. When I saw one or two students nodding in agreement, I raised my

hand. I believed ... there is a considerable distinction. American soldiers, in uniform, did not have a policy of specifically targeting civilians; suicide bombers, who wear plainclothes, do. The professor didn't call on me. The people who did get a chance to speak cited various provocations for terrorism; not one of them questioned its morality.[133]

Along with its overarching dismal consequences, postmodernism has one monumental philosophical problem: It cannot possibly be true. Because God is truth, postmodernism is false. Man did not create God. Postmodernism is the belief that truth is created by man, not discovered. This is the logical equivalent of saying that the painting created the painter. God created man; man did not create God.

While moral relativism is the belief that there is no absolute standard of right or wrong or good or evil, God is always the same, always good, and always opposed to evil. That means truth is truth.

4.6— The National Education Association's (NEA's) primary goal has always been the education of children in academic subjects. *False.* (Test question #42)

The best explanation for this question is found in one of my previous books, *One Nation Under Man?*. Here's the key passage in its entirety:

> The NEA is so liberal it refuses to give quarter to any opinions of the conservatives who are forced to join in order to receive the necessary teacher liability insurance. Phyllis Schlafly notes:
>
> > The NEA accords no rights to the 30 percent of NEA members who are Republicans. Since 1976 when the NEA became a big player in national politics by supporting Jimmy Carter, the NEA has endorsed a Democrat for President in every election.[134]
>
> Bill Bennett, the former U.S. Secretary of Education, made this comment regarding the NEA: "You're looking at the absolute heart and center of the Democratic Party."[135]

Both the NEA and the ACLU work closely with the DNC to further liberal policies in America. David Limbaugh observes:

> It would be ludicrous for the NEA to deny its political activism. In 1996, it employed more political operatives than both major political parties combined. It would be just as ridiculous for it to deny its liberalism, but it does, claiming to be bipartisan. But since the NEA established its Political Action Committee in 1972, it has supported and endorsed every Democratic presidential candidate and has overwhelmingly supported Democratic candidates at the congressional level as well.[136]

In January 1999, *Investor's Business Daily* published an article delineating the NEA's liberal agenda and commitment to the liberal Democratic party:

> The nation's largest teacher union wants the U.S. to nationalize health care, start a nuclear freeze, adopt national energy policies and pass more gun-control laws. Yet it doesn't want teachers tested or schools privatized...The NEA has long backed a left-wing political agenda. Many of its proposals seem far removed from improving teachers' working conditions...The NEA's political action committee spent $6 million in the '96 election cycle, ninety-nine percent of its political action committee donations to candidates went to Democrats.[137]

Another test to see where an organization stands is to note who they consider to be their enemies. While the NEA is supposedly the great preserver of "the 3 R's" in American education, its "public enemy number 1" is the "2 R's." Yes, the NEA considers the Religious Right its nemesis. In 1997, the NEA published a guide for its members that explained how to oppose the "Radical Right" (as the NEA calls the Religious Right). So, allow me to say it clearly: The NEA, the ACLU, Americans United for the Separation of Church and State, and the Democratic National Committee are specifically opposed to a Christian worldview.[138]

4. Follow-up—For Further Thought about Education

1. Name of five dead humanists that still have an impact on America's educational system.

2. John Dewey wrote that the purpose of the government schools is not academics and the obtaining of cognitive knowledge. What did he claim to be the purpose?

3. Write down four facts about Benjamin Bloom and what he believed.

4. What is the goal of outcome-based education?

5. What are the four pillars for the Chinese model for life-long learning?

6. If fully implemented on a national level, what will the future hold for Christian and God-fearing students that believe in moral absolute truth if they don't conform to the humanist worldview?

7. What is the goal of values clarification courses?

8. What does Karl Marx in the Tenth Plank of the Communist Manifesto call for, and how are America's humanistic liberals implementing this policy?

EDUCATION

SECTION 5—FAMILY

5.1— Individual freedoms would be advanced and protected through a one-world government under the authority of the United Nations. *False.* (Test question #43)

The Bible and the Gospel of Jesus Christ are based upon moral absolutes. As a result, many individuals and organizations—including the United Nations—go to great lengths to suppress this truth for which they have such hatred. In 1995, for instance, the United Nations Educational Scientific and Cultural Organization prepared the International Declaration of Principles on Tolerance that stated: "Tolerance is respect, acceptance and appreciation of the rich diversity of our world's cultures...it is not only a moral duty, it is also a political and legal requirement."

There is actually a desire by the United Nations to make laws enforcing "tolerance." That means if you were charged with being intolerant, you could be found guilty of a crime punishable by the state. The UN document goes on to say:

- "Intolerance is a global threat."

- "Tolerance involves the rejection of dogmatism, and absolutism."

- "Tolerance means that one's views are not to be imposed on others."

Note the use of the word "impose." If the UN ever accomplishes its goal of making tolerance a legal standard, sharing the Gospel of Jesus Christ could become illegal. In fact, many nations have already adopted this UN policy.

"Protecting children" becomes another doorway for UN incursion on individual freedoms. As a former board member of the radically liberal Children's Defense Fund, now Senator Hillary Clinton actively supports the United Nations Convention on the Rights of the Child. While the idea of "children's rights" may sound nice, this is just one more effort by liberal agents of change to demean and negate traditional family values. In November 1973, *The Harvard Educational Review* published then Hillary Rodham's radical views of children's rights in an article entitled, "Children Under the Law." In her article, Ms. Rodham (now Clinton) stated that some children "may have interest independent of their parents or the state."[139] Senator Clinton disapproves of "the belief that families are private, non-political units whose interests subsume those of children."[140] In other words, she prefers to view the child as distinct from the family.

With that in mind, it is no wonder Hillary suggests that age restrictions on children's activities must be legally justified:

> The state should no longer be allowed to assume the rationality of regulations based upon age, and should at least be required to justify its action on the basis of modern legislative or administrative findings.[141]

And what does that mean? Dr. Dennis Cuddy, nationally syndicated columnist and former U.S. Department of Education official, explains that Senator Clinton is really saying, "If individuals can vote at eighteen years of age, drive at sixteen, and have sex and abortions at a particular age, then the state should have to justify why they're not allowed to do those things at earlier ages."[142]

In an article in the October 1992 issue of *Harper's* magazine, Christopher Lasch defined Senator Clinton's opinion this way:

> The traditional family is, for the most part, an institution in need of therapy, an institution that stands in the way of children's rights—an obstacle to enlightened adults.... She condemns the State's assumption of parental responsibilities, not because she has any faith in parents themselves but because she is opposed to the principle of parental authority in any form....Her writings leave the unmistakable impression that it is the family that holds children back; it is the state that sets them free.[143]

Why all this emphasis on the "state"? Could it be that Hillary plans to use the federal government to set children free from parental authority? Why would she want to do that?

Similarly, what is the purpose for the United Nations Convention on the Rights of the Child, and who came up with this idea anyway? The pretext for the convention was provided by Poland in 1979 as their contribution to the Year of the Child. And remember: In 1979, Poland was controlled by a Marxist-Leninist, socialistic government. Does that give you an idea of why this treaty is so dangerous—and why Hillary is no friend of the family?

Let's be clear about what constitutes some of the legal "rights" that would be guaranteed by the UN Convention on the Rights of the Child. Consider this sweeping statement proposed by the treaty: "The right of every child to a standard of living adequate for the child's physical, mental, spiritual, moral, and social development." Again, it may sound good at first blush, but who will determine the adequacy of these intangible factors? On what basis will judges and social workers determine what is "adequate"? Social workers certainly are a likely candidate for the job. Yet consider the track record they display. An Alabama social worker once testified under oath that even if she received anonymous complaints against the governor himself, she would need to inspect his home, no matter what evidence was offered to rebut the allegations.[144]

What if your sixteen-year-old son demands his own car upon receiving his driver's license, and you won't provide him one? He could claim that he is not living in an environment adequate for his physical, mental, or social development and bring the state into the argument against you. What if your family only has one car and your son is unable to go out with his friends on a Friday night because you are using the car? Will you have hindered his "social development"? Not to mention that you may also have deprived him of his "right to freedom of association and peaceful assembly," according to Article 15 of the UN Convention on the Rights of the Child.

Does this sound far-fetched? Not if you are aware of what is taking place in courts across America today. The Supreme Court of Washington state recently ruled that it was *not* a violation of parents' rights to remove a child from her family because she objected to the parents' "reasonable rules which were reasonably enforced." The parents had grounded their eighth-grade daughter because she wanted to smoke marijuana and sleep with her boyfriend. She objected, and the court removed her from the home.[145] That alone should take your breath away, but the implications of the UN action are far more sweeping. Article 13 of the Convention lists the right of every child (any individual under 18) to be:

> The right of freedom of expression; this right shall include freedom to seek, receive and impart information and ideas of all kinds, regardless of frontiers,

FAMILY

either orally, in writing or in print, in the form of art, or through any other media of the child's choice.

This article would give the child the *right* to view pornography whether in print or through the computer. You would be in violation of the law if you tried to prevent it. Every child would have the right of "access to information and material from a diversity of national and international sources," and the state must "encourage the mass media to disseminate information and material of social and cultural benefit to the child" as well as "encourage the production and dissemination of children's books" (Article 17).

Again: Who will decide the content of these "children's books" to be produced and disseminated by the state? Can we trust the same government who funds blasphemous and homo-erotic art through the National Endowment for the Arts to decide what is of "social and cultural benefit"? What about parents who don't want their children reading books the state has deemed as "information"?

Just so you'll know, other "rights" provided for under the UN Convention include:

- The right of "freedom of thought, conscience, and religion" (Art. 14);

- The right of the child to "education" (Art. 28);

- The "right . . . to benefit from child-care services" (Art. 18);

- The "right of the disabled child to special care" (Art. 23).

I have no problem with the right of every child to receive an education, or for the disabled to receive necessary care. Potential problems arise, however, from the vague wording of many of these rights. Hillary Clinton believes that some families can go "to the point of depriving [children] of an advanced worldly education."[146] Most of the Christians I know are doing everything they can to keep their kids from having a "worldly" education!

The question then becomes: How do Hillary, the UN, and other "agents of change" define education? If you home school your child or send him or her to a private school that does not fit the government definition of an "education," will you then be guilty of depriving your child of an education? Obviously, the UN and company are not opening the doors to greater freedom but to more totalitarian-style control.

What about Article 23, which provides for the rights of the disabled child? Who will determine which children are disabled? Liberal educators regularly hand out new disability labels. What if your child is determined to have dyslexia or have ADD (attention deficit disorder)—or any of myriad other so-called disorders? What if you don't want your child to take Ritalin or some other mind-altering drug to control his or her hyperactivity? Suppose you refuse to allow your child to take part in special classes, programs, or courses—many of which are filled with psycho-babble, New Age thinking, and humanistic garbage. Will you then be depriving your "disabled" child from special services?

Consider this frightening real-life example. A school guidance counselor examined a first grader and diagnosed the child as hyperactive. The counselor recommended psychotherapy. In response, the mother took her daughter to four sessions but stopped after concluding that the little girl's problems were due to the classroom environment at school and not the result of any personal or emotional issues. It was also apparent that counseling was not helping her daughter. When the mother refused to take the daughter back to therapy, social workers removed the child from the home. The court, claiming the right to intervene whenever "medical intervention will have a beneficial effect," ruled the mother guilty of child neglect.[147]

There are children in this country and around the world who do not receive the kind of love and nurture that every child craves and needs. And there are parents who do not take the responsibility of parenting seriously, some of whom should have children removed from their custody because of physical or sexual abuse. Nevertheless, this does not mean the problem in our nation is so great that *all* parents should have the rights of parenting taken from them. Why strip the constitutional freedoms of the majority in order to get at an irresponsible minority? There is no cause or justification for such action.

Article 37 of the UN Convention on the Rights of the Child provides every child "deprived of his or her liberty" with the right of free legal counsel and access to the courts to let his or her case be heard. Will children be encouraged by their public school teachers, guidance counselors, school nurses, school phychologists, or friends to sue you the next time you deprive them of their liberty? Under the right of freedom of religion, you could be sued by your child for forcing him or her to go to church with you. Under the right of freedom of expression, you could be sued by your child if you refuse to let her pierce her nose or deny him the "right" to wear a T-shirt with profanity written on it.

In a report for the Family Research Council, Dr. Lucier, a former congressional staffer, explains how these "rights" could be used against parents:

> The child is guaranteed these rights, no matter what the parents' religion, political, or other opinion. If the parents, on the basis of their religion or political views, or even ethical views, object to the so-called "rights" guaranteed in the Constitution, the state must step in and uphold those rights "irrespective" of the parents' opinion. The state, or agency acting on behalf of the child, can sue in court against the parents so that the child can think what it pleases, and associate with whomever it pleases....If parents refuse to grant these rights, even on the basis of conscientiously held religious or other opinions, the child may be removed from the parents "when competent authorities subject to judicial review determine, in accordance with applicable law and procedures, that such separation is necessary for the best interests of the child."[148]

Common sense tells us that any treaty built on ideas from the the one-time communist regime of Poland cannot be good for America, Americans, or U.S. Constitutional freedoms. So why do liberals want such a treaty? The answer is clear: To undermine parental authority and to take all power, control, and influence away from moms and dads.

Author and syndicated columnis Thomas Sowell provides this warning:

> Parents are the greatest obstacle to any brainwashing of children...if parents cannot be gotten out of the picture or at least moved to the periphery, the whole brainwashing operation is jeopardized.[149]

Such brainwashing is not new. In the 1940s, Nazi Germany tried to do away with parental influence. In her book, *The Story of the Von Trapp Family Singers,* Maria von Trapp recalls her childhood experience with the Nazis:

FAMILY

> This morning we were told [by the Nazis] at the [school] assembly that our parents are nice, old-fashioned people who don't understand the new Party. We should leave them alone and not bother. We are the hope of the nation, the hope of the world. We should never mention at home what we learn at school now.[150]

The United Nations Convention on the Rights of the Child gives children the right to do almost anything. Why do I say *almost* anything? Because there is one very important right that this treaty does not grant every child: It does not give a child the right to say, "I was wrong."

When, in a moment of anger and rebellion, a child picks up the phone and files a complaint against his or her parents for supposedly violating one of the "liberties" given by the UN, this treaty does not give the child the right to say later, "I was wrong." The treaty does not allow the child to change his or her mind and have the complaint withdrawn.

Your child is sure to receive at school or through radio or television the proper number to call when he feels his liberties have been violated. How many parents will find themselves embroiled in a court case or being subjected to the regular visits of a social worker simply because their child got angry and made a call which the child later regrets but cannot reverse? Who will provide the official interpretation of this treaty? A group of parents? Certainly not. Even the interpretation will be up to the UN—through its Committee on Children.

In Great Britain and some European countries, the committee has already determined that it is in the best interests of the child to outlaw corporal punishment and conduct public education campaigns to accept the prohibition of corporal punishment. That means it becomes illegal for parents to spank their children.

The Associated Press reported in August 1995 that a Norwegian father who smacked his four-year-old daughter on the bottom was fined $470 for violating Norway's strict child protection law. The law bars corporal punishment—even in the privacy of a family's home.

But the UN goes even further. The committee wants to limit the rights of parents to withdraw their children from sex education classes and intends to change laws so as to increase the ability of children to participate in their parents' decisions concerning them.[151]

The socialist, liberal agenda, with their one-world viewpoint, seeks to take away America's pride, prestige, and prosperity. They know the best way to do that is to remove any influence that traditional family values may have on children. When all else fails, they must resort to removing children from homes that are not politically and socially correct. In order to do that, they need laws on the books that will give social workers, teachers, judges, and psychologists the authority to determine whether you are a fit parent and whether or not your child's "rights" are being denied.

And what is the present status of the UN Convention on the Rights of the Child? It was "approved by the UN General Assembly on November 20, 1989, and entered into force on September 2, 1990, after the 20th nation ratified."[152] So far, liberals and social engineers in the United States have done a fine job of sugar-coating this bitter pill that they hope Americans will swallow. During the first years of the Clinton Administration, 47 U.S. Senators in the 103rd Congress co-sponsored the U.S. proposal in the Senate, called for the president to sign the treaty and send it to the Senate to be ratified.

If the United Nations Convention on the Rights of the Child is ever ratified by a two-thirds majority vote by the U.S. Senate, it would become the law of the land—as the U.S. Constitution Article 6, paragraph 2 states:

> This Constitution and the laws of the United States which shall be made in Pursuance thereof; and all treaties made, or which shall be made, under the authority of the United States, shall be the supreme law of the land; and the judges in every state shall be bound thereby, any Thing in the Constitution or Laws of any State to the contrary notwithstanding.

If this treaty is passed, Christian parents in America will find themselves on the wrong side of the law of the land. It will represent the greatest restriction of freedoms yet foisted on the American people.

5.2— The federal government should fund school-based health clinics which would include safe-sex counseling. *False.* (Test question #44)

Liberals claim that America needs school-based clinics for children whose parents who cannot afford medical treatment, but this is a groundless argument. Nearly every state requires a student

FAMILY

to have a physical exam before a child can enter school, and any parent—regardless of economic circumstances—can take his or her child to the doctor, thanks to both state and federal programs which provide medical treatment and examinations for underprivileged children.

The real motive behind encouraging school-based clinics is to foster the illicit sexual worldview of those who promote them. Already, the problem of school prerogative in student healthcare is out of control in some places. In Nebraska, for example, minor girls can be taken from school *without their parent's permission or knowledge* by school officials to receive an abortion. Although schools cannot give a child an aspirin without a permission slip signed by the parent, school authorities can take her to an abortionist without parental consent or knowledge. Citizens in Nebraska are working to rectify this absurdity by making it illegal for school officials to take a minor to an abortion provider, but meanwhile, the illogic of the situation demonstrates the true motives behind school-based care. It's not about student health but about the liberal agenda to "normalize" all manner of sexual behavior and to make sure the younger generation grows up feeling that any form of sexual deviancy is "OK."

Liberals advocate for school-based clinics (SBC) where students receive everything from abortion counseling to contraceptives to forced genital exams. In March 1996 I received a phone call from concerned parents in East Stroudsburg, Pennsylvania. Knowing that I was the education reporter and periodic guest host of *The Michael Reagan Show*, these angry parents believed that if more people were aware of what had happened to their eleven- and twelve-year-old daughters their tragedy would not be repeated in another city or state. Let me explain what happened.

Katie and Paul Tucker, the parents of one child involved, told me that the girls coming out of the school nurse's office were crying and telling the other girls standing in line in their underclothes, waiting their turn, that the nurse was performing genital exams. Many of the girls, including the Tuckers' daughter, began to cry and requested to call their mothers. One or two girls attempted to climb out of the window in order to avoid the procedure. The Tuckers' daughter was told to lie down on the table and stop fighting the nurse or they would call in school security to hold her down.

Upon confirming the details, I took the story to Michael Reagan, and that night we broke the story on his national radio show. For the next several days Mike and I reviewed the developing facts and national reaction to the abuse of these 59 little girls. I invited Katie and Paul

FAMILY

Tucker to join the program by phone so listeners could hear the agony and righteous anger of one of the girls' parents. I then contacted the *Washington Times* and invited one of their reporters to interview Katie and Paul Tucker about the East Stroudsburg incident and the national trend of school-based clinics where such activity would become commonplace. The *Washington Times* reported the story as follows:

> [The girls] were marched to the school nurse's office, ordered to take off their clothes and then examined by a female pediatrician. The girls were scared. They were crying and trying to run out the door, but one of the nurses was blocking the door so they couldn't leave. "My daughter told the other nurse that, 'My mother wouldn't like this. I want to call her. And they said no.' And my daughter said, 'I don't want this test to be done.' And the nurse said, 'too bad.'"[153]

> A May 6, 1996, *Washington Times* article reported: The physician reportedly put the girls in a room and had them lie down on a table, spread-eagle, with nothing covering them. In a fax received from the East Stroudsburg Area School District they claim that all parents were notified. Some of the parents admit that they were notified of the physical but there was absolutely no mention of any type of genital exam. According to The Rutherford Institute in a press release dated May 10th, 1996, "One girl's parents even sent the permission slip back to the school denying it permission to examine their child—but the school examined her anyway."[154]

> According to the March 22, 1996, issue of the *Pocono Record* newspaper, a community doctor commenting on the situation told the paper that, "Even a parent doesn't have the right to say what's appropriate for a physician to do when they're doing an exam."[155]

Yes, parental authority is under assault.

After The Rutherford Institute sued on behalf of several of the girls and their families, justice to some degree was rendered:

> U.S. District Judge A. Richard Caputo ruled....that the

East Stroudsburg School District violated the Fourth Amendment rights of 59 6th grade girls.....The judge ruled that the exams constituted "unreasonable searches," and said he "could not identify a compelling government reason to examine the genitals."[156]

Two days later, the jury returned a verdict against the district, awarding a total of $60,000 in damages, or $7,500 for each of the eight student plaintiffs in the lawsuit. The jury did not award damages to the parents. The physician who performed the exams reached an out-of-court settlement with the girl's families.[157]

When parents asked why the exams were done, some were told the school was looking for evidence of sexual abuse. The real abuse, of course, was exacted on the girls by those looking for evidence of sexual abuse.

Similar stories have been reported all over the nation and will only become more frequent as parental authority breaks down and school-based clinics become more commonplace. Attorney John Eldredge reveals yet another tragic story involving young girls victimized by school counselors and abortion doctors:

> Abortion has been one of the most emotionally charged issues in America since it was legalized in 1973. While it may be legal, not everything that is legal is moral, and abortion is clearly immoral. We have a tendency to forget that the statistics we read in our newspapers and the reports we hear on the nightly news represent the lives of real people.
>
> Numbers like 1.6 million abortions every year can be overwhelming. For many of us, figures like these are too much to comprehend. Perhaps we can relate to one woman and one child whose life is in question.
>
> Rachel was 17 when she learned she was pregnant. Her high school counselor recommended she have an abortion and arranged for state funding and recommended a particular abortion clinic. No other alternatives were discussed. Rachel was afraid to tell her parents that she had become pregnant. Unaware of any alternatives, she consented to the abortion.
>
> Several days later she developed flu-like symptoms in her chest. She went to her family doctor, but she

125

did not tell him about the abortion because she did not think the symptoms were related. Sometime later, Rachel became so sick her father took her to a local hospital. The next morning she was found in a comatose condition.

Subsequently, it was discovered that she had developed bacterial endocarditis — a condition directly attributable to a post-abortion surgical infection. The bacterial endocarditis had caused blood clots to develop and become lodged in the vascular system of her brain, causing a stroke. When Rachel recovered from her coma, she was left permanently wheelchair-bound. Why was it not required by law that her parents know before the procedure ever happened?

Rachel's story is not uncommon, although the consequences for her were particularly extreme. Consider also the millions of women and girls who undergo deep physical and emotional distress as a result of abortion. Add to that all of the butchered children who if allowed to live would have been starting kindergarten this year, or playing on the varsity team, or going off to college, but were never given a chance.[158]

With school-based clinics, the only winners are the champions of that cause in their quest to undermine American life.

5.3— Christians should love themselves and have a healthy and positive self-image according to contemporary standards. *False.* (Test question #45)

Joel Osteen, Robert Schuler, and many of today's postmodern pastors preach and teach the need to love yourself or to grasp a positive self-image. But is this Biblical? Should our focus be on our own self-worth?

Those who argue that self-love, self-esteem, or having a healthy self-image are Biblical often justify their teaching by using Leviticus 19:18, which Jesus quotes in Luke 10:27—"you shall love your neighbor as yourself." In the Leviticus passage, God's instructions include a list of ways we should treat other individuals respectfully in our daily conduct. The direction never shifts from social interaction to descriptions of inner worship or affirmation of one's own goodness.

FAMILY

When Jesus uses the passage, He clearly is saying that Christians should automatically look out for the best interests of others and not simply to think of their own well-being, even though self-interest would be the natural (but in many instances sinful) reflex of every human. Jesus' instruction is an admonishment to avoid being selfish or self-centered.

Self-love in Leviticus and Luke refers to a person's natural compulsion to watch out for his or her own welfare. In the physical realm, this allows people to survive. It is an instinctive, basal motivation that does not require a lengthy decision-making process. The impulse seeks to gain pleasure and avoid pain. It compels a person to eat when he is hungry and sleep when he is tired. It is the kind of self-love that causes you to look both ways before crossing the street, to brush your teeth so they do not rot, to wear a helmet when mountain-biking through rough terrain, or to get out of the pool when you hear thunder so as not to be struck by lightning. It is that unlearned, intuitive prompting that gives human beings enough sense to "get in out of the rain."[159]

Biblical self-love is common to all people—Christians as well as non-Christians—and in neither is it based on a conscious understanding of a person's value to God or the *imago Dei*. This self-love is instinctive, spontaneous, and effortless. It needs no lessons, encouragement, or therapy. Impulse drives it, and consistency characterizes it. Esteem, on the other hand, takes us into another category of thinking altogether.

It is difficult to justify contemporary notions of self-love when we are called to *die* to self, to pick up our crosses, and hate our own lives (Luke 14: 26, 27). The Bible tells us to boast only in Christ and the work of the cross (Galatians 6:14), to have confidence in the Lord and not in our own works or abilities apart from Christ (Proverbs 14:6). In 2 Corinthians 12:9 we are told to boast in our weaknesses so the power of Christ may be seen in us.

To teach self-esteem—or its corollary, mankind's basic goodness—is to say that man really was not 100% in need of Jesus Christ and His sacrifice on the cross. People were pretty much good enough to face judgment, and perhaps all the cross really did was to shore up our natural human failings, shortcomings, or flaws—not redeem some overwhelming condition like *depravity*.

The truth is, we are not good, honorable, or deserving of respect based on self. Only in and through Christ Jesus do the fruit and actions of my life have merit. And that merit is not about *my*self

FAMILY

but about Christ Jesus and His saving work. The action or work that is worthy of merit can only happen when I die to self as described in Romans 6 and 8.

This dying to self is so complete that it may even require the giving up of the self-preservation style of love I said earlier is legitimate. The Christian that has surrendered his or her life to Christ may be called to reject even this natural reflex and accept places and positions that are not safe, secure, comfortable, and free of danger.

If the martyrs of Christian history had put the natural reflex of self-love before their Christian calling, they would have done what was in the best interest of self-preservation rather than submit to premature death. But by preaching the gospel when it was illegal, punishments, torture, and death were often assured. The martyrs denied the reflex of self-preservation because they placed a higher priority on fulfilling the will of God through their lives.

The challenge for the true convert of Christ in today's postmodern world is to be quick to recognize and reject the false teaching of self-love as taught by its humanistic and psychological proponents. We also must be willing to reject the natural reflex of self-comfort and self-preservation when it comes in conflict with God's desire for us and our living out Biblical truth.

5.4— Elementary-aged children cannot understand Christian doctrine, and thus it would be a waste of time to teach them such things until junior high school.
False. (Test question #46)
— **By training the heart of a child to obey God, parents train him or her to be pleasers of God, not of men, whereas if parents teach children to obey so they avoid punishment, a scolding, or to receive an award, parents are training them to jump through hoops so as to keep the parents happy.** *True.* (Test question #47)

The Bible instructs parents to "train up a child in the way he should go, and when he is old he will not depart from it" (Proverbs 22:6). But is this business of training just so our children will be well-behaved and make us look good in public? Or is it so they will seek God? In his excellent book *Shepherding a Child's Heart*, Tedd Tripp outlines why we must intently train our children:

Therefore, your parenting goal cannot simply be well-behaved children...your concern is to unmask your child's sin, helping him to understand how it reflects a heart that has strayed. That leads to the cross of Christ. It underscores the need for a Savior.[160]

The central focus of childrearing is to bring children to a sober assessment of themselves as sinners. They must understand the mercy of God, who offered Christ as a sacrifice for sinners. How is that accomplished? You must address the heart as the fountain of behavior and the conscience as the God-given judge of right and wrong. The cross of Christ must be the central focus of your childrearing... the focal point of your discipline and correction must be your children seeing their utter inability to do the things that God requires unless they know the help and strength of God.[161]

The vast necessity of training children can be summarized in five central goals for a Christian parent. We train our children so they will do these things:

1. Seek God
• Although King Jehoshaphat of Judah—according to 2 Chronicles 19:3—was not saved, he had taken steps to prepare his heart to seek God: he removed idols from his land. Just as the non-believing king prepared himself for God, we can prepare the hearts of our children early on to seek God by making sure they have no idols in the way.

2. Acknowledge their sinfulness, repent, and follow Jesus Christ as Savior and Lord of their life.
• 1 Thessalonians 5:23—"...and may your whole spirit, soul, and body be preserved blameless at the coming of our Lord Jesus Christ."

3. Live a life centered around pleasing God, not men, by doing His will *from the heart*, not as a legalistic compulsion.
• Ephesians 6:6-7—"...as bondservants of Christ, doing the will of God from the heart, with goodwill doing service, as to the Lord, and not to men..."

FAMILY

• Romans 6:17—"...you obeyed from the heart that form of doctrine to which you were delivered..."
• Matthew 22:37—"Jesus said to him, "'You shall love the Lord your God with all your heart, with all your soul, and with all your mind." This is the first and great commandment.'"

4. Fulfill the Great Commission: To make disciples who follow Jesus Christ.
• Ezra 7:10—"...For Ezra had prepared his heart to seek the Law of the Lord, and to do it, and to teach statutes and ordinances in Israel." Here is an example of preparing the heart to seek God and His laws and to teach them to others.
• 1 Peter 3:15—"But sanctify the Lord God in your hearts, and always be ready to give a defense to everyone who asks you a reason for the hope that is in you, with meekness and fear..."

5. Have a comprehensive Biblical worldview so as to understand the times and know what God would have them do.
• 1 Chronicles 12:32 tells us that in Israel there were men "who had understanding of the times, to know what Israel ought to do..."

Unless our children know the Bible, they will not be thoroughly equipped for every good work. It is impossible to apply a Biblical worldview to our laws, science, economics, history, families, government, religion, and social issues unless we know the doctrines of Scripture.

Doctrine is all about the will of God and the Gospel—Jesus taught doctrine during His earthly ministry. To ignore doctrine is to ignore God's commandments, the teachings of Jesus Christ, and what the Bible reveals concerning salvation. In order for children to understand God, we must teach them the moral law, because moral law is a reflection of God's character and nature. Everything consistent with the character and nature of God is truth, and everything contrary is untruth.

Parents must connect the Word of God, the moral law, and Christian doctrine with the character and nature of God. It gives a very

FAMILY

skewed picture simply to tell a child to do or not to do something ONLY because the Bible says so. The Bible "says so" because of God's nature. If we teach our children that the Bible is a book of rules for behavior, then we are leading them down the road to legalism and rebellion. Rather, we must be clear that the Word of God reveals God Himself. He wants us to model His character so we can bring honor and glory to Him, be witnesses to the unsaved, and enter a deeper relationship with Him. The moral law reveals the disease as well as the need for the cure, which is only found in salvation through Jesus Christ.

Remember: the purpose of our training is to prepare the soil of our children's hearts so they will seek God for themselves and be convicted of sinfulness and the need to repent. Forcing or coercing children to "pray a sinner's prayer" will not save them but only make false converts. I know this well from personal experience. At the age of five, I prayed a "sinner's prayer," and at seven I walked the aisle to join our church and be baptized. For years, I used these acts to affirm my salvation. I learned to "perform," to do what was expected of me, or to do what I knew would make other Christians respect and accept me.

I played the "game" even though I didn't know I was playing a game. I thought I was saved because I had prayed the right prayer, walked the aisle, and was baptized. It was not until I read *Revival's Golden Key* by Ray Comfort that I understood my total depravity and need for Biblical repentance. (Ray Comfort's book is now titled *Way of the Master* and is available in our online bookstore at www.worldview-weekend.com). Ray reveals Biblical teachings about the moral law— the lost key to understanding why we need salvation. Subsequently, I worked out my salvation with "fear and trembling" and went from false to true conversion.

Studies show that, before they graduate from college, 70 to 88 percent of young people from *Christian* homes end up rejecting the faith they claimed to possess. When you consider the foundation of sand upon which worldviews are often built, it becomes evident why theirs collapses when secular winds and waves of skepticism, criticism, unbelief, and doubt undermine them.

Regrettably, the worldview of a typical Christian parent, Sunday School teacher, youth leader, and even pastor in America has been far too influenced by the thinking of the world. As a result, it is not really hard to understand why students graduate from our church youth groups and move on from Christian homes doctrinally illiterate, only to become easy prey for the enemy waiting to devour them. They have not truly opened their minds and hearts to sound doctrine. They have

FAMILY

not repented of their sins and yielded to Christ.

If we have not trained the hearts and minds of our children to love sound doctrinal teachings, then we should not be surprised that three-fourths of them eventually walk away from the faith in college. Unlike some of us, writers of Scripture were not in denial on this point. They warned that drifting from faith could happen:

> Beware lest anyone cheat you through philosophy and empty deceit, according to the tradition of men, according to the basic principles of the world, and not according to Christ. (Colossians 2:8)

One of the greatest rewards as a parent is watching children live committed, godly lives. Christians should commit to rise above the world's standard of *good* parenting and make their goal *godly* parenting so Christ can be glorified in their lives and families.

5. Follow-up—For Further Thought about Family

1. List some of the goals of the United Nations that would damage Christian families and freedom.

2. What do Secular Humanists hope to accomplish by having school-based clinics?

3. What did Jesus mean by "love your neighbor as yourself"?

4. What is the Biblical definition of self-love?

5. From where does man gain his real worth and value?

6. If a low-self esteem is not man's deepest problem, what is man's real problem and how can that problem be solved?

7. How does the Bible verse, "When I am weak, then He is strong" apply to this discussion?

8. What is the world's definition of self-love, and how is it contrary to fulfilling the commandment to love your neighbor as yourself?

9. What is the goal of the moral law?

10. Why is it important that parents train the heart of their child?

11. How can a parent prepare the heart of a child to follow Christ?

12. What is Biblical doctrine?

13. List three of the foundational doctrines of Christianity.

FAMILY

SECTION 6—RELIGION

6.1— Adam and Eve were mythical characters who never really lived. *False.* (Test question #48)

Skeptics commonly complain that so many bad things happen in the world that it must be that God does not care. Often the "bad things" are used as an argument for atheism.

While there is great evil in the world, people who blame it on God have it backwards. None of the bad is God's fault. It is *our* fault. *People* do the bad things, and it started with the first two people, Adam and Eve. They are clearly described in the Bible as historical characters whose actions had consequences for all people who have come after them. The account of what happened follows directly from the creation narrative and leads seamlessly into the chronological record that follows.

To see why evil is really our fault, you have to pay attention to what happened when Adam and Eve committed the first sin. Eve bought the lie of Satan that she could become like God Himself by eating the fruit God had told Adam and Eve not to eat. It set people up to think they could be in charge of everything—both good and evil.

Adam and Eve now had to suffer the consequences of their sin. The consequence was based straightforwardly on their choice to "do things their own way," not God's. This is how what we know as sin entered into the world. You could say that because of Adam and Eve, all humanity "wanted it this way." And so came death, disease, suffering, and all sorts of evil. God had planned to provide everything they needed, but because Adam and Eve decided they didn't want God around, they were forced to work hard to have food to eat, shelter, and clothes. Adam and Eve's sin caused all of us to miss out on God's plan that there would never have to be such evil in the world. Evil has its roots in the earliest history of mankind.

6.2— Jesus Christ was crucified on the cross but was *not* physically raised from the dead.
False. (Test question #49)

Roman executioners were very good at their job—too good to overlook a major point like leaving a capital criminal alive after being crucified. They were so brutally thorough, in fact, that it was common practice for them to break the legs of any victims who wouldn't die fast enough. With legs broken, they could not push themselves up to breathe and would at last die of suffocation.

The Bible reports that when these Roman death experts examined Jesus, intending to break His legs, He was already dead. To confirm their observation, a guard stabbed Jesus with a spear, and blood and water poured out, the sure sign of a victim's demise. Nevertheless, there are skeptics whose predispositions against the possibility of resurrection compel them to argue that Jesus might not really have died on the cross. So it becomes necessary for us to recognize exactly how untenable that argument really is.

Numerous medical experts agree that the description of Jesus' crucifixion presents unmistakable medical evidence that Jesus was dead when He was taken down from the cross. In *The Journal of the American Medical Association*, W. D. Edwards, W. J. Gabel, and F. E. Hosmer describe the pertinent medical factors:

> Jesus of Nazareth underwent Jewish and Roman trials, was flogged and was sentenced to death by crucifixion. The scourging produced deep stripe-like lacerations and appreciable blood loss, and it probably set the stage for hypovolemic shock as evidenced by the fact that Jesus was too weakened to carry the crossbar (patibulum) to Golgotha. At the site of crucifixion his wrists were nailed to the patibulum and after the patibulum was lifted onto the upright post (stipes) his feet were nailed to the stipes.
>
> The major pathophysiologic effect of crucifixion was an interference with normal respirations. Accordingly death resulted primarily from hypovolemic shock and exhaustion asphyxia. Jesus' death was ensured by the thrust of a soldier's spear into his side. Modern medical interpretation of the historical evidence indicates that Jesus was dead when taken down from the cross.[162]

The Edwards/Gabel/Hosmer article concludes:

> Clearly, the weight of historical and medical evidence indicates that Jesus was dead before the wound to his side was inflicted and supports the traditional view that the spear, thrust between his right ribs, probably perfo-

rated not only the right lung but also the pericardium and heart and thereby ensured his death. Accordingly, interpretations based on the assumption that Jesus did not die on the cross appear to be at odds with modern medical knowledge.[163]

Besides this evidence to the contrary, it is hardly plausible that if Jesus had not died and was revived by the cool air in the tomb (as some suggest) that in His condition He was able to roll away a stone from the tomb's opening that took more than twenty healthy men to put into place. Further, if others—the disciples, for instance—had somehow moved the heavily guarded stone, allowing Jesus to walk out, would they have been inspired by this half-dead man? Would such a weak and near-death Jesus have caused the disciples to snap out of their fear and depression and run about advocating a strong and mighty Savior? Again, the contention simply isn't believable.

Some claim the disciples stole Jesus' body to make it look as though He had risen from the dead, but that raises some pretty hard issues:

1. How could the disciples have moved a stone away from the tomb without waking up the guards (assuming they were sleeping—which they probably weren't, since guards could be executed for falling asleep while on duty)?

2. Disturbing a tomb was punishable by death, so it is unlikely the disciples would risk being killed for raiding the tomb just to pull off a fake resurrection. At the point of Jesus' death, the disciples were a discouraged group.

3. Even if the disciples had wanted to steal Jesus' body and if they could have gotten by the guards, how would they have moved the stone that blocked the tomb? In his Biblical studies, Josh McDowell discovered an early copy of the Bible says the stone was so big that not even 20 men together could move it! Scripture indicates the stone was moved by an angel from heaven, not by the disciples or the women.

4. If the Jewish or Roman leaders really believed the disciples had stolen the body of Jesus, they would have had the disciples executed for disturbing a grave. If the body of Jesus was still in the tomb and the disciples were lying about the resurrection, the authorities would have put the body on display to end the story. Or if the rulers had taken the body of Jesus to a secret location, they could have brought it out for everyone to see.

5. If the body of Jesus had been stolen, why were the grave clothes still in the tomb, folded neatly, just as you would expect if Jesus had slipped out of them supernaturally? They wouldn't be.

Perhaps the greatest evidence for the resurrection of Jesus Christ is that more than *five hundred* eyewitnesses saw Him. And Jesus not only appeared to His followers but to one of the first century's greatest enemies of Christianity, Saul of Tarsus.

Saul was a Jewish leader who was responsible for killing numerous Christians for their faith. Yet, when Jesus, after His resurrection, appeared to Saul on the Damascus road, Saul was transformed and became one of the all-time greatest defenders of Christianity.

In Acts 26:4-5, 9-23 Saul (who upon his conversion became known as Paul) gives his own testimony:

> My manner of life from my youth, which was spent from the beginning among my own nation and at Jerusalem, all the Jews know. They knew me from the first, if they were willing to testify, that according to the strictest sect of our religion I lived a Pharisee....
>
> Indeed, I myself thought I must do many things contrary to the name of Jesus of Nazareth. This I also did in Jerusalem, and many of the saints I shut up in prison, having received authority from the chief priests; and when they were put to death, I cast my vote against them. And I punished them often in every synagogue and compelled them to blaspheme; and being exceedingly enraged against them, I persecuted them even to foreign cities.
>
> While thus occupied, as I journeyed to Damascus with authority and commission from the chief priests,

at midday...along the road I saw a light from heaven, brighter than the sun, shining around me and those who journeyed with me. And when we all had fallen to the ground, I heard a voice speaking to me and saying in the Hebrew language, "Saul, Saul, why are you persecuting Me? It is hard for you to kick against goads."

So I said, "Who are You, Lord?"

And He said, "I am Jesus, whom you are persecuting. But rise and stand on your feet; for I have appeared to you for this purpose, to make you a minister and a witness both of the things which you have seen and of the things which I will yet reveal to you. I will deliver you from the Jewish people, as well as from the Gentiles, to whom I now send you, to open their eyes, in order to turn them from darkness to light, and from the power of Satan to God, that they may receive forgiveness of sins and an inheritance among those who are sanctified by faith in Me."

Therefore...I was not disobedient to the heavenly vision, but declared first to those in Damascus and in Jerusalem, and throughout all the region of Judea, and then to the Gentiles, that they should repent, turn to God, and do works befitting repentance. For these reasons the Jews seized me in the temple and tried to kill me. Therefore, having obtained help from God, to this day I stand, witnessing both to small and great, saying no other things than those which the prophets and Moses said would come—that the Christ would suffer, that He would be the first to rise from the dead, and would proclaim light to the Jewish people and to the Gentiles.

It is a fact of history that Saul of Tarsus was a leader of his day who persecuted Christians. It is also true that Saul changed radically, became known as Paul, and was a pivotal leader of the early church. So what would cause a man to change from hating, persecuting, and killing Christians to becoming a Christian and a defender of Christianity? Paul's own answer is the most logical conclusion: an encounter with the risen Lord.

In 1 Corinthians 15:6, Paul directed skeptics or critics to ask the eyewitnesses who had seen the resurrected Christ. Those who saw Jesus were changed and became willing to die rather than to say they had not seen Him alive after His crucifixion. Those who did die for their faith would have only had to say, "Jesus really is dead," and they could have lived.

Former skeptic and critic Frank Harber correctly points out that people are not willing to die for something they know to be a lie:

> Many people have died for a cause they believed was true even though it was false; however, no one ever eagerly dies for a cause knowing it to be false. Christianity could have never endured had these first Christians not believed in the Resurrection. The tenacity of these early eyewitness in the face of death testifies to the truth that the Resurrection must have occurred.[164]

Ten of Jesus' original disciples died a martyr's death (Judas betrayed Jesus and killed himself; of the remaining eleven only John was spared martyrdom). Peter, for example, was crucified upside down at his own request because he considered himself "unworthy" to be crucified in the same way his Lord had been. Thomas, who had been a "doubter" until he saw Jesus alive after death, carried the gospel all the way to India, where he ministered for many years before being martyred. After several long imprisonments, Paul—a latecomer to witnessing the resurrection—died a martyr's death in Rome.[165]

Would these men die for a known lie or a hoax they orchestrated by stealing the body of Jesus Christ and then reporting Him as risen from the dead? It is simply not credible that all of the disciples would willingly die as martyrs for a lie. The disciples and eyewitnesses spoke the truth and refused to change their story in the face of persecution, torture, and death. As author Tim LaHaye has said, "They signed their testimony in blood."[166]

6.3— The Bible, rightly divided, should be the foundation for all our beliefs, actions, and conduct.
True. (Test question #50)
— **Believers should not only base their philosophy in Christ, but they should know how to respond to critics and skeptics of Christianity with the reasoning and basis of our Biblical worldview.** *True.* (Test question #51)
— **A Christian can develop a Biblical worldview for every major area of life by studying the Bible from beginning to end in context.** *True.* (Test question #52)
— **The Bible is God's revealed Word and should be the**

basis of our worldview. *True.* (Test question #53)

— **God had no beginning and has no end.**
True. (Test question #54)

— **God is the Creator of the universe.**
True. (Test question #55)

— **Your worldview is the foundation of your values, and your values are the foundation of your actions.**
True. (Test question #56)

A worldview is the lens—the glasses—through which you view the world. It's the foundation of your values, and your values determine how you act and how you live your life. Whether conscious of it or not, every person has a worldview. You are surrounded by people who have their own way of looking at things, and many of these hold views that oppose Christianity.

This book spells out the Biblical viewpoint on issues as varied as America's free enterprise system, evolution, and same-sex marriage. Every area of life is subject to a worldview, and whatever you think about anything should be based on Biblical teachings because the Bible is the basis for all Christian beliefs.

The Bible is a remarkable book. There is literally none other like it. It was written over a period of 1,600 years, and there were more than 40 different authors from three continents (Africa, Asia, and Europe) who wrote in three different languages. Despite the varied backgrounds of the writers, Scripture tells a consistent story from beginning to end.

One way we know the Bible can be trusted is that it is full of "predictive prophecy." Predictive prophecy occurs when the Bible tells about things that are going to happen years in advance of when the events actually occur, and then the whole prediction comes true. Scripture records many such prophecies. Take the nation of Israel, for example. The Bible predicted Israel would become a nation again after centuries of the Jewish people having no place for their own country. Israel had not been a nation for more than 2,000 years, but in 1948, it became a nation just as predicted in the Old Testament:

- Ezekiel 45:12 even tells what kind of money would be used in the new Israel. Modern Jewish money is called the shekel.

- Ezekiel 37:21 explains that the Jewish people would

RELIGION

return to Israel from all over the world—just as they have.

• Zephaniah 3:9 foretells that the official language of Israel will be Hebrew, and today, newspapers in Israel are printed in Hebrew.

• Ezekiel 36:26-35 and Isaiah 27:6 prophesy that the desert of Israel will become like a garden. Today an Israeli farmer, working desert land, produces four to six times as much food as an average farmer in America. Israel actually sends large amounts of fruit and flowers to other countries—all from a desert!

• Ezekiel 37:10 says the nation of Israel will have a great army. During the last 50 years, Israel's army, air force, and intelligence agency have proven to be among the best trained and most powerful in the world.

The Bible also makes predictions about things other than Israel. For instance, Daniel 12:4 suggests that technology will produce a huge increase in knowledge, speed of transportation, and worldwide communications. Consider these examples of progress:

• Experts estimate that in the last 50 years, there has been more scientific progress than in the previous 5,000 years!

• High rates of speed? Before 1830, people traveled only by horse, foot, or sailboat. From 1830 to 1890, we invented steam engines, which gave us trains and ships. From 1890 to today, people have developed cars and jets, as well as spacecraft capable of traveling to the moon. We have even landed unmanned spacecrafts on the planet Mars.

• You see examples of worldwide communications every day. On television, you can watch live events taking place on the other side of the earth, and you can talk on the phone or e-mail people that live thousands of miles away.

RELIGION

Archeology provides further evidence for the veracity of the Bible. Archeologists have made more than 25,000 discoveries related to the Old Testament and found exactly what the Bible talks about in every case.

Although some people claim the Bible isn't accurate because it has been copied so many times by different people, this amounts to a smokescreen. Between 1947 and 1956, handwritten copies of every book of the Old Testament except one were found in caves in Israel (the Dead Sea Scrolls). These copies of Bible books reflect the same thing we read in our Bibles today.

Similarly, the New Testament is the most documented work of antiquity. Although there are no original versions of New Testament books, there are more manuscripts of the New Testament than of any other ancient book ever written—24,286 to be exact. Like the Dead Sea Scrolls, these copies prove that the Bible of today is just as it was originally written 2,000 years ago.

So the Christian angle on things begins with a belief in God—a theistic worldview—based on the unassailable authenticity of Scripture. The God we believe in is the One described in the Bible. Other viewpoints differ on this central truth. Cosmic Humanism (also known as New Age), for instance, believes in pantheism, the belief that everything is God. It (not He) is a force you can use to your advantage through the power of your mind (the "force" in *Star Wars* is a fictional, but logical, extension of this idea). Yet another alternative is Secular Humanism—the belief that there is no God. In this view, people are the highest order of creature.

Christian theism says there are both spiritual and natural worlds. At the other extreme, by contrast, Secular Humanists believe in naturalism, which means they think all that exists is the natural world. There is no spiritual side.

A Christian believes people are in need of redemption, and that can happen only through repenting of sins, believing in the death, burial, and resurrection of Jesus Christ, and accepting Him as Lord and Savior. A Cosmic Humanist believes mankind is saved through reincarnation—the belief that a person's soul passes repeatedly from one body to another until his or her good deeds (good karma) outweigh bad deeds (bad karma). A Secular Humanist believes people die, and that's it—there is nothing beyond the grave.

Christians believe the world was created by God through His spoken word and that He is the source of all truth. He has always existed and is the source of all creation. A Secular Humanist believes in naturalistic Darwinian evolution, that the cosmos came about at random.

While Christianity holds that God is the source of all truth (Jesus called Himself "the truth"), both forms of humanism believe truth is relative, not a fixed reference point. Scripture teaches that people have a soul that will live forever in either heaven or hell, depending on whether or not they have accepted the atonement of Christ, because they are accountable to God's absolute truth. A Christian believes mankind is born with a sin nature but that each person has a free will and can choose to be a slave to sin or a servant of Jesus Christ.

A worldview impacts every area of life. Christians are to love the Lord their God with all their heart, soul, strength, and mind, and it is each person's responsibility to sharpen his or her mind to think and live according to a Christian worldview.

6.4— Both Secular Humanism and Marxism are religious worldviews. *True.* (Test question #57)

While theirs is not the God Christians worship, both Marxists and Secular Humanists have created their own substitutes. Liberals in our culture generally adopt some version of one or the other.

Since liberals believe abortion and same-sex marriage are morally acceptable, that all religions are equal, all truth is relative, and that the Bible is not the inspired Word of God, they are responding to something other than the God presented in the Christian Scriptures. They've imagined a way of being that serves humanist desires and purposes of all kinds. Their god is really nothing more than a worldview in which man is the center and measure of all things.

The battle that rages in America today between radical liberals and traditional conservatives is a battle between two opposing *religious* worldviews—Secular Humanism and its Marxist progeny, and Christian theism. Sadly, most Americans believe only what they've been programmed to think—that humanism is a "neutral" position and belief in God is somehow a skewed perspective. This nonreligious mask of humanism is why it is the only religion funded and promoted in America's public schools. Teaching "non-God" is OK; teaching "God" is not.

Humanist organizations like the ACLU and other liberal groups and individuals file lawsuit upon lawsuit to keep students from praying over their lunches, mentioning God or Jesus Christ in their graduation speeches, singing Christmas carols, having Christmas parties, or

RELIGION

observing Thanksgiving as an occasion to show gratitude to a Deity. While liberals fight to remove the religion of Christianity from our schools, colleges, courtrooms, city halls, city seals, or from the city square, their "dirty little secret" is that they don't want a religion-free zone. They simply want to replace the Judeo-Christian faith and acknowledgement of God's place in our history with their religion of Secular Humanism.

If Americans in large enough numbers would recognize that humanism *is* a religion, religious liberals would not be allowed to usher Christianity out the back door of our schools while the religion of humanism is ushered in the front. To make sure you understand how "religious" humanism actually is, take note of several telling facts.

In their 2003 *New York Times* bestseller *Mind Siege,* Dr. David Noebel and Dr. Tim LaHaye explain:

> The truth is, humanism is unmistakably and demonstrably a religion. One need merely visit the second edition of *A World Religions Reader* to note the prominence given to Secular Humanism as one of the world's religions. Indeed, in a list of the world's religions—Hinduism, Buddhism, Shintoism, Judaism, Christianity, Islam, and Sikhism—Secular Humanism is at the top.[167]

Some argue that humanism, unlike Christianity, does not force a specific set of religious positions and beliefs on people, but Dr. Noebel points out:

> Humanists preach a faith every bit as dogmatic as Christianity. Moral relativism is foundational for Secular Humanist ethics; spontaneous generation and evolution are basic to their biology; naturalism is foundational to their philosophy; and atheism is their theological perspective.[168]

No less a source than the U.S. Supreme Court also validates the claim that humanism is a religion. Again, Dr. Noebel explains:

> In 1961, the Supreme Court handed down the *Torcaso v. Watkins* decision regarding a Maryland notary public who was initially disqualified from office because he would not declare a belief in God. But the Court ruled in

his favor. It argued that theistic religions [religions that believe in one God] could not be favored by the Court over non-theistic religions. In a footnote it clarified what it meant by non-theistic religions. [169]

The footnote to which Dr. Noebel refers was written by Justice Hugo L. Black and elaborates the point: "Among religions in this country which do not teach what would generally be considered a belief in the existence of God are Buddhism, Taoism, Ethical Culture, Secular Humanism, and others."

So the next time you hear of ACLU president Barry Lynn and other high priests of humanism attacking a cross on a city seal, the singing of a Christmas carol in a school program, or a prayer spoken at a graduation ceremony, be prepared to speak out against their true goal. They're in an all-out campaign to eradicate Christianity in favor of the religion of humanism.

6.5— All religions are equally true. *False.* (Test question #58)
— **Jesus Christ lived a sinless life.** *True.* (Test question #59)
— **There is more than one way to God.**
     False. (Test question #60)

Whether or not all religions are equally true can be determined by examining the character of the One who founded Christianity. Jesus makes the difference, and a fascinating story from Erwin Lutzer explains why.

Dr. Erwin Lutzer is the pastor of the historic Moody Church in downtown Chicago. He has spoken for the Worldview Weekend and is an outstanding author. In 1994, he attended in Chicago a major symposium on the religions of the world. Dr. Lutzer walked the convention center, visiting with some of the 7,000 attendees. He describes his experience in his superb book, *Called*:

> I walked through the display area in search of a sinless prophet/teacher/Savior. I asked a Hindu Swami whether any of their teachers claimed sinlessness. "No," he said, appearing irritated with my question, "If anyone claims he is sinless, he is not a Hindu!"
>
> What about Buddha? No, I was told, he didn't claim sinlessness. He found a group of ascetics and preached sermons to them. He taught that all outward things are

RELIGION

146

only distractions and encouraged a life of discipline and contemplation. He sought enlightenment and urged his followers to do the same. He died seeking enlightenment. No sinlessness here.

What about Baha ullah? He claimed he had a revelation from God that was more complete and more enlightened than those before him. Though he was convinced of the truth of his teachings, he made few personal claims. He thought his writings were "more perfect" than others, but he never claimed perfection or sinlessness for himself.

When I came to the representatives of the Muslim faith, I already knew that in the Koran the prophet Mohammed admitted he was in need of forgiveness. They agreed. "There is one God, Allah, and Mohammed was not perfect." Again, no sinlessness there.

Why was I searching for a sinless Savior? Because I don't want to have to trust a Savior who is in the same predicament as I am. I can't trust my eternal soul to someone who is still working through his own imperfections. Since I'm a sinner, I need someone who is standing on higher ground.

Understandably, none of the religious leaders I spoke with even claimed to have a Savior. Their prophets, they said, showed the way, but made no pretense to be able to personally forgive sins or transform so much as a single human being. Like a street sign, they gave directions, but were not able to take us where we need to go. If we need any saving, we will have to do it ourselves.

The reason is obvious: No matter how wise, no matter how gifted, no matter how influential other prophets, gurus, and teachers might be, they had the presence of mind to know that they were imperfect just like the rest of us. They never even presumed to be able to reach down into the murky water of human depravity and bring sinners into the presence of God.[170]

What did Jesus and those who knew Him have to say about His sinless life?

• He pointed out hypocrisy in the lives of His critics, but none of them returned the compliment: "Which of you convicts Me of sin? And if I tell the truth, why do you not believe Me?" (John 8:46).

• Judas, an apparent friend turned enemy, testified, "I have sinned by betraying innocent blood" (Matthew 27:4).

• Pilate, who badly needed to come up with a charge against Christ, confessed, "I find no fault in this man" (Luke 23:4).

• Peter, who lived with Him for three years, said He "committed no sin, nor was deceit found in His mouth" (1 Peter 2:22).

• The apostle Paul explained that God the Father "made Him who knew no sin to be sin for us, that we might become the righteousness of God in Him" (2 Corinthians 5:21).

Not all religions are created equal because not all founders of religions are.

6.6— Good people can earn their way to heaven if their good deeds outweigh their bad deeds. *False.* (Test question #61)

Most followers of New Age thinking do not believe in heaven or hell, but in reincarnation—the belief that a person's soul repeatedly passes from one body to another at death. The process continues until the soul reaches a state of perfection when the soul's good karma (good deeds) outweighs its bad karma (bad deeds). Accumulating good karma results in a soul being reincarnated into a desirable state. If someone accumulates bad karma, he or she will be reincarnated into a less desirable state.

An inconsistency arises when you discuss "good" and "bad" karma. According to the New Age Movement, there is no right or wrong, only interaction of forces. Dostoevsky has said, "Anything is permissible if there is no God, but anything is also permissible if everything is God."[171] The faulty thought process—earning your way to heaven, happy reincarnation, or whatever—is the same.

If Cosmic Humanism claims there is no good or evil, no right or wrong, then how can there be good and bad karma? In order to have good and bad karma, there must be a standard by which to determine what is good and what is bad. This is just one of many contradictions within New Age philosophy.

New Age leader J.Z. Knight claims to have a 35,000-year-old spirit that speaks or channels through her. On the ABC News program *20/20*, Knight claimed, "If you believe in reincarnation, how could murder be wrong?" If someone is murdered, it happened because they wanted it to happen or their "bad karma" caught up with them. (Just to set the record straight: I submit that J.Z. Knight is not channeling a 35,000-year-old spirit but a demon from the dark side of the spiritual world.)

Similarly, New Ager Kevin Ryerson says killers can actually turn out to be great people, thanks to reincarnation:

> Criminals and murderers sometimes come back around to be murdered themselves, or perhaps to become a saint. For instance, Moses was a murderer...He beat the fellow to death out of rage, which was not exactly the most ethical decision. But he went on to become a great intellect, a great law-giver, and is considered a saint by many people. So basically, you get many chances. Your karma is your system of judgment. There is justice.[172]

A look at the inconsistencies in this one paragraph points out again why "earning points" to get to heaven just doesn't wash—even in a system of thought which teaches so. Ryerson claims that Moses did not act ethically when he got mad and killed the Egyptian for beating the Israelite slave. But how could a New Ager judge the actions of Moses as unethical if there is to be no personal judging and no absolute standard exists? Ryerson also says karma is "your" system of judgment, and there is justice. If there are no absolutes, if evil and good are all part of each other because all is part of God and God is part of everything, then an idea such as "justice" has no meaning. The more you read and listen to these various New Agers, the more you realize they talk in circles and contradict themselves every time they turn around. They're really getting nowhere—let alone to heaven.

6.8— The Bible is a consistent revelation from beginning to end. *True*. (Test question #62)

— **The Bible is a reflection of God's character and nature.**
True. (Test question #63)

To hammer out the U.S. Constitution, several dozen men met, debated, and disagreed for weeks on end, yet ultimately produced a cohesive document to govern a nation. But what do you think the chances of their producing a unified work would have been if roughly the same number of men had never known each other, been separated in many cases by centuries of time, had generally not shared a common profession, and had each written with little knowledge of what the others had to say? Obviously, very little. Yet such a diversity is exactly what produced the miracle of The Holy Bible as we know it today.

Despite being penned by more than 40 authors from some 20 different walks of life during a timespan of over 1,600 years, the Bible presents a consistent message from beginning to end.[173] That wonder itself is evidence of its truthfulness. It represents a feat beyond any human ability to accomplish. The Bible has stood up to thousands of years of scrutiny. Despite being hated and vilified by untold numbers, critics have yet to prove the Bible false.

Yet there is an even greater reality behind why the Bible is true. The source of all truth is God, and the Bible is a reflection of God's character and nature.

In John 14:6 we read that Jesus Christ, who came to earth as God incarnate, declared, "I am the way, the truth and the life." We understand that it is wrong to lie, steal, murder, cheat, commit adultery, or covet because those things are against God's character and nature.

Why do you suppose so many liberals and humanists are threatened by Mel Gibson's movie, *The Passion of the Christ*? It is because Jesus, the central character in the movie, made the most politically incorrect statement of all time when He said, "No one comes to the Father except through Me." Yes, He meant that following, serving, and believing in Buddha, Krishna, Mohammed, or any other spiritual leader would not guarantee eternal life. Any attempt to gain salvation or reach heaven apart from Him is futile—a message clearly branded as "intolerant" in today's world. Liberals find this offensive largely because it means their definitions of truth are wrong.

Those who maintain a genuine desire to discover truth, though, will eventually find it. Josh McDowell, for example, set out to disprove Christianity and became one of the world's greatest Christian thinkers and defenders. He summarizes the search for truth this way:

RELIGION

God is the original. He is the origin of all things that are in existence. And if we wish to know if anything is right or wrong, good or evil, we must measure it against the person who is true. "He is the Rock," Moses said, "His work is perfect...a God of truth and without iniquity, just and right is he" (Deuteronomy 32:4, KJV). You see, it is the very person and nature of God that defines truth. It is not something he measures up to. It is not something he announces. It is not even something he decides. It is something he is. [174]

This means that moral and spiritual truth isn't abstract philosophy. It is, rather, very concrete, innate within Creation. Why? Because *truth is a Person.* It is best understood as a "Who," not a "what." And when we acknowledge that personal nature of truth, it changes everything in the minds and hearts of our young people and the whole postmodern generation![175]

This shift from "what" to "Who" mandates a change in how we think of Christianity. Relating to or obeying moral and spiritual truth should not be thought of as a response to philosophical concepts but rather as how we relate to a person.[176]

God is truth and has been since before time began: "In the beginning was the Word, and the Word was with God, and the Word was God." (John 1:1) *Logos* is Greek for "word," a title for God. So the verse is saying that in the beginning all that existed was God.

God is always the same, He is always good, and He always opposes evil. Moral relativism, on the other hand, is the belief that there is no absolute standard of right or wrong, good or evil. Morals and ethics are autonomous and can evolve and change to fit the needs and desires of an individual and society. Therefore, moral relativism and situational ethics are false.

James 1:17-18 offers a crystal clear perspective on this understanding of truth:

Every good gift and every perfect gift is from above, and comes down from the Father of lights, with whom there is no variation or shadow of turning. Of His own will He brought us forth by the word of truth, that we might be a kind of firstfruits of His creatures.

RELIGION

God is the source of goodness, and the Bible presents this truth consistently throughout.

6.7— Christians should never speak publicly about what someone has said or written publicly before first talking to them in private. *False.* (Test question #64)

People who object to Christians publicly taking issue with other public Christian teachers generally cite Matthew 18:15-17 as evidence for why public criticism is wrong:

> Moreover if your brother sins against you, go and tell him his fault between you and him alone. If he hears you, you have gained your brother. But if he will not hear, take with you one or two more, that by the mouth of two or three witnesses every word may be established. And if he refuses to hear them, tell it to the church. But if he refuses even to hear the church, let him be to you like a heathen and a tax collector.

However, these people strip Matthew 18:15-17 from its context in order to force their "nonjudgmental" view on Christians who challenge unBiblical beliefs, doctrine, or worldviews. In context, it is clear the verses address how to handle a private issue or a personal offense. The three verses detail steps that should be taken for church discipline of an individual who has sinned. If the offending person does not repent when you confront him or her privately, then you are to take one or two people with you. If the individual still will not repent, take the issue before the church. If even that doesn't work, the person is to be removed from fellowship until he or she does admit to the sin and repents.

To the contrary, the great apostle Paul himself publicly denounced false teachers by name *without* first going to them in private. That is necessary in order to correct *public* false teaching. It is crucial that Christians be committed to publicly pointing out erroneous teaching whenever it is promoted in books, television, radio, websites, and other public forums.

6.9— Christians should present the Gospel in a seeker-friendly, non-offensive manner that avoids using terms such as hell, sin, the wrath of God and judgment day. *False.* (Test question #65)

— **Repentance is necessary for salvation.**
True. (Test question #66)

Some of what people attempt to pass off these days as the Gospel is overwhelmingly syrupy, Christian happy-talk. Sometimes the "good news" sounds more like it came from the pages of *Oprah* magazine or a Dr. Phil book than from the Bible. The real motive, I believe, for preachers who promote this form of Christianity is simply that they want to be liked by all and offensive to none. They shrink from the hard edges of the Gospel Jesus preached.

Some even consider "sin" to be a controversial subject. For example, on the June 20, 2005 edition of *Larry King Live*, King probed popular teacher Joel Osteen on some provocative issues, but Rev. Osteen would not take a stand on Biblical teachings:

> **KING:** How about issues that the church has feelings about? Abortion? Same-sex marriages?
>
> **OSTEEN:** Yeah. You know what, Larry? I don't go there. I just ...
>
> **KING:** You have thoughts, though.
>
> **OSTEEN:** I have thoughts. I just, you know, I don't think that a same-sex marriage is the way God intended it to be. I don't think abortion is the best. I think there are other, you know, a better way to live your life. But I'm not going to condemn those people. I tell them all the time our church is open for everybody.
>
> **KING:** You don't call them sinners?
>
> **OSTEEN:** I don't.
>
> **KING:** Is that a word you don't use?
>
> **OSTEEN:** I don't use it. I never thought about it. But I probably don't. But most people already know what they're doing is wrong. When I get them to church I want to tell them that you can change. There can be a difference in your life. So I don't go down the road of condemning.

RELIGION

153

Not even the loosest of modern paraphrases offers any notion that the Bible says the problem of sinful humanity is a lack of self-esteem. Joel Osteen is one of a number of "evangelists" who don't discuss atonement, dying to self, picking up your cross, hell, the wrath of God, God's jealousy, or the death, burial, and resurrection of Jesus Christ.

The same interview by Larry King also gives insight into the inclusiveness promoted by such people:

KING: What if you're Jewish or Muslim, you don't accept Christ at all?

OSTEEN: You know, I'm very careful about saying who would and wouldn't go to heaven. I don't know...

KING: If you believe you have to believe in Christ? They're wrong, aren't they?

OSTEEN: Well, I don't know if I believe they're wrong. I believe here's what the Bible teaches, and from the Christian faith this is what I believe. But I just think that only God will judge a person's heart. I spent a lot of time in India with my father. I don't know all about their religion. But I know they love God. And I don't know. I've seen their sincerity. So I don't know. I know for me, and what the Bible teaches, I want to have a relationship with Jesus.

Suggestions such as Rev. Osteen's sound better to many American ears than warnings from Jesus about being hated by most people for His sake. But it remains that in large measure, anything less than Jesus' straightforward teaching is heretical.

Unfortunately, this sort of approach to the Gospel is all too common among churches that attempt to be "seeker friendly." Most such churches avoid talking about sin, the wrath of God, repentance, the cross, self-denial and dying to self. Setting out to make a church comfortable for sinners is as foolish as making a police station comfortable for criminals. The job of the police is to go out and catch criminals. No matter how we disguise the police station it will never attract lawbreakers. Likewise, the church needs to go out and apprehend sinners for Christ.

While we certainly should welcome the unsaved into our churches, the purpose of the New Testament church is for Christians to gather to use their spiritual gifts for the edification of the saints. The church is to be a place where we disciple, encourage and challenge the followers of Christ. It should challenge and equip members to go out, grab hold of the lost through Biblical evangelism, and bring new converts into the body. There they can be discipled and, in turn, go out and apprehend more of the lost.

If we want to evangelize like Jesus Christ, then we must learn to use the moral law as He did. That means we cannot be afraid to use the word "sin." According to 1 John 3:4, sin is the transgression of the law. According to Romans, the moral law is written on the heart and mind of every person—thus the conscience ("con" means with and "science" means knowledge). Because of the conscience, every time people sin or rebel against God, they know it is wrong. Romans 7:7 assures us that the law convicts people of their sin.

Through the Word of God we come to understand that we don't murder fellow human beings because murder goes against the character of God. Neither are we to lie, steal, or break any of the other Ten Commandments because doing so would go against who God is.

Romans 1:21 reminds us, "although they knew God, they did not glorify Him as God, nor were thankful, but became futile in their thoughts, and their foolish hearts were darkened." And Romans 2:15 points out that people "show the work of the law written in their hearts, their conscience also bearing witness, and between themselves their thoughts accusing or else excusing them."

People can either accept the guilty feeling of the law that accuses them of their transgression when they sin, or they can excuse the guilty feeling and learn to ignore it. If people ignore the guilt long enough or often enough, they will become liars whose "consciences are seared with a hot iron" (1 Timothy 4:2). Norm Geisler explains how this works out in a person's life:

> [T]he root cause of the character disorders (moral corruption)...is directly associated with a person's refusal to acknowledge and act upon what is morally right and reject what is morally wrong. It becomes harder and harder for the individual to get help with his character disorder because of the increased moral depravity. This increase is associated with greater levels of insensitivity in that person's conscience. For example, during

RELIGION

155

the progressive moral deterioration in the life of the person who uses pornography, his sequence of feeling-to-thought-to-deed proceeds with less and less intervention of the inhibitory mechanism of conscience and guilt.

Even if a person's conscience is seared, though, no one will have an excuse at judgment for rejecting God. Romans 3:19-20 explains:

> Now we know that whatever the law says, it says to those who are under the law, that every mouth may be stopped, and all the world may become guilty before God. Therefore by the deeds of the law no flesh will be justified in His sight, for by the law is the knowledge of sin.

Everyone has broken the law. No one can claim to warrant entry into heaven because they have "lived a good enough life." God's standard is that people must keep the complete moral law, and no one has done that. The purpose of the law is not to save us. It is to condemn us, to show us our true state, to reveal our sin, and to show us we deserve God's wrath. Romans 3:20 explains that the purpose of the law is to get people to stop justifying their sin.

Further, 1 John 3:4 says, "Whoever commits sin also commits lawlessness, and sin is lawlessness." And Romans 3:10 explains, "There is none righteous, no, not one." Finally, Romans 3:23 concludes: "...all have sinned and fall short of the glory of God." Because everyone but Jesus Christ has broken the law, any who have not repented of their sins and trusted in the death, burial, and resurrection of Jesus Christ will not be pardoned for breaking the moral law.

To repent means to turn from sin and to stop practicing sin as a lifestyle. This does not mean a person will never sin again, but there is a big difference between stumbling into sin and willingly jumping in.

A repentant heart is born out of an awareness of a person's deep-seated sinfulness and the understanding that everyone deserves the wrath of God. A repentant person who surrenders his or her life to Christ receives eternal life with Christ. Eternal life is theirs at the moment of salvation because Christ fully paid for sin by dying in place of sinners. 2 Corinthians 7:9-10 says:

> Now I rejoice, not that you were made sorry, but that

your sorrow led to repentance. For you were made sorry in a godly manner, that you might suffer loss from us in nothing. For godly sorrow produces repentance leading to salvation, not to be regretted; but the sorrow of the world produces death.

True repentance is a "godly sorrow" for sin. It is turning and going in the opposite direction of a willfully sinful lifestyle. True repentance leads to a change in a person's life as he or she grows in relationship with Jesus Christ.

My friend Mark Cahill speaks for the Worldview Weekend and wrote an outstanding book entitled *One Thing You Can't Do in Heaven*. In his book, Mark offers a superb explanation of the real meaning and result of repentance:

> One topic that I believe we must talk about when we discuss sin is repentance. It seems to be a word that we don't use much in witnessing, and a word that some people don't want to use at all. Yet the word "repent" and its various forms is used over one hundred times in the Bible. It must be a very important word then, and something that we must understand.
>
> The apostle Paul tells us in 2 Corinthians 7:10, "For godly sorrow produces repentance to salvation, not to be regretted; but the sorrow of the world produces death."
>
> John the Baptist preached in the wilderness, "Repent, for the kingdom of heaven is at hand!" (Matthew 3:2).
>
> Jesus preached this same message of repentance. Mark 1:14, 15 says, "Now after John was put in prison, Jesus came to Galilee, preaching the gospel of the kingdom of God, and saying, 'The time is fulfilled, and the kingdom of God is at hand. Repent, and believe the gospel.'"
>
> In Mark 6, Jesus sends out the twelve disciples two by two. Verse 12 states, "So they went out and preached that people should repent." If Jesus sent the disciples out preaching that people must repent of their sins, we ought to do the same.
>
> Repentance is not when we feel bad because we got caught doing something wrong. True repentance is when we change our mind about our sin so our actions

RELIGION

will not continue to be the same....

I was sitting around talking one night with a young man I had met at a camp. He was telling me about his life and confessed that he had been using cocaine for the past thirty days. About forty-five minutes into the conversation he asked, "Is this the point where you are going to start talking to me about Jesus?"

I said, "No." He looked rather surprised. "You're not?" I told him that he was not ready for Jesus, and that it was not his day to get saved. He did not hate his sin enough to want to repent and walk away from it. He loved the world way too much. It was very interesting that he didn't argue one bit with me. He didn't want to get saved that day. He wanted to use drugs. He had gone to a Christian high school, so he knew all the right answers. The issue was repentance, and he didn't want to do that....Repenting means to make a turn, and that is what you see in the true Christian life.

Did you catch the meaning of the word repentance? Mark describes precisely why we must use the moral law to reach people. God's law teaches them they are guilty sinners needing a new heart. God's Holy Spirit uses His law to teach us we are guilty sinners deserving hell. God's saving grace by God's mercy opens our hearts to surrender our will to Christ. The moral law has the power to create *a heart that hates evil*. As Proverbs 8:13 says, "To fear the Lord is to hate evil."

In Galatians 3:24, Paul tells us that the law is the schoolmaster to bring us to repentance. Many seeker-friendly churches use a man-centered form of evangelism that simply creates false converts. Man-centered evangelism encourages people to say a "sinner's prayer" before the individual understands what he or she has done that has offended God for which repentance is necessary. As Ray Comfort has explained to me, "People need to understand they are lost before they can be saved. We must preach the disease before we preach the cure."

The false converts that are created through today's man-centered evangelism efforts often are people that see grace as a way to justify their sinful lifestyles. They believe they can live however they want because they are under God's grace and God has to forgive them. Tragically, such individuals are still workers of iniquity. A worker of iniquity is someone who willfuly breaks the moral law. The Bible is very clear that God's grace or forgiveness is only extended to those who repent.

The great preacher John Wesley said we need to preach 90% law and 10% grace. Ray Comfort in his presentation, "Hell's Best Kept Secret," explains that when we use the moral law in our churches and evangelism efforts, we create converts who:

1. Understand the reason for God's wrath

2. Understand God's grace and mercy

3. Understand their sinful condition

4. Have gratitude to God for salvation

5. Understand they don't deserve the hope of heaven based on their own merit

6. Have gratitude that creates zeal for sharing the moral law with the lost.[177]

And *that* leads to repentance.

Oswald Chambers offers a perspective on the kind of thing seeker-friendly "happy talk" teaching does to Christians: "Satan's great aim is to deflect us from the center. He will allow us to be devoted to the death to any cause, any enterprise, to anything but the Lord Jesus."[178] Hebrews 13:9 instructs us to not be carried away by all sorts of strange teachings (deflected from the center), but, sadly, that is exactly what is happening for many.

RELIGION

6. Follow-up—For Further Thought about Religion

1. List two verses that command us to defend the claims of Christ.

2. All religions might be false, but they cannot all be _____.

3. What is pluralism?

4. Why can we not earn our way to heaven?

5. List three prophecies that have already been fulfilled.

6. List ten of 109 messianic prophecies that Jesus fulfilled.

7. The Bible is a reflection of what?

8. How do we know Jesus was dead when He was taken down from the cross?

9. What evidence is there for the resurrection of Jesus Christ?

10. How is Matthew 18 misused, and what is the real meaning of this verse?

11. List three prophecies concerning Israel that have come true.

12. What did Jesus and those who knew Him have to say about His sinless life?

13. Define truth.

RELIGION

SECTION 7—SOCIAL ISSUES

7.1— Ideas have consequences. *True.* (Test question #67)

The results that derive from a given set of ideas in any area of life are demonstrable. This pattern is exceptionally evident, though, in how the realm of ideas—in this case, educational and political philosophy—have wrought havoc in our public schools. Let me explain by telling several stories.

In the early 1990s, I met two education leaders from the former Soviet Union. They had come to the United States to ask American Christian Schools International, America's largest association of Christian schools, to train Russian teachers and students in Biblical worldview principles. As a result, ACSI sent hundreds of Christian schoolteachers and administrators, as well as thousands of Christian worldview books, to the former Soviet Union.

Along with many friends and colleagues, I told the one-time Soviet officials that they now had more religious freedom in their schools than we do in America. After hearing the facts about our situation, they were not only shocked but fearful for our country. They desperately wanted us to understand that America is following the path of Secular Humanism that had led their nation into godlessness and communism.

An element of their fear was legitimately self-serving. These Russian leaders were afraid that if America does not reject Secular Humanism and socialist ideals, the former Soviets would no longer have a strong, free, and virtuous America to assist them in the years to come as they seek to secure their freedoms and rebuild from the destruction of atheism and communism.

In sharing with our Russian friends how the Secular Humanist worldview is taught in our schools and how religious liberties are being stripped from American culture, we explained that many years ago humanistic liberals strategized about how to inculcate their worldview into the hearts and minds of as many Americans as possible. Their primary target became school children because of the long-term effect of changing the thinking of young people.

Just to give you a taste of how humanism and its spinoff ideas inevitably bring about the persecution of anyone who does not acquiesce to that viewpoint, let me highlight another especially significant case.

SOCIAL ISSUES

161

In 1997, federal judge Ira DeMent issued a sweeping order that eliminated virtually all voluntary religious speech in Alabama's public schools. Judge DeMent's detailed dictate was repressive, to say the least. It barred student-led prayer in almost any form and dictated that student commencement speakers could make only a "brief" reference to God and could not ask any audience member to join in. The judge threatened students and school officials with disciplinary action if they violated his order. In addition, Judge DeMent specifically banned prayer in a time of national emergency. The judge added the final draconian touch by establishing undercover school "monitors" in the DeKalb County school system to check for violations. Incensed, then-governor of Alabama Fob James called the monitors "secret police."

There is a direct correlation between America's academic decline and the humanists' successful expulsion of God from America's schools. While the United States once had an educational system that was the envy of the world, today we consistently rank toward the bottom of all industrialized nations in academic scores. Recognizing the problem as early as 1981, President Reagan ordered a study of America's educational system. Released two years later, the report, entitled *A Nation at Risk*, stated:

> Our Nation is at risk...We report to the American people that...the educational foundations of our society are presently being eroded by a rising tide of mediocrity that threatens our very future as a nation and a people...If an unfriendly foreign power had attempted to impose on America the mediocre educational performance that exists today, we might well have viewed it as an act of war. As it stands, we have allowed this to happen to ourselves....Our society and its educational institutions seem to have lost sight of the basic purposes of schooling, and of the high expectations and disciplined effort needed to attain them.

In this realm of ideas and their consequences, legendary radio broadcaster Paul Harvey has a unique gift of explaining the important issues of our day with clear and laser-like accuracy. In a reading entitled "If I Were the Devil," he shares this view:

> If I were the devil: I would gain control of the most powerful nation in the world; I would delude their

minds into thinking that they had come from man's effort, instead of God's blessings; I would promote an attitude of loving things and using people, instead of the other way around;

I would dupe entire states into relying on gambling for their state revenue; I would convince people that character is not an issue when it comes to leadership;

I would make it legal to kill unborn babies; I would make it socially acceptable to take one's own life, and invent machines to make it convenient; I would cheapen human life as much as possible so that the life of animals are valued more than human beings;

I would take God out of the schools, where even the mention of His name was grounds for a lawsuit;

I would come up with drugs that sedate the mind and target the young, and I would get sports heroes to advertise them;

I would get control of the media, so that every night I could pollute the mind of every family member with my agenda;

I would attack the family, the backbone of any nation. I would make divorce acceptable and easy, even fashionable. If the family crumbles, so does the nation;

I would compel people to express their most depraved fantasies on canvas and movie screens, and call it art;

I would convince the world that people are born homosexuals, and that their lifestyles should be accepted;

I would convince the people that right and wrong are determined by a few, who call themselves authorities and refer to their agenda as politically correct;

I would persuade people that the church is irrelevant and out of date, and the Bible is for the naive; I would dull the minds of Christians, and make them believe that prayer is not important, and that faithfulness and obedience are optional;

Hmmm... I guess if I were the devil, I'd leave things pretty much the way they are. *Good day.*[179]

The Bible says Satan is "like a roaring lion, seeking whom he may devour" (1 Peter 5:8). Satan wants to consume as many souls

SOCIAL ISSUES

163

as he can, and I believe the worldview battle in American today is a spiritual battle between those who want to follow God and those who follow the lies—the ideas—of Satan.

The consequences of ideas also play out in our social problems. David Barton reveals in his book, *To Pray or Not to Pray*, the consequences of banishing God from America's schools. Starting in 1962, the U.S. Supreme Court handed down numerous anti-God and anti-Christian rulings, and, according to the U.S. Departments of Education, Commerce, Health and Human Services, and Justice, the increase in violence, crime, and immorality showed a sharp upturn at about that time. Since then, these are some of the tragic statistics among our young people:

- Assaults by girls ages 13-14—up 377%;

- Assaults among 16-year-old girls—up 535%;

- Murders among 15-year-old girls—up 450%;

- Rapes by boys ages 13-14—up 186%.

Crime rates for boys and girls of other ages are equally shocking. Further, in 1962, suicide ranked 12th in the cause of death among young people, but by 1990, it ranked third. Suicide among youth age 15 to 24 has increased 253%. Estimates of the number of attempted suicides among adolescents now range from 400,000 to nearly two million per year.

Pregnancy rates among teenage girls also have exploded with resultant problems for academic achievement. Of those who give birth before age 18, only half complete high school, compared with 96 percent of those who abstain from sexual activity. Problems come at ever younger ages, too. Pre-marital sexual pursuits, among 15-year-old girls, for example, has increased 1000% since 1962.

This rise in sexual involvement has brought about a dramatic increase in sexually transmitted diseases. AIDS, a latecomer to the STD world, has increased 62 percent among teens since 1990, and the number of teenagers with AIDS is doubling *every 14 months*. It is now the sixth leading cause of death among young adults. Sexually transmitted diseases cost more than $2 billion annually in healthcare.[180]

In all of these categories, increases occurred after years of low, stable levels before 1962. And the increases have come at rates many

SOCIAL ISSUES

magnitudes greater than our population growth. Any freedom gained by eliminating Christianity from schools and substituting humanist ideas appears to be the freedom to pursue personal and social destruction.

Ideas have consequences.

7.2— There must be absolutes if there is to be moral and legal order. *True.* (Test question #68)

The loss of a fixed moral standard as the basis for law means there is no standard that society can use to judge good and bad behavior. As I noted in the answer in section 7.1 ("Ideas have consequences"), after the 1962 and 1963 U.S. Supreme Court rulings that outlawed prayer and the Bible in America's public schools, cheating, stealing, rape, murder, and assault increased dramatically throughout the culture. After the 1980 U.S. Supreme Court ruling that outlawed the posting of the Ten Commandments in our nation's public schools, the increase in deviant behavior went even higher, and that trend continues to this day.

With no fixed moral standard, government has no moral purpose for its existence. As we've already discussed, Romans 13 explains that the God-given purpose of civil government is to protect the righteous and punish the wicked. Without a moral foundation, the laws by which government judges and punishes evil doers are arbitrary.

If there is no fixed moral standard as the basis for law, our rights are not God-given but are merely granted to us by government. More and more people live as if they believe the state grants rights to American citizens, but this is an extremely dangerous twist in thinking. According to the Declaration of Independence, all people begin with an innate collection of individual rights. The government's rightful job is to protect and uphold those rights that we *already have.* You see the difference? Not all governments do this, of course, but ours is supposed to. While others may suppress these rights, America is to honor them. Government is not God, to create rights, but is, rather, God's minister to protect the rights God has given man.[181]

The loss of a fixed moral standard as the basis for law means that might does indeed make right. When that perception is in place, the groundwork has been laid for anarchy or for our nation to be governed by the feelings, opinions, agenda, and worldview of an elitist group of immoral judges who dominate from the bench, or a dictator who rules from the end of a gun. Attorney John Whitehead offers a sobering description of the results:

SOCIAL ISSUES

165

Those who do not favor taking God's law as the ultimate standard for civil morality and public justice will be forced to substitute some other criterion of good and evil for it. The civil magistrate cannot function without some ethical guidance, without some standard of good and evil. If that standard is not to be the revealed law of God (which, we must note, was addressed specifically to perennial problems in political morality), then what will it be? In some form or expression it will have to be a law of man (or men)—the standard of self-law or autonomy. And when autonomous laws come to govern a commonwealth, the sword is certainly wielded in vain, for it represents simply the brute force of some men's will against the will of other men. "Justice" then indeed becomes a verbal cloak for whatever serves the interests of the strongmen in society (whether their strength be that of physical might or of media manipulation). Men will either choose to be governed by God or to be ruled by tyrants.[182]

If we ignore a fixed moral standard as the basis for law, Lady Justice is not blind, and those that have money and influence have a greater chance of getting what they want—to the detriment of the middle class and the poor.

The loss of a fixed moral standard means there is no deity to which people are ultimately accountable. If men and women will not engage in morals-based self-restraint, they must be constrained by external sources—namely, a larger, more intrusive government presence in our lives.

Without a fixed moral standard, injustice will naturally follow, and many people will suffer and die unjustly. Gary DeMar outlines the destructive consequences of believing that law and morality evolve rather than reflect absolute standards:

Darwinian evolution has placed law in the arena with evolving man. If man has evolved, then the standards primitive man once held must change along with him. When the higher law is abandoned, another law takes its place. The humanistic doctrine of evolution allows man to create for himself the law he believes will most benefit evolving man. Law then is what men or the

SOCIAL ISSUES

courts say it is. Wrongs are defined in terms of what hurts man. There is no appeal to a law-order outside man. For example, abortion is made legal because it is convenient for the mother. For some women, having a baby is "harmful" because it restricts their freedom. These women are "wrongfully" curtailed in their desire to live as they wish. Laws are then passed to alleviate the "problem." The developing fetus is termed a "non-person" without protection from the morally powerful. There is no consideration that God has defined the nature of life, or that freedom should be defined in terms of submission to the commandments of God. Nor are the necessarily destructive and suicidal long-term consequences of such legal thought and practice seriously considered.[183]

Of course, the denial of moral absolutes flies in face of two other fundamental realities of our world. First, people throughout history have generally held that certain acts—stealing, murder, lying—are wrong, while others—honesty, kindness, faithfulness—are right. It is reasonable to believe this general agreement comes from somewhere, and that "somewhere" is God. Second, we accept certain physical laws as immutably governing the physical world, so it is appropriate to think there could (and perhaps should) be similarly definitive laws that govern the "unseen" world of morals. So the existence of moral absolutes underpinning our laws is very likely and so needs to be honored.

7.3— One of the greatest virtues one can possess is the virtue of tolerance as defined by our postmodern world— namely, we accept everyone's lifestyles and beliefs as equal. *False.* (Test question #69)

People of faith are often attacked for their belief in absolutes which we desire to see maintained in our nation's schools, legal system, and public policy. Strangely, though, while attackers make their claims under the banner of tolerance and moral relativism, they are at the same time trying to force their "new absolutes" on everyone.

In a review of William Watkins' book *The New Absolutes*, Rick Wade explains how the new absolutes compete with the old:

SOCIAL ISSUES

Though these new beliefs might not be "absolutes" in a strict, philosophical sense, they *function* as absolutes in contemporary society. According to Watkins, the *old* absolute was: "Human life from conception to natural death is sacred and worthy of protection." The *new* absolute is: "Human life, which begins and ends when certain individuals or groups decide it does, is valuable as long as it is wanted."

Two issues that bring this new belief to the fore are *abortion* and *physician-assisted suicide*. Few practices are as fiercely opposed or defended as abortion. Opponents say abortion is morally wrong for all people. Proponents say it is a matter of individual choice. Physician-assisted suicide draws similar responses... they think of it as a right not to be tampered with. It is rooted, they say, in a Constitutional "right to privacy."

In claiming this right, however, any foundation in relativistic thinking must be abandoned. For the very "right" proponents claim is itself an *absolute*. They think the right of individuals to decide for themselves should be observed by everyone else. When they say it is wrong for pro-lifers to try to press their beliefs on others, they are stating an absolute. If they say that the value of human life is a matter of its quality rather than of intrinsic worth, they are stating another absolute.[184]

Wade also explains the impact of these new absolutes on religious freedom in America:

It used to be held that "religion is the backbone of American culture, providing the moral and spiritual light needed for public and private life." Now, according to Watkins, we have a *new* absolute: "Religion is the bane of public life, so for the public good it should be banned from the public square."[185]

One significant reason this has happened is a popular, gross misconstruing of the First Amendment. Countless legal and media sources repeat *ad nauseum* that the separation of church and state prohibits the government from any involvement with religious matters. Public policy, we hear, should be kept separate from "religious matters."

The hypocrisy of the new absolutism is seen most clearly in "political correctness." To be politically correct is to be in line with certain ideals—abortion rights, multiculturalism, feminism, homosexual rights. To say or do anything which goes against these is politically *in*correct. And thinking that way, PC proponents believe, is absolutely wrong.

Consider, too, the logical problem with saying there are no absolutes. The statement "there are no absolutes" is itself a statement of an absolute truth. But if a statement claiming that there are no absolutes is true, then the statement itself can't be true. That is a logical impossibility. There simply is no way to conclude we live in a world of no absolutes.

Liberal arguments are rife with statements that contradict their assertion of moral relativism. To discern the convolutions, you need only to listen to what they are saying. When you catch one, use it as an opportunity to help the person examine the faulty foundation on which the non-absolute, "tolerant" worldview is built.

7.4— The Bible says, "Judge not, that you be not judged," which means we are not to judge the choices or behavior of a person as right or wrong. We all make mistakes, and thus we should not judge someone's actions or behavior according to any particular standard.
False. (Test question #70)

Tolerance advocates seem to have found the one absolute truth they are willing to live by: "Judge not, that you be not judged." The statement has become the great cry for open-mindedness when anyone has the courage to declare that someone else's belief, actions or lifestyle is morally amiss.

Another form of the same non-judgmental judgment is "that may be true for you, but it's not true for me." The logic behind the statement goes something like this: "Your truth is your truth, and my truth is my truth. We are both right, and I hold to my opinion of truth." This is like saying two chairs can occupy the same space around the dining room table at the same time, but it doesn't work.

Postmodernism's anti-rational concept of truth argues that even two opposite and wholly contradictory claims can both be true. Again, to draw a simple analogy: It's like saying black and white are the same color. But this is the absurdity of postmodernism. Yet it is often blithely accepted as the fundamental principle by which we should

SOCIAL ISSUES

respond to each other's ideas. In his book, *True for You, But Not for Me*, Paul Copan expands on the fallacy in this all-too-common thinking:

> It has been said that the most frequently quoted Bible verse is no longer John 3:16 but Matthew 7:1: "Do not judge, or you too will be judged." We cannot glibly quote this, though, without understanding what Jesus meant. When Jesus condemned judging, he wasn't at all implying we should never make judgments about anyone. After all, a few verses later, Jesus himself calls certain people "pigs" and "dogs" (Matt 7:60) and "wolves in sheep's clothing" (7:15)....What Jesus condemns is a critical and judgmental spirit, an unholy sense of superiority. Jesus commanded us to examine ourselves first for the problems we so easily see in others. Only then can we help remove the speck in another's eye—which, incidentally, assumes that a problem exists and must be confronted.[186]

If Americans don't start to judge and punish evil instead of accepting all ideas and beliefs as equal, we will become a nation that welcomes same-sex marriage, polygamy, pedophilia, incest, euthanasia, and likely a host of moral aberrations. I believe, though, that Americans had better start getting comfortable with politically incorrect, non-humanistic forms of making intelligent judgments on moral issues because God will hold us accountable for what we allow.

7.5— Homosexual marriages should be legalized.
False. (Test question #71)

Homosexual and lesbian activists are trying to redefine marriage to include same-sex couples. Although "redefining" something sounds simple enough, the proposition of redefining marriage is ludicrous and as a result should not be given legal sanction. Author and family expert Bob Knight explains why marriage cannot be redefined but only destroyed:

> The term "marriage" refers specifically to the joining of two people of the opposite sex. When that is lost, "marriage" becomes meaningless. You can no more leave an entire sex out of marriage and call it "marriage" than

you can leave chocolate out of a "chocolate brownie" recipe. It becomes something else. Giving non-marital relationships the same status as marriage does not expand the definition of marriage; it destroys it. For example, if you declare that, because it has similar properties, wine should be labeled identically to grape juice, you have destroyed the definitions of both "wine" and "grape juice." The consumer would not know what he is getting.[187]

Same-sex marriage should not be legalized because of the impact, both legally and culturally, that it will have, not only on the institution of marriage, but also on the family of which marriage is the foundation. Tony Perkins, president of the Family Research Council, explained the problem to a gathering of 20,000 people in the Seattle, Washington, area:

> Let me tell you another reason the policy of same-sex "marriage" will affect you. If you have not discovered this yet, you will. For those pushing the homosexual agenda, tolerance is not a two-way street. It is a one-way street: "their way."
>
> Just north of us in Canada, a measure currently in parliament, C-250, is about to become law. Known as the "chill bill," the law is targeted at churches and would ban publicly expressed opposition to same-sex "marriage" or any other political goal of homosexual groups. The quoting of Scripture will soon be hate speech.
>
> Already in Sweden sermons are explicitly covered by an anti-hate speech law passed to protect homosexuals. In England, the "Gender Recognition Bill," which was passed by the House of Lords last month, allows people to declare their gender and makes it illegal for a clergyman to refuse to conduct a marriage between two people of the same sex if they say they are not of the same sex.

In an article in *The Weekly Standard,* Stanley Kurtz offered another current example of what happens when marriage is corrupted:

SOCIAL ISSUES

Marriage in Scandinavia is in deep decline, with children shouldering the burden of rising rates of family dissolution. And the mainspring of the decline—an increasingly sharp separation between marriage and parenthood—can be linked to gay marriage.[188]

Peter Sprigg offered this caution in his address to the 2004 World Congress of Families in Mexico City:

And so, as one part of our broad-based efforts to support the traditional family, we oppose what is sometimes called "the gay agenda." It is an agenda that demands the full acceptance of the practice of homosexuality: morally, socially, legally, religiously, politically, and financially. Indeed, it calls for not only acceptance, but affirmation and celebration of this behavior as normal. It even demands that homosexuality be seen as desirable for those who desire it. This is "the gay agenda"—and we are against it.

This agenda has already made remarkable progress. Homosexual activists knew that their behavior would never be accepted as "normal" if doctors considered it a form of mental illness. Therefore, in 1973 they forced a resolution through the American Psychiatric Association to remove homosexuality from the Diagnostic and Statistical Manual of Mental Disorders. It is important for everyone to realize that the 1973 decision was *not* the result of new clinical research or scientific evidence. It was, rather, a *political* decision made in response to a vicious campaign of harassment and intimidation by homosexual activists.

Indeed, studies actually continue to show that homosexuals experience high rates of mental illness. For example, the Netherlands Mental Health Survey and Incidence Study, reported in the *Archives of General Psychiatry* in 2001, found that "people with same-sex sexual behavior are at greater risk for psychiatric disorders."[189] The fact that this is true even in one of the most "gay-friendly" nations on earth—indeed, the first nation to grant same-sex civil marriage—undermines any argument that such mental illnesses are merely a reaction to society's alleged "discrimination."

Peter Sprigg continued to click off the devastating impact that legalizing same-sex marriage will have on families in America:

> The final harm done by same-sex marriage would undoubtedly be a slide down the proverbial "slippery slope." Advocates of same-sex marriage seek to remove the potential for procreation from the definition of marriage, making gender irrelevant in the choice of a spouse, and re-defining marriage only in terms of a loving and committed relationship. If that happens, then it is hard to see how other restrictions upon one's choice of marriage partner can be sustained. These include the traditional restrictions against marrying a child, a close blood relative, or a person who is already married.
>
> While pedophile or incestuous marriages may be further off, polygamous marriages have much stronger precedents in history and culture than do even homosexual ones. Lawsuits have already been filed in American courts—with the support of the American Civil Liberties Union—demanding recognition of plural marriages. And—I am not making this up—news reports in recent weeks have carried stories of an Indian girl being married to a dog, and a French woman who was legally permitted (with the approval of the president of France) to marry her boyfriend—who is already dead. [190]

Lesbian activist Paula Ettelbrick, currently the executive director of the International Gay and Lesbian Human Rights Commission, has said that homosexuality "means pushing the parameters of sex, sexuality, and family, and in the process transforming the very fabric of society," but the truth is, homosexuality and homosexual civil marriage would *rip* the fabric of society in ways that may be difficult, if not impossible, to mend.[191]

Perhaps the most telling aspect of the legalization debate, though, is that gays are not interested so much in marriage as they are in their agenda. Numerous studies document that the average homosexual has hundreds of sexual relationships. Given this reality, it stands to reason that homosexuals are not interested in getting married and having one life partner but in using the marriage issue to further a liberal, anti-family, anti-Christian political agenda. Consider the following facts:

• The number of registered same-sex unions in Sweden is reported to be about 1,500 (for a total of 3,000 individuals) out of the estimated homosexual and lesbian population of 140,000.[192] This indicates that only about two percent of Swedish homosexuals and lesbians choose to enter into legally recognized unions. Put another way, about 98 percent of Swedish homosexuals and lesbians do not officially register as same-sex couples.[193]

• A news report by the Gay Financial Network predicted that "some 10,000 gay couples could be married" in the first year following the legalization of gay "marriage" in the Netherlands. In reality, far fewer chose to solemnize their relationships. The Office of Legislative Research released a report in October 2002 stating: "The Dutch Ministry of Economic Affairs reports that 3,383 of the 121,776 marriages licensed between April 1, 2001, and June 30, 2002, involved people of the same sex."[194]

The Dutch study of partnered homosexuals, which was published in the journal *AIDS*, found that men with a "steady" partner had an average of eight sexual partners per year.[195] Bell and Weinberg, in their classic study of male and female homosexuality, found that 43 percent of white male homosexuals had sex with 500 or more partners, with 28 percent having one thousand or more sex partners.[196]

In their study of the sexual profiles of 2,583 older homosexuals published in the *Journal of Sex Research*, Paul Van de Ven, et al, found that "the modal range for number of sexual partners ever [of homosexuals] was 101-500." In addition, 10.2 percent to 15.7 percent had between 501 and 1,000 partners. A further 10.2 percent to 15.7 percent reported having had more than one thousand lifetime sexual partners.[197]

A survey conducted by the homosexual magazine *Genre* found that 24 percent of the respondents said they had had more than one hundred sexual partners. The magazine noted that several respondents suggested including a category for those who had had more than one thousand sexual partners.[198]

Homosexual activist Michelangelo Signorile acknowledges the way the homosexual world operates and has said concerning the desire of homosexuals to get married and live in a monogamous relationship:

> For these men the term "monogamy" simply doesn't necessarily mean sexual exclusivity....The term "open relationship" has for a great many gay men come to have one specific definition: A relationship in which the partners have sex on the outside often, put away their resentment and jealousy, and discuss their outside sex with each other, or share sex partners.[199]

Former homosexual William Aaron explains why homosexuals are not interested in monogamy:

> In the gay life, fidelity is almost impossible. Since part of the compulsion of homosexuality seems to be a need on the part of the homophile to "absorb" masculinity from his sexual partners, he must be constantly on the lookout for [new partners]. Consequently the most successful homophile "marriages" are those where there is an arrangement between the two to have affairs on the side while maintaining the semblance of permanence in their living arrangement.[200]

To those who would suggest that restricting marriage to opposite sex couples is discriminatory, Bob Knight explains the fallacy in that thinking:

> Marriage laws are not discriminatory. Marriage is open to all adults, subject to age and blood relation limitations. As with any acquired status, the applicant must meet minimal requirements, which in terms of marriage, means finding an opposite-sex spouse. Same-sex partners do not qualify. To put it another way, clerks will not issue dog licenses to cats, and it is not out of "bigotry" toward cats. Comparing current laws limiting marriage to a man and a woman with the laws in some states that once limited inter-racial marriage is irrelevant and misleading. The very soul of marriage—the

joining of the two sexes—was never at issue when the Supreme Court struck down laws against inter-racial marriage.

Requiring citizens to sanction or subsidize homosexual relationships violates the freedom of conscience of millions of Christians, Jews, Muslims and other people who believe marriage is the union of the two sexes.

Civil marriage is a public act. Homosexuals are free to have a "union" ceremony with each other privately, but they are not free to demand that such a relationship be solemnized and subsidized under the law.

Homosexual activists say they need legal status so they can visit their partners in hospitals, etc. But hospitals leave visitation up to the patient, except in very rare instances. This "issue" is a smokescreen to cover the fact that, using legal instruments such as power of attorney, drafting a will, etc., homosexuals can share property, designate heirs, dictate hospital visitors and give authority for medical decisions. What they should not obtain is identical recognition and support for a relationship that is not equally essential to society's survival.[201]

Bob goes on to describe the legal and social fallout of redefining marriage to include same-sex couples:

If same-sex relationships acquire marital-type status in the law, several things will occur:

• Businesses that decline to recognize non-marital relationships will increasingly be punished through loss of contracts and even legal action. This is already occurring in San Francisco and in Canada.

• Other groups, such as bisexuals and polygamists, will demand the right to redefine marriage to suit their own proclivities. Once the standard of one-man, one-woman marriage is broken, there is no logical stopping point.

• As society rewards homosexual behavior, more young

people will be encouraged to experiment and more will be discouraged from overcoming homosexual desires.

• Popular understanding of what marriage is and what it requires will undergo change. Homosexual relationships, which usually lack both permanence and fidelity, are unlikely to change to fit the traditional model of lifelong, faithful marriage. Instead, society's expectations of marriage will change in response to the homosexual model, thus leading to a further weakening of the institution of marriage. Some homosexual activists have acknowledged that they intend to use marriage mainly as a way to radically shift society's entire conception of sexual morality.[202]

Dr. Timothy J. Dailey also describes why same-sex marriage is not a civil rights issue:

Defining marriage as the union of a man and a woman would not deny homosexuals the basic civil rights accorded other citizens. Nowhere in the Bill of Rights or in any legislation proceeding from it are homosexuals excluded from the rights enjoyed by all citizens—including the right to marry.

However, no citizen has the unrestricted right to marry whoever they want. A parent cannot marry their child (even if he or she is of age), two or more spouses, or the husband or wife of another person. Such restrictions are based upon the accumulated wisdom not only of Western civilization but also of societies and cultures around the world for millennia.[203]

Finally, America's Founders also proclaimed a crucial reason same-sex marriage should not be legalized. They told us that under our constitutional republic, we are not to make laws that contradict the laws of nature and nature's God. Homosexuality and lesbianism are against the laws of God and nature. God calls homosexuality an abomination, and He set marriage apart in the Garden of Eden when He said "Therefore a man shall leave his father and mother and be joined to his wife, and they shall become one flesh" (Genesis 2:24).

SOCIAL ISSUES

7.6— Since it is her body, a woman should be free to end her pregnancy with an abortion. *False.* (Test question #72)

— The Bible is not clear on whether abortion is right or wrong, so the individuals involved should be free to make their own choices. *False.* (Test question #73)

The idea that a woman should be free to end her pregnancy because "it is her body" begs the question of whether or not a woman even has a right to do whatever she wants with her body. Having the "right to choose" sounds seductively appealing to American ears, but the fact is that it is not now nor has it ever been true that any woman has a right to do anything she wants with herself. Is it legal, for instance, for a woman to commit suicide? No, women who try it are regularly arrested and taken to jail or a mental hospital. Can a woman lawfully shoot her veins up with methamphetamines or use her nose to snort cocaine? No. Is a woman allowed to sell her body for sex? Walk naked at a shopping mall? No again. Laws apply every day that prohibit women from doing certain things society deems unacceptable with their bodies. So to forbid the aborting of a child comes with plenty of legal precedence.

The idea that abortion is doing something with a woman's "own body" begs another serious question of whether or not an in-utero baby is part of the mother's body. Before the days of contemporary science, it may have been possible to intelligently assert that the baby and the woman are one. Nowadays, though, the idea is ludicrous in light of what we know. Kerby Anderson points out the unmistakable separate identity of a fetus:

> At conception the embryo is genetically distinct from the mother. To say that the developing baby is no different from the mother's appendix is scientifically inaccurate. A developing embryo is genetically different from the mother. A developing embryo is also genetically different from the sperm and egg that created it. A human being has forty-six chromosomes (sometimes forty-seven chromosomes). A sperm and an egg each have twenty-three chromosomes. A trained geneticist can distinguish between the DNA of an embryo and the DNA of a sperm and egg. But that geneticist cannot distinguish between DNA of a developing embryo and the DNA of a full-grown human being.[204]

SOCIAL ISSUES

In Exodus 21:22-25, we read there was punishment for causing harm or death to an unborn child, and Psalm 51:5 explains that a baby even has a sin nature. It is also noteworthy that the Biblical Greek word for "baby" is the same whether referring to a child inside or outside of his or her mother, clearly suggesting that God views the born and unborn baby equally. The Biblical worldview argues that abortion is murder, and the Ten Commandments is clear on that one: "Thou shalt not."

7.7— Christians should be directly opposed to a state lottery for numerous Biblical and economic reasons.
True. (Test question #74)
— **There is a Biblical basis for prohibiting various forms of gambling.** *True.* (Test question #75)

Since the Bible includes more than 1,700 verses that deal with finances, there is much that can be discerned about the Biblical view of gambling—particularly state-sponsored gambling. As we noted earlier, Romans 13:1-4 says the purpose of civil government is to protect the righteous and punish the wicked. Government officials are ministers of God. However, states that sponsor gambling are encouraging a vice that God says to avoid. Gambling encourages laziness, greed, and covetousness, and it takes advantage of the poor. A civil government does not fulfill its God-given purpose to protect and defend righteousness when it promotes unrighteous habits and wrong living

Casinos (riverboat and otherwise), lotteries, pull-tabs at the local bar, online gambling, horse tracks, and neighborhood poker games have become an American obsession. Despite the glitz and glowing promises of the gambling industry, the facts about its effect on our lives are not pretty:

> • Legalized gambling siphons off money from the economy. More money is wagered on gambling than is spent on elementary and secondary education ($286 billion versus $213 billion in 1990). Historian John Ezel concludes in his book *Fortune's Merry Wheel*, "If history teaches us anything, a study of over 1,300 legal lotteries held in the United States proves...they cost more than they brought in if their total impact on society is reckoned.[205]

• In one year, more than $550 billion is spent in legal-ized gambling. Each day, $88 million is spent on lotter-ies alone, more money than is spent on food.

• Ten million Americans have a gambling addiction. Six percent of all adolescents are addicted to gambling. Three-fourths of high school students are involved in some form of gambling. When gamblers come to the point of seeking help, their debts usually range between $18,000 and $50,000.

• When legalized gambling enters a new area, there is a 100 to 500 percent rise in compulsive gamblers, and at least two-thirds of these turn to crime to finance their addiction.

• A Colorado city realized a six-fold increase in child protection cases the year after a casino arrived.

• Domestic violence and child abuse dramatically increase.

• 20 percent of compulsive gamblers attempt suicide.

• *U.S. News* reports, "Crime rates are higher in places with gambling: 1,092 incidents per 10,000 population in 1994, compared with 593 per 10,000 for the entire nation."[206]

• In a testimony before a U.S. Congressional Committee on Small Businesses, the statement was made that for every $1.00 a state receives from gambling revenue, it costs at least $3.00 in increased services such as crimi-nal justice and welfare.

• About half of the college students surveyed in the United States and Canada said they had gambled at a casino during the previous year.

• In New Jersey, "gambling is festering in every high school and college," said Edward Looney, director of the New Jersey Council on Compulsive Gambling. "It's absolutely epidemic. Just about any college in the country has students who gamble at racetracks and casinos."[207]

• A veteran judge for some 25 years in the Municipal Courts of Chicago and the Circuit Court of Cook County, Illinois, Jacob M. Brande includes gambling as one of fifteen key causes of juvenile delinquency.[208]

Despite the devastating impact of gambling on Americans, many lawmakers continue to support legislation that allows the industry to proliferate. There are, however, conservative lawmakers who oppose legislation that expands gambling. They understand the economic liability, and they see the gambling issues through the lens of their Christian worldview.

Gambling is wrong from a Christian worldview for the following reasons:

(1) The Lottery: deception and legalized robbery. State-sponsored gambling is wrong because gambling is by its very nature deceptive in its marketing tactics and is really "legalized robbery." The next time you see a TV commercial or hear a radio commercial promoting a state lottery or a casino, listen carefully to what they present. It is not the truth. Do these commercials tell you that your chances of winning are so remote that you have a better chance of being struck by lightning or of a woman having triplets? Do the lottery commercials explain the devastating consequences of gambling on marriages and children? Not hardly. The commercials promise you a great time, lots of fun and happiness, and imply that you will get rich. This is outright deception, which the Bible condemns.

Numerous verses warn against deception and deceptive tactics, but let me just list a few:

• Leviticus 6:2— "When a person sins and acts unfaithfully against the LORD, and deceives his companion in regard to a deposit or a security entrusted *to him,* or through robbery, or *if* he has extorted from his companion."[209]

• Proverbs 6:19—God hates a "false witness *who* utters lies, and one who spreads strife among brothers."[210]

• Proverbs 11:18—"The wicked man earns an empty wage."

(2) Do not take advantage of the poor. National studies reveal that people who pay the dearest price for the vice of gambling are those in low-income families:

> Lotteries "are more aggressive than most other forms of gambling, since individuals in lower income brackets spend proportionally more money on them than do persons with higher income," according to the National Policy on Gambling.
>
> In Georgia, those who make less than $25,000 a year spend three times as much on lottery tickets than those who make $75,000 or more per year. On the national average, lottery gamblers with household incomes under $10,000 bet nearly three times as much on the lottery as those with incomes of more than $50,000.[211]

Economics professor and lottery expert Robert Goodman says that after three to five years, many people stop playing the lottery because they can no longer afford it.[212] You have a one in 12,912,583 chance of winning the lottery; you have a one in 705,000 chance of having quadruplets.[213]

First Timothy 5:8 warns: "But if anyone does not provide for his own, and especially for those of his household, he has denied the faith and is worse than an unbeliever." Many low-income people who play the lottery are taking money that should be used for milk, food, housing, healthcare, clothes, and other basics of life and squandering it on gambling.

Second Corinthians 12:14 also instructs: "Now for the third time I am ready to come to you. And I will not be burdensome to you; for I do not seek yours, but you. For the children ought not to lay up for the parents, but the parents for the children."

Paul did not burden the Corinthian church financially by depending on them to pay for his daily support. Rather, parents are responsible to provide for their children. Gambling takes away resources parents should be using to provide for their children.

(3) Do not covet. Exodus 20:17 says we are not to covet that which belongs to others, but when people gamble, they are coveting that which is not rightfully theirs and that which they have not earned through work or investing. Christians are to put their hands "to the plow" and *earn* money through hard work, not by pursuing get-rich-quick schemes or ill-gotten gains.

Proverbs 12:11 notes that "He who tills his land will be satisfied with bread, but he who follows frivolity is devoid of understanding."

Proverbs 28:20 observes, "A faithful man will abound with blessings, but he who hastens to get rich will not go unpunished."

The New Testament picks up the theme this way:

- 2 Thessalonians 3:10-12—"For even when we were with you, we commanded you this: If anyone will not work, neither shall he eat. For we hear that there are some who walk among you in a disorderly manner, not working at all, but are busybodies. Now those who are such we command and exhort through our Lord Jesus Christ that they work in quietness and eat their own bread."

- Ephesians 4:28—"Let him who stole steal no longer, but rather let him labor, working with his hands what is good, that he many have something to give him who has need."

Gambling should not create a moral dilemma for a Christian. It is clearly wrong.

7.8— The federal government should pass legislation that allows doctors and family members to decide when a loved one should be put to death based on the individual's quality of life. *False.* (Test question #76)

Although they may sound different, euthanasia and doctor-assisted suicide are actually two forms of the same issue. Some people even argue that euthanasia is consistent with a Biblical worldview, and it actually can be. It all depends on how you define the terms.

In *Moral Dilemmas,* Kerby Anderson explains the various forms of euthanasia:

SOCIAL ISSUES

- **Voluntary, passive euthanasia:** This form of euthanasia assumes that medical personnel, at the patient's request, will merely allow nature to take its course.... the physician did nothing to hasten death....[214]

- **Voluntary, active euthanasia:** This means that the physician, by request, hastens death by taking some active means (e.g., lethal injection).[215]

- **Involuntary, passive euthanasia:** This assumes that the patient has not expressed a willingness to die or cannot do so. The medical personnel do not go to any extraordinary measures to save the patient and often withhold food (by removing nasogastric tubes), antibiotics, or life-support systems (respirators).[216]

- **Involuntary, active euthanasia:** ...In this case the physician does something active to hasten death, regardless of the patient's wishes, for humanitarian reasons, economic considerations, or genetic justifications.[217]

Passive forms of euthanasia are not problematic in most cases because nothing is done to hasten the end of a person's life. Medical personnel keep a terminal patient as comfortable and pain-free as possible while allowing nature to take its course. It is the active forms of euthanasia that are of serious concern.

Active, involuntary euthanasia includes what is called "mercy killing" in which a family member or doctor takes the life of a terminally ill patient or a patient that has no "quality of life." In the past few years there have been several cases in which a wife or husband has shot and killed a sleeping spouse that was terminally ill or severely disabled by Alzheimer's or Parkinson's Disease. These spouses rightly have been prosecuted for murder.

In other forms of active involuntary euthanasia, family members convince a doctor to use drugs to terminate a patient, much as a veterinarian would put an ailing dog to sleep. Or at times a doctor simply does so without the family's knowledge or consent. Either situation is unacceptable.

Allowing even slight flexibility in favor of active forms of euthanasia has chilling results, as evidenced by what has happened in the euthanasia-friendly country of Holland:

SOCIAL ISSUES

The Dutch experience is instructive. A survey of Dutch physicians was made in 1990 by the Remmelink Committee. They found that 1,030 patients were killed without their consent. Of these, 140 were fully mentally competent and 110 were only slightly mentally impaired. The report also found that another 14,175 (1,701 of them were mentally competent) were denied medical treatment without their consent and died.[218]

The consequences of legalizing active euthanasia would impact every American—whether you agree with it or not—because of the inconceivable danger of doctor-assisted suicide being forced on those who do not want to be killed. Kerby Anderson describes the consequences as follows:

> First, physician-assisted suicide would change the nature of the medical profession itself. Physicians would be cast in the role of killers rather than healers. The Hippocratic Oath was written to place the medical profession on the foundation of healing, not killing. For twenty-four hundred years patients have had the assurance that doctors have taken an oath to heal them, not kill them. This would change with legalized euthanasia.
>
> Second, medical care would be affected. Physicians would begin to ration healthcare so that elderly and severely disabled patients would not be receiving the same quality of care as everyone else.
>
> Legalizing euthanasia would result in less care for the dying, rather than better care. Legalizing physician-assisted suicide would open the door to anyone wanting the "right" to kill themselves. Soon this would apply not only to voluntary euthanasia but also to involuntary euthanasia as various court precedents began to broaden the application of the right to die to other groups in society, like the disabled or the clinically depressed.[219]

While you will not find the word "euthanasia" in Scripture, the Biblical position on the issue is absolute. While many scriptures that address abortion also can be applied to euthanasia, there are scriptures that focus specifically on taking the life an adult. The death of King Saul is an important example:

SOCIAL ISSUES

Now it came to pass after the death of Saul,...behold, it happened that a man came from Saul's camp with his clothes torn and dust on his head....Then David said to him, "How did the matter go? Please tell me." And he answered, "The people have fled from the battle, many of the people are fallen and dead and Saul and Jonathan his son are dead also." So David said to the young man who told him, "How do you know that Saul and Jonathan his son are dead?" The young man who told him said, "As I happened by chance to be on Mount Gilboa, there was Saul, leaning on his spear; and indeed the chariots and horsemen followed hard after him. "Now when he looked behind him, he saw me and called to me. ...And he said to me...'Please stand over me and kill me, for anguish has come upon me, but my life still remains in me.' So I stood over him and killed him, because I was sure that he could not live after he had fallen."...So David said to him, "How was it you were not afraid to put forth your hand to destroy the LORD's anointed?" Then David called one of the young men and said, "Go near, and execute him." And he struck him down so that he died. So David said to him, "Your blood is on your own head, for your own mouth has testified against you, saying, 'I have killed the LORD's anointed.'" (2 Samuel 1:1-16, selected verses)

Here we see the issues of euthanasia and capital punishment in the same verses. Saul was injured on the battlefield and requested that the young man kill him. Instead of a doctor doing the killing, it was a soldier involved in active euthanasia. When the young man tells the new King David what he had done, David announces that the "mercy" killing was an act of murder and orders a death sentence. David's judgment makes clear that even *voluntary* active euthanasia is not to be tolerated.

As the king, David was the head of government, and he exercised his Biblical authority to wield capital punishment on one who had committed a capital crime. He adjudged that Saul had been murdered, not innocently "euthanized." In most cases, euthanasia is the deliberate taking of innocent life, and Biblical teaching renders that morally unacceptable[220] (see also Exodus 20:13, Matthew 5:21; 19:18, Mark 10:19, Luke 18:20, Romans 13:9).

7. Follow-up—For Further Thought about Social Issues

1. Define pluralism.

2. Define the Secular Humanist meaning of tolerance.

3. What did Jesus mean by "Judge not lest you be judged"?

4. What does the world mean by "judge not lest you be judged"?

5. Why should homosexual marriages not be legalized?

6. What does the Bible say about abortion?

7. Give two examples of how Secular Humanists' ideas have serious consequences?

8. What is the difference between active euthanasia and passive euthanasia?

9. When discussing abortion, why is it a fallacy for people to say that it is justifiable because a women can do what she wants with her body?

10. Why should Biblically minded Christians be opposed to state sponsored gambling?

11. What are seven consequences of rejecting a fixed moral standard as the foundation for law?

SOCIAL ISSUES

SECTION 8—HISTORY

8.1— The Founding Fathers had no Biblical reason in mind when they made America a constitutional republic instead of a pure democracy. *False.* (Test question #77)
— The more a government resembles a pure democracy the more disorder and confusion occur.
True. (Test question #78)
— The original intent of our Founding Fathers was to create a form of government that was free to set its own policy only if God had not already ruled in that area. Our Founders believed that manmade laws were not to contradict the laws of God. *True.* (Test question #79)

The Founders lived at a time when debating social philosophy was especially fashionable among intellectuals, and they could have chosen from a wide range of governmental forms in creating the American Consitution. However, they deliberately chose a system of government based on a standard that never changes even if—and particularly if—it is not consistent with what a deviant majority of the populace might desire.

Most Americans believe the United States originated as and now is a democracy, yet we are not. Our country was founded very intentionally as a constitutional republic. There are democratic elements in our system, to be sure, but the Founding Fathers were extremely determined that we not be a pure democracy. The pledge of allegiance states, "and to the republic for which it stands...." Yet, few Americans understand the critical distinctions between a democracy and a constitutional republic.

In his book *The Church at the End of the 20th Century*, the late Christian philosopher Francis Schaeffer called democracy "the dictatorship of the 51 percent."

U.S. War Department Training Manual No. 2000-25 explains in its definition of democracy why this is so:

Democracy: A government of the masses. Authority derived through mass meeting or any other form of "direct" expression. Results in mobocracy [mob rule]. Attitude toward property is communistic—negating property rights. Attitude toward law is that the will of the

HISTORY

majority shall regulate, whether it be based upon delib-
eration or governed passion, prejudice, and impulse,
without restraint or regard to consequences. Results
in demagogism [trying to stir up people by appeals to
emotion or prejudice in an attempt to establish a new
leader], license, agitation, discontent, anarchy.[221]

The framers of the U.S. Constitution so believed in the dangers
of democracy that they included a provision in the Constitution requiring that "each State maintain a republican form of government."[222]

Many of the individual Founders also wrote about the dangers
of a democracy:

> • Fischer Ames—"A democracy is a volcano which con-
> ceals the fiery materials of its own destruction. These
> will produce an eruption, and carry desolation in their
> way."[223]

> • Benjamin Rush—"A simple democracy is the devil's
> own government."[224]

> • John Adams—"Remember, democracy never lasts
> long. It soon wastes, exhausts, and murders itself.
> There never was a democracy yet that did not commit
> suicide."[225]

> • Noah Webster—"In democracy...there are commonly
> tumults and disorders . . .Therefore a pure democracy
> is generally a very bad government. It is often the most
> tyrannical government on earth."[226]

> • John Witherspoon—"Pure democracy cannot subsist
> long nor be carried far into the departments of state...it
> is very subject to caprice and the madness of popular
> rage."[227]

By contrast, the same military training manual cited earlier
explains the strength and benefits of a republic:

> **Republic:** Authority is derived through the election by
> the people of public officials best fitted to represent

them. Attitude toward property is respect for laws and individual rights and a sensible economic procedure. Attitude toward law is the administration of justice in accord with fixed principles and established evidence, with a strict regard to consequences. A greater number of citizens and extent of territory may be brought within its compass. Avoids the dangerous extreme of either tyranny or monocracy... results in statesmanship, liberty, reason, justice, contentment, and progress ...Our Constitutional fathers, familiar with the strength and weakness of both autocracy and democracy, with fixed principles definitely in mind, defined a representative form of government. They made a very marked distinction between a republic and a democracy and said repeatedly and emphatically that they had founded a republic.[228]

Noah Webster explained what the firm foundation and fixed principles of this republic must be:

[O]ur citizens should early understand that the genuine source of correct republican principals is the Bible, particularly the New Testament, or the Christian religion.[229]

In his book *Keys to Good Government,* historian and author David Barton outlines the distinction between the two forms of government:

The difference between a republic and a democracy is the source of its authority. In a democracy, whatever the people desire is what becomes policy. If a majority of the people decides that murder is no longer a crime, in a democracy, murder will no longer be a crime. However, not so in our republic: in our republic, murder will always be a crime, for murder is a crime in the Word of God. It is this foundation which has given our republic such enduring stability.[230]

John Adams adds to our understanding, "The very definition of a republic is 'an empire of laws and not of men.'"[231]

The Founders chose a constitutional republic because they understood that the heart of man was inclined toward evil, and that left to their own desires over time, people would naturally choose to do wrong. Their understanding of human nature was based, of course, on Scripture. The Bible clearly tells us that "every way of a man is right in his own eyes" (Proverbs 21:2), that "the heart is deceitful above all things, and desperately sick" (Jeremiah 17:9), and that "evil men and imposters will grow worse, deceiving and being deceived" (2 Timothy 3:13).

On the subject of mankind's inclination to do wrong, Alexander Hamilton in *The Federalists* answers the question of why government is a necessity:

> Why has government been instituted at all? Because the passions of men will not conform to the dictates of reason and justice without constraint... [T]he infamy of a bad action is to be divided among a number, than...to fall singly upon one.[232]

So just what is the "constraint" the American fathers set as the foundation of our republic? It is overwhelmingly documented that the foundation is the Bible. There we find the principles and standards for every area of life. As I noted in section 1.9, William Blackstone was the foremost legal authority of the Founders' day. His monumental *Blackstone's Commentaries on the Laws*, introduced in 1766, became the law book of the Founding Fathers, an authoritative source for the U.S. Supreme Court, and the basis of American law until 1920. Regarding the need to keep our laws consistent with God's laws, *Blackstone's Commentaries* states:

> To instance in the case of murder: this is expressly forbidden by the Divine...If any human law should allow or enjoin us to commit it, we are bound to transgress that human law...But, with regard to matters that are...not commanded or forbidden by those superior laws such for instance, as exporting of wool into foreign countries; here the...legislature has scope and opportunity to interpose.[233]

Other Founders supported this same Christian worldview. Alexander Hamilton, for instance, explained:

[T]he law...dictated by God Himself is, of course, superior in obligation to any other. It is binding over all the globe, in all countries, and at all times. No human laws are of any validity if contrary to this.[234]

Rufus King argued:

[T]he...law established by the Creator...extends over the whole globe, is everywhere and at all times binding upon mankind...[T]his is the law of God by which He makes His way known to man and is paramount to all human control.[235]

Unfortunately, most of this escapes modern Americans. In his report, *Practical Outcomes Replace Biblical Principles as the Moral Standard*, George Barna recounts:

In several instances there is a large gap between what people say is morally acceptable and what they say should be legal. This reflects the shift away from biblical principles and Christian values as the basis of modern law. Increasingly, Americans are looking for the law to reflect their personal preferences and desires rather than a universal set of absolutes based on God's dictates. If this trend continues then it stands to reason that we will inevitably experience increased instability in our laws, relationships and marketplace experiences.[236]

Even Christians fail to grasp the significance of God's Word in our society. Explaining why this shift in understanding has occurred, Barna states that religious institutions have failed to present a compelling case for Bible-based moral truth:

Most people do not believe there is any source of absolute moral truth. Even [self-professing] born-again individuals are abandoning the notion of law based on scriptural principles. Families, who hold a major responsibility for shaping the moral values and attitudes of children, are ill-equipped to do that job in relation to a Christian worldview or on the basis of a comprehensive and coherent notion of faith-based truth. The result is that busy people, regardless of their faith affiliation, wing it when it comes to moral decisions.[237]

Barna further reveals that many Americans do not comprehend how God desires for us to conduct the affairs of our nation. In another report, *Americans Are Most Likely to Base Truth on Feelings,* Barna writes:

> The virtual disappearance of this cornerstone of the Christian faith—that is, God has communicated a series of moral principles in the Bible that are meant to be the basis of our thoughts and actions, regardless of our preferences, feelings or situations—is probably the best indicator of the waning strength of the Christian Church in America today.[238]

The result of our misunderstanding is a downward spiral into lawlessness and disorder. The deterioration of America's freedoms will continue because we now lack the key component to sustain such freedom and liberties—knowledge and understanding of Biblical truths. In his book, *Original Intent,* David Barton expands on this reality:

> The Founders understood that Biblical values formed the basis of the republic and that the republic would be destroyed if the people's knowledge of those values should ever be lost...Understanding the foundation of the American republic is a vital key toward protecting it. Therefore, in analyzing public policy remember to ask, "Is this act consistent with our form of government?" and support or oppose the policy on that basis.[239]

The battle to display the Ten Commandments in America's public buildings is not just a religious battle but a battle to maintain the very foundation of America's form of government. Without the moral law of the Bible and without a Christian worldview, there is no foundation for America's constitutional republic.

To separate the Biblical worldview from our republican form of government means that we abolish the form of government given us by the Founders. Clearly, that is the goal of such groups as the American Civil Liberties Union, Americans United for the Separation of Church and State, and numerous socialistic, humanist organizations.

Contrary to the "neo-patriotic" position, Benjamin Rush believed the Bible should be a textbook in America's schools. He believed Christianity is the only worldview consistent with perpetuating our form of government:

> We profess to be republicans, and yet we neglect the only means of establishing and perpetuating our republican forms of government; that is, the universal education of our youth in the principles of Christianity by means of the Bible. For this Divine Book, above all others, favors that equality among mankind, that respect for just laws, and those sober and frugal virtues which constitute the soul of republicanism.[240]

In a similar vein, Noah Webster wrote a textbook entitled *History of the United States* in which he explained:

> The brief exposition of the Constitution of the United States will unfold to young persons the principles of republican government; and it is the sincere desire of the writer that our citizens should early understand that the genuine source of correct republican principles is the Bible, particularly the New Testament or the Christian religion.[241]

Dr. Jedidiah Morse warned about the possibility of allowing our foundation to be undermined: "Whenever the pillars of Christianity shall be overthrown, our present republican forms of government, and all the blessings which flow from them, must fall with them."[242]

The Founders cautioned repeatedly that we could not expect God's blessing or protection and could very well face His wrath if we made a practice of violating His principles. Engraved on the Jefferson Memorial in Washington, D.C., are these famous words of Thomas Jefferson (the author of the Declaration of Independence and our third president):

> God who gave us life gave us liberty. And can the liberties of a nation be thought secure when we have removed their only firm basis, a conviction in the minds of the people that these liberties are the gift of God?

That they are not to be violated but with His wrath? Indeed, I tremble for my country when I reflect that God is just; that His justice cannot sleep forever.

Similarly, George Washington wrote: "We ought to be no less persuaded that the propitious smiles of Heaven can never be expected on a nation that disregards the eternal rules of order and right which Heaven itself has ordained."[243]

George Mason, the Father of the Bill of Rights, speaking at the Constitutional Convention, also declared: "As nations cannot be rewarded or punished in the next world, so they must be in this. By an inevitable chain of causes and effects, Providence punishes national sins by national calamities."[244]

David Barton drives home the important point that a nation's laws, legislation, and policy will reflect its theology and belief (or non-belief) in God:

Of course, considering the spiritual implications of a policy is important only if there is a God, only if He has established transcendent rights and wrongs, and only if He responds on that basis. However, if one accepts these "ifs," then public policy must be analyzed accordingly.[245]

Regardless of what any majority of Americans may want, every law, every piece of legislation, and all public policy, must be consistent with the teachings of the Divine or we are not operating under the rules of a constitutional republic. The basis of our freedom lies not in the whims of the majority but in holding the will of the people in check. That is done by measuring our national will against God's unchanging standard and measuring whether we are being just or unjust, good or evil, right or wrong.

8.2— American Founding Fathers violated New Testament principles when they founded America.
False. (Test question #80)
- **Family, church and state are institutions ordained by God.** *True.* (Test question #81)

A nationally known pastor (that I appreciate and agree with most of the time) has written that the founding of America was a sin:

Over the past several centuries, people have mistakenly linked democracy and political freedom to Christianity. That's why many contemporary evangelicals believe the American Revolution was completely justified, both politically and scripturally. They follow the arguments of the Declaration of Independence, which declares that life, liberty, and the pursuit of happiness are divinely endowed rights.

Therefore those believers say such rights are part of a Christian worldview, worth attaining and defending at all cost including military insurrection at times. But such a position is contrary to the clear teachings and commands of Romans 13:1-7. So the United States was actually born out of a violation of New Testament principles, and any blessings God has bestowed on America have come in spite of that disobedience by the Founding Fathers.[246]

When you combine a lack of knowledge about the American Revolution with a false interpretation of Romans 13, you end up with well-meaning conservative Christians disagreeing with each other about our Founders and believing that America was *not* established under God but by an unChristian rebellion. My friend and regular Worldview Weekend speaker David Barton has written a paper entitled "Was the American Revolution a Biblically Justified Act?" in which he notes:

> The Presbyterians, Lutherans, Baptists, Congregationalists, and most other Christian denominations during the American Revolution believed that Romans 13 meant they were not to overthrow government as an institution and live in anarchy. This passage does not mean they had to submit to every civil law. Note that in Hebrews 11, a number of those who made the cut in the "Faith Hall of Fame" as heroes of the faith were guilty of civil disobedience—including Daniel, the three Hebrew Children, the Hebrew Midwives, Moses, etc....[247]

If the Founding Fathers had removed themselves from under the authority of Great Britain because they were choosing anarchy over an established government, that would have been a violation of

Romans 13. The Romans passage is not an endorsement of every government. It is a description of what God defines as the proper role of civil government.

In Scripture, God initiates several realms of authority in society: family, church, and state. We take these to be the normal pattern of social interaction, and civilizations throughout history have reflected these in some form. Simply because the presence of these institutions is normative, however, does not mean we should expect every instance of them to be acceptable.

Fathers are the God-ordained head of the family, but those who abuse their children and wives deserve to be removed from their positions of authority. Wives and children should not passively accept daily beatings just because the concept of family government gives the father a role as head of the home. God has created family order, but that does not mean the leader of every family is endorsed by God.

Few people disagree that a pastor or elder should be removed from leadership in the church—a God-ordained position of authority—if the leader is guilty of grave moral and ethical failures. Christians who attend a church where a leader remains even though violating God's standards should remove themselves from that church and find one that complies with God's principles.

Which brings us to the arena of civil government. Romans 13 articulates God's specific plan and purpose for state authorities. But as with church and family, God does not necessarily sanction every leader or every civil government that comes to power. God gives government the responsibility to punish wrongdoers and reward and protect the righteous, but it doesn't always work that way. Nazi Germany failed spectacularly in that calling. Likewise, Stalinist Russia. These modern examples are easy to judge. Yet the picture becomes similarly clear for America's early history when we understand the nature of eighteenth-century British rule over the colonies.

For eleven years, our Founders petitioned the King of England to cease his unlawful, unBiblical actions against the colonials. Although the monarch ignored their grievances, they remained dutifully under his authority until he sent 25,000 troops into the colonies for the purpose of seizing property, invading homes, and imprisoning people without trials. The king's actions violated his own British common law, the English Bill of Rights, and the centuries-old Magna Carta.

Once King George III started down the path of violent suppression, the Founders announced their intention to separate from Great Britain. They wrote at length that they were taking a stand for self-defense, which they correctly believed was Biblical. British troops fired the first shot in every confrontation leading up to the Revolutionary War—the Massacre of 1770, the bombing of Boston in 1774, and the Lexington and Concord engagements of 1775.

Unless you are a thoroughgoing pacifist, there is no basis for saying the Founders sinned in defending themselves against King George's troops and their terrorist tactics against colonists. The Founders' fight was not a "military insurrection." Our early leaders took seriously their standing before God and believed He could bless a war of defense but not a war of offense. They fought to protect their own lives and those of their families and friends.

Many Christians get queasy over the subject of "civil disobedience" (for further discussion of civil disobedience, see section 1.5) and invoke Romans 13 to avoid the responsibility of standing up to a deviant government. While I agree it is crucial that Christians pursue civil disobedience only when obeying government requires us to disobey God, Scripture offers clear direction on when such action is acceptable. Kerby Anderson points out the following Biblical principles for civil disobedience:

1. The law or injunction being resisted should clearly be unjust and unbiblical.

2. The means of redress should be exhausted.

3. Christians must be willing to accept the penalty for breaking the law.

4. Civil disobedience should be carried out in love and with humility.

5. Civil disobedience should be considered only when there is some possibility of success.[248]

Our nation was founded under God's guiding hand—not in *spite* of it.

8.3— The Bible and a Biblical worldview played an instrumental role in building American civilization, our original laws, and our form of government.
True. (Test question #82)

In December 1982, *Newsweek* ran a cover story about the influence of the Bible on America. The article discussed the declaration by Ronald Reagan and the U.S. Congress of 1983 as the year of the Bible and explored the question: Was America founded as a nation under God? The article noted:

> For centuries [the Bible] has exerted an unrivaled influence on American culture, politics, and social life. Now historians are discovering that the Bible, perhaps even more than the Constitution, is our founding document: The source of the powerful myth of the United States as a special, sacred nation, a people called by God to establish a model society, a beacon to the world.[249]

While I don't agree that it is a *myth* of any kind that America was founded by men called by God, I am pleased that *Newsweek* acknowledged that the Bible was "perhaps" the foundation upon which the nation was founded.

Not to be outdone, the May 25, 1987, issue of *Time* featured an article entitled, "Looking to Its Roots" which explained:

> Ours is the only country deliberately founded on a good idea. That good idea combines a commitment to man's inalienable rights with the Calvinist belief in an ultimate moral right and sinful man's obligation to do good. These articles of faith, embodied in the Declaration of Independence and in the Constitution, literally govern our lives today.

Anyone who wonders whether or not America was founded as a nation under God need only spend a few hours reading the writings of the Founders to answer this question. They were such prolific writers that, even today, some of their letters and diaries have still not been studied. The thousands upon thousands of personal writings, letters, journals, and speeches that have been examined, however, reveal a far different picture than liberal revisionist historians want you to know.

After reviewing some 15,000 items—newspaper articles, pamphlets, books, monographs, etc.—written between 1760 and 1805 by the 55 men who wrote the Constitution, Professors Donald S. Lutz and Charles S. Hyneman reported in the 1984 *American Political Science*

Review that the Bible contributed 34 percent of all quotations used by our Founding Fathers.[250] Other significant sources for the Founders' writings include: Baron Charles Montesquieu (8.3%), Sir William Blackstone (7.9%), John Locke (2.9%), David Hume (2.7%), Plutarch (1.5%), Beccaria (1.5%), Trenchard and Gordon (1.4%), Delolme (1.4%), Samuel von Pufendorf (1.3%), Cicero (1.2%), Hugo Grotius (0.9%), Shakespeare (0.8%), and Vattel (0.5%).

It is noteworthy that of these additional citations, *sixty percent* were quotations from Scripture used in the writings cited. When you add the direct and indirect citations together, you find that nearly *three-quarters* of all quotations referenced by the Founding Fathers come from the Bible![251] Here are a few samples:

- **John Jay,** the original Chief Justice of the U.S. Supreme Court and one of the men most responsible for the Constitution wrote: "Providence has given to our people the choice of their rulers, and it is the duty—as well as the privilege and interest—of our Christian nation to select and prefer Christians for their rulers."[252]

- **George Washington** in his "Farewell Address" discussed the vital role that religion and morality should play in our nation: "Of all the dispositions and habits, which lead to political prosperity, religion and morality are indispensable supports. In vain would that man claim the tribute of patriotism, who should labor to subvert these great pillars."[253] He also noted that "without such a firm foundation, liberties and freedoms were at risk: Let it simply be asked, 'Where is the security for life, for reputation, and for property, if the sense of religious obligation desert?'"[254]

- **Benjamin Franklin** was one of America's least religious founders. Yet on June 28, 1787, frustrations were running high at the Constitutional Convention when the aging Franklin rose to his feet and declared: "If a sparrow cannot fall to the ground without His notice, is it probable that an empire can rise without His aid? We've been assured in the sacred writing that 'Except the Lord build the house, they labor in vain that build it'."[255]

If our Founders had actually intended to found America as a secular nation, as liberals claim, why did they reference God and Holy Scriptures so readily in our founding documents? In the Declaration of Independence, God is mentioned four times:

1) "[T]he Laws of Nature and of Nature's God...." The "Laws of Nature" refer to the natural laws God built into man and creation. The laws of "Nature's God" references God's laws found in the Bible.

2) "[A]ll Men are created equal, they are endowed by their Creator with certain unalienable Rights...." "Creator" is a reference to the Creator God.

3) "[A]ppealing to the Supreme Judge of the World for the Rectitude of our Intentions...." The Supreme Judge of the World is God.

4) "[W]ith a firm Reliance on the Protection of Divine Providence...." A reference to God's power, wisdom, and sovereignty.

Many skeptics point out that neither God nor the Bible are mentioned in the U.S. Constitution. But the Declaration of Independence had already established the role of God and the Bible, so further reference was not necessary. The Declaration of Independence and the U.S. Constitution are equally important, and it is the Declaration that lays the foundation for the Constitution. As Constitutional historian and legal expert John Eidsmoe points out:

The Declaration has been repeatedly cited by the U.S. Supreme Court as part of the fundamental law of the United States of America. The *United States Code Annotated* includes the Declaration of Independence under the heading "The Organic Laws of the United States of America" along with the Articles of Confederation, the Constitution, and the Northwest Ordinance. Enabling Acts frequently require states to adhere to the principles of the Declaration; in the Enabling Act of June 16, 1906, Congress authorized Oklahoma Territory to take steps to become a state. Section 3 provides that the

Oklahoma Constitution "shall not be repugnant to the Constitution of the United States and the principles of the Declaration of Independence."[256]

Eidsmoe also describes the relationship between the Declaration and the Constitution:

The Declaration is a statement of the basic American values or principles: equality, God-given rights. The Constitution is the means by which these rights are to be secured: a federal republic consisting of a federal government and state governments, with certain powers delegated to the federal government and others reserved for the states, with those powers separated into legislative, executive, and judicial branches. The Declaration is the foundation; the Constitution is the structure built on that foundation.[257]

And later:

The Constitution is built on the Declaration of Independence, and the Declaration finds practical expression in the Constitution. Neither can be fully understood without the other.[258]

Each of our states, in order to be admitted to the Union, had to establish a constitutional republic as the basis of their state government. Thus it was natural for every state constitution to acknowledge God. Let's look at a few examples:

- **Maryland,** 1776, Preamble: "We the people of the state of Maryland, grateful to Almighty God for our civil and religious liberty...."

- **Pennsylvania,** 1776, Preamble: "We, the people of Pennsylvania, grateful to Almighty God for the blessings of civil and religious liberty, and humbly invoking His guidance...."

- **South Carolina,** 1778, Preamble: "We the people of the State of South Carolina...grateful to God for our liberties, do ordain and establish this Constitution...."

- **Minnesota,** 1857, Preamble: "We, the people of the State of Minnesota, grateful to God for our civil and religious liberty, and desiring to perpetuate its blessings...."

- **Alabama,** 1901, Preamble: "We the people of the State of Alabama...invoking the favor and guidance of Almighty God, do ordain and establish the following Constitution...."

- **Alaska,** 1956, Preamble: "We, the people of Alaska, grateful to God and to those who founded our nation and pioneered this great land...."

Not only was America founded by men who had a strong belief in God, but America was founded by men who had a strong commitment to applying God's principles in creating our form of government. The Founders set up our government based on a Biblical understanding of man's relationship to God and man's struggle with his sinful nature.

8. Follow-up—For Further Thought about History

1. Describe the difference between a constitutional republic and a pure democracy.

2. How did the Bible and a Biblical worldview influence America's founding? Give specific examples.

3. List the four times that God is mentioned in the Declaration of Independence.

4. Why was the founding of America by the Founding Fathers not a violation of New Testament principles?

EPILOGUE

What Now?

By reading this book, you've already demonstrated your desire to think like a Biblically minded Christian, and that in itself is a great service to our Lord. The world desperately needs more people who hold firm an uncompromising commitment to Biblical truth. Now that you're through *Put Your Beliefs to the Test*, I would ask you to take our free online worldview test again (at www.worldview-weekend.com) and see how much your score improves over how you did before reading the book. Be encouraged that any improvement means you're growing in living out a Biblical worldview, wherever you find yourself.

High school and college students: be aware that your beliefs will be tested over and over again, but stand strong. Be ready to give a reason for the hope that you profess and an answer for why you believe what you profess. As 1 Peter 3:15 reminds us: "sanctify the Lord God in your hearts, and always be ready to give a defense to everyone who asks you a reason for the hope that is in you, with meekness and fear." Every high school student, before going to college, should attend Dr. David Noebel's two-week worldview program. For further details visit www.summit.org.

Adults, please consider leading a worldview class in your community with other adults and/or students. If you can push "play" on a CD and DVD player, then you can lead a worldview class with our curriculum, *Developing a Christian Worldview*. It's available in our online bookstore at www.worldviewweekend.com.

Also, the Worldview Weekend online institute offers family and group rates. You can check out the free demo at www.worldviewtraining.com.

In conclusion, let me also challenge you with the following three points:

1. **Live a life centered around pleasing God, not men, by doing His will *from the heart*, not as a legalistic compulsion.**

• Ephesians 6:6—"...as bondservants of Christ, doing God's will from your heart."

• Romans 6:17—"...you obeyed from the heart that form of doctrine to which you were delivered."

• Matthew 22:37—"Jesus said to him, 'You shall love the Lord your God with all your heart, with all your soul, and with all your mind.'"

2. Fulfill the Great Commission: To make disciples who follow Jesus Christ.

Many people believe the Great Commission directs us solely toward evangelizing the lost, but that is not the case. The Great Commission is a call to *make disciples*. Yes, we have to lead people to Jesus Christ first, but then we have to disciple them so they can grow in their Biblical knowledge and wisdom. Worldview training and Worldview Weekends is all about making disciples for Jesus Christ.

• Ezra 7:10—"...Ezra had prepared his heart to seek the Law of the Lord, and to do it, and to teach statutes and ordinances in Israel."

Ezra was committed to making disciples in Israel. Are you committed to making disciples in your city, state, and nation?

3. Have a comprehensive Biblical worldview so you'll understand the times and know what God would have you do.

In addition to watching the news, reading the newspaper, and surfing the internet news, be sure to read your Bible so you can understand the times in light of God's Word. Nothing is happening in our world today that is a surprise to God, and Scripture addresses every major issue facing our world today. Read your Bible to have a wise perspective on the times and to find out what God would have you do.

• 1 Chronicles 12:32 tells us that in Israel there were men "who had understanding of the times to know what Israel ought to do."

Thank you for reading this book and for endeavoring to love the Lord with your heart, soul, strength, and *mind*.

APPENDIX 1—TOPICAL SCRIPTURES

Gambling, the Lottery, and Taking Advantage of the Poor
Exodus 20:17
Leviticus 6:2
Proverbs 6:19; 11:18; 12:11; 14:21,31; 22:16; 28:20
Isaiah 3:14
Amos 5:11-12.
1 Timothy 5:8
2 Corinthians 12:14
2 Thessalonians 3:10-12
Ephesians 4:28

Pornography
Proverbs 23:71
Matthew 5:27-28
Corinthians 6:18
Romans 13:14
1 Peter 2:11

Capital Punishment
Genesis 9:5-6; 6-8; 18-19
Exodus 11; 14; 22
Leviticus 20
Numbers 13-14; 16
Deuteronomy 18-19
Romans 13:1-7

Abortion
Exodus 21:22-25
Psalm 139:13-16

Divorce
Deuteronomy 24:1-4
Malachi 2:10-16
Matthew 5:31-32; 19:8-9
1 Corinthians 7:10-15
1 Timothy 3:2

Polygamy
1 Timothy 3:2

Cohabitation/Pre-Marital Sex
Genesis 2:18,24
Deuteronomy 22:30
Leviticus 18:8
Mark 7:21-23
Romans 13:1,13

1 Corinthians 5:1-3; 6:16,18; 7:2,36-37
Ephesians 5:3,31; 6:1-2
1 Thessalonians 4:3-5
Hebrews 13:4
1 Peter 2:13

Drunkenness/Drugs
Deuteronomy 21:20-21
Proverbs 20:1
Isaiah 5:11
Amos 6:1
Habakkuk 2:15-16
1 Corinthians 6:9-10
Galatians 5:19-21
Ephesians 5:18

Civil Disobedience
Exodus 1; 2
Proverbs 24:11-12
Daniel 6
Matthew 24:45
Acts 4; 5
James 4:17

Movies, Music, Media and Video Games
Romans 13:13
Philippians 4:8
Colossians 3:8
2 Timothy 2:22
Hebrews 5:14

Homosexuality
Genesis 19
Leviticus 18:22; 20:13
Romans 1:26-27
1 Corinthians 6:9-10
1 Timothy 1:10

Murder
Proverbs 6:16-17

Same-Sex Marriage
Genesis 2:24
1 Timothy 3:2

Divorce
Deuteronomy 24:1-4
Malachi 2:10-16
Matthew 5:31,32; 19:8-9

1 Corinthians 7:10-15
1 Timothy 3:2

Adultery
Exodus 20:14

Active Euthanasia
Genesis 1:26
Exodus 20:13
Deuteronomy 32:39
2 Samuel 1:9-16
Job 1:21; 42:2-3
Psalm 139:16
Ecclesiastes 3:2
Isaiah 55:8-9
Matthew 22:39
1 Corinthians 15:26,56
Galatians 6:2
Ephesians 5:29

Radical Environmentalism
(Verses that show nature is not to be worshipped because God stands outside of His creation)
Genesis 1; 2
Job 38-41
Psalms 19; 24; 104; 139:13-16
Romans 1:18-20
Colossians 1:16-17

(Verses addressing the need to take care of God's creation)
Genesis 2:15
Leviticus 25:1-12
Deuteronomy 22:6; 25:4
Job 38:25-28
Psalm 104:27-30
Isaiah 5:8-10

Appendix 1

The Qualifications and Duties of a Ruler

(Adapted from: Swanson, J., & Nave, O., *New Nave's* (Oak Harbor: Logos Research Systems, 1994).)

Character and Qualifications

Genesis 41:33	Proverbs 16:10-13; 17:7;	28:6; 60:17
Exodus 18:21-22; 23:8	19:12; 20:8,26,28; 21:1;	Jeremiah 13:18
Deuteronomy 1:13;	24:23–26; 25:2,3,5;	Romans 12:8; 13:1–7
16:18-20; 27:19	28:2,16; 29:2,4,14;	1 Timothy 2:1-2
2 Samuel 23:3-4	31:4,5,8,9	1 Peter 2:13-14
Ezra 7:25	Ecclesiates 8:4; 10:16-17	
Psalms 2:10-11; 72:1-17	Isaiah 5:22-23; 16:5;	

Duties

Exodus 18:16,20,21;	19:18-19; 24:16; 25:1	Jeremiah 2112; 22:1-3
23:3,6,7,9	Joshua 1:7-8	Zechariah 7:9-10; 8:16
Leviticus 19:15; 24:22	2 Chronicles 9:8; 19:6-7	Romans 13:3
Numbers 27:16-7;	Ezra 7:25-26	1 Timothy 2:2
Deuteronomy 1:16-17;	Psalms 82:2-4; 148:11, 13	1 Peter 2:14
16:18-20; 17:16-20;	Isaiah 58:6	

The Free Enterprise System

(Adapted from: Swanson, J., & Nave, O., *New Nave's* (Oak Harbor: Logos Research Systems, 1994).)

Bribery
Exodus 23:8
Deuteronomy 16:18-19; 27:251
Samuel 8:1-3
Job 15:34
Psalm 26:9-10
Proverbs 15:27; 17:8,23; 18:16; 21:14; 25:14; 28:21; 29:4
Ecclesiastes 7:7
Isaiah 1:23; 5:22-23; 33:15-16
Ezekiel 13:19; 22:12-13
Amos 2:6; 5:12
Micah 7:3

Collateral or Surety
Genesis 44:32
Exodus 22:26-27
Deuteronomy 24:10-13
Job 24:3
Proverbs 6:1-5; 11:15; 17:18; 20:16; 22:26-27; 27:13
Ezekiel 18:7,12; 33:15

Amos 2:8

Creditors
Exodus 21:2-6; 22:25-27
Leviticus 25:14-17, 35-37 Deuteronomy 15:2-3; 23:19-20; 24:6,10-13,17
Matthew 5:42
Luke 6:34
Oppressions of:
2 Kings 4:1
Nehemiah 5:1-13
Job 20:18-20; 22:6; 24:3, 9-10
Proverbs 22:26-27
Matthew 5:25-26; 18:28-35
Luke 12:58,59
Merciful:
Psalm 112:5
Matthew 18:23-27
Luke 7:41-43

Debtors
Exodus 21:2-6; 22:10-15
Leviticus 25:14-17, 25-

41,47-55
2 Kings 4:1-7
Nehemiah 5:3-5; 10:31
Job 20:18-19
Matthew 5:25-26,40; 18:23-33
Luke 20:9-16

Dishonesty
Leviticus 6:2-7; 19:13, 35-36; 25:13, 15-16
Job 24:2-11
Psalms 37:21; 50:18; 62:10
Proverbs 3:27-28; 11:1; 20:10,14,17,23
Isaiah 32:7
Jeremiah 7:8-10; 9:4-6,8; 22:13
Ezekiel 22:29
Hosea 4:1-2; 12:7
Amos 3:10; 8:5
Micah 6:10-11
Nahum 3:1
Zephaniah 1:9
Zechariah 5:3-4
Luke 16:1-8

1 Thessalonians 4:6
James 5:4

Extortion
Genesis 25:31; 47:13-26
Psalm 109:11
Isaiah 16:4
Ezekiel 22:12
Micah 3:2-3
Matthew 23:25
Luke 18:11
1 Corinthians 5:10-11;
6:10

Honesty
Leviticus 19:35-36
Deuteronomy 16:20;
25:13-16
Job 27:6
Psalm 7:3-4; 15:5; 24:4
Proverbs 4:25; 11:1; 12:22;
16:11; 20:10,23
Isaiah 33:15-16
Ezekiel 45:10
Mark 10:19
Luke 3:12-13; 6:31
Matthew 7:12
Acts 24:16
2 Corinthians 4:1-2; 7:2;
8:21
Philippians 4:8
Colossians 3:22
1 Thessalonians 4:11-12
Hebrews 13:18
1 Peter 2:12

Idleness and Sloth
Forbidden:
Romans 12:11
Hebrews 6:12
Produce apathy: Proverbs
12:27; 26:15
Akin to extravagance:
Proverbs 18:9
Accompanied by conceit:
Proverbs 26:16
Lead to poverty:
Proverbs 10:4; 20:4,13;
24:34;
Hunger:
Proverbs 19:15

Bondage:
Proverbs 12:24
Disappointment:
Proverbs 13:4; 21:25
Ruin:
Proverbs 24:30,31
Ecclesiastes 10:18
Tattling and meddling:
1 Timothy 5:13
*Effects of, afford
instruction to others:*
Proverbs 24:30-32
Remonstrance against:
Proverbs 6:6,9
False excuses for:
Proverbs 20:4; 22:13
Illustrated:
Proverbs 26:14
Matthew 25:18,26

Interest
Exodus 22:25
Leviticus 25:36-37
Deuteronomy 23:19-20
Nehemiah 5:1-13
Psalm 15:5
Proverbs 28:8
Isaiah 24:2
Ezekiel 18:8-9,13,17;
22:12

Laziness
Proverbs 6:6,9-11;
10:4,5,26; 12:9,24,27;
13:4; 14:23; 15:19;
18:9; 19:15,24; 20:4,13;
21:13,25,26; 23:21; 24:30-
34; 26:13-16
Ecclesiastes 4:5; 10:18
Isaiah 56:10
Ezekiel 16:49
Matthew 20:6-7; 25:26-27
Luke 19:20-25
Acts 17:21
Romans 12:11
2 Thessalonians 3:10-11
1 Timothy 5:13
Hebrews 6:12

Lending
Exouds 22:25-27

Leviticus 25:35-37
Deuteronomy 15:1-11;
23:19-20; 24:6,10-13,17
Nehemiah 5:1-13
Psalms 37:25-26; 112:5
Proverbs 19:17; 22:7; 28:8
Isaiah 24:1-2
Ezekiel 18:13
Matthew 5:42
Luke 6:34-35

The Need to Work
Genesis 2:15; 3:19
Exodus 20:9-11; 23:12;
34:21; 35:2
Leviticus 19:13; 23:3
Deuteronomy 5:13; 24:14-
15; 25:4
Proverbs 10:4-5;
12:11,24,27; 13:4,11,23;
14:4,23; 16:26; 20:13;
21:5; 22:29; 27:23-27;
28:19; 30:25-28; 31:13-27
Ecclesiastes 1:3; 2:10-
11,17-22; 5:12; 9:10;
11:4,6
Jerermiah 22:13
Malachi 3:5
Matthew 20:1-15
Luke 10:7
Acts 20:35
Romans 12:11
1 Corinthians 9:9
Ephesians 4:28
1 Thessalonians 4:11-12;
3:7-13
Thessalonians 3:10-12
1 Timothy 5:8,18
James 5:4

**The Poor and Our Duty
to the Poor**
Exous 22:25-27; 23:11
Leviticus 19:9-10; 23:22;
25:25-28,35-37,39-43
Deuteronomy 14:28-29;
15:2-14; 24:12-21;
26:12-13
Nehemiah 8:10
Psalms 37:21,26; 41:1-3;

112:4-5,9
Proverbs 28:27; 29:7;
31:9,20
Isaiah 1:17; 16:3-4;
58:7,10
Ezekiel 18:7,16,17
Daniel 4:27
Zechariah 7:10
Matthew 5:42; 19:21;
25:35-36
Mark 14:7
Luke 3:11; 6:30; 11:41;
12:33; 14:12-14;
18:22; 19:8
Acts 20:35
Romans 12:8,13,20
1 Corinthians 13:3; 16:1-2
2 Corinthians 6:10; 8:9;
9: 1-15
Galatians 2:10; 6:10
Ephesians 4:28
1 Timothy 5:9-10,16
Hebrews 13:3
James 1:27; 2:2-9,
15-16; 5:4
1 John 3:17-19

Private Contract
Genesis 21:25-32; 23:18;
26:3,15,31; 29:15-20,23-
30; 30:28-34,37-43;
31:7,44-54
Exodus 4:18
Numbers 18:19
Joshua 9:15,20
Ruth 4:1-2,6-8
1 Samuel 18:4
1 Kings 5:9-11; 9:11
1 Chronicles 16:16
Proverbs 6:1; 11:21;
17:18; 22:26
Jeremiah 32:10-15
Ezekiel 17:18
Colossians 2:14
Hebrews 6:16,17

**The Responsibilities of
the Employee and the
Employer**
Leviticus 19:13; 25:6,43
Deuteronomy 5:14; 15:18;

24:14-15
Ruth 2:4
Job 7:1-3; 14:1,6;
31:13-15
Proverbs 22:16; 29:21
Jeremiah 22:13
Malachi 3:5
Matthew 10:10; 20:1-15;
21:33-41
Luke 10:7; 15:15-16,17,19
John 10:12-13
Romans 4:4
Ephesians 6:9
Colossians 4:1
1 Timothy 5:18
Philemon 15,16
James 5:4-5

Restitution
*To be made for injury to
life, limb, or property:*
Exodus 21:30-36
Leviticus 24:18
For theft:
Exodus 22:1-4 Prov. 6:30-
31 Ezekiel 33:15
For dishonesty:
Leviticus 6:2-5
Numbers 5:7
Job 20:18
Ezekiel 33:15
Luke 19:8

The Rich
Deuteronomy 6:10-12;
8:10-18; 31:20; 32:15
1 Samuel 2:7
Psalm 37:16
Proverbs 10:2,22; 11:4,28;
13:7-8; 14:24; 15:6,16-17;
16:8; 19:4; 21:6; 23:4-
5; 27:23-24; 28:8,20,22;
30:8-9
Ecclesiastes 5:9-20; 6:1-2;
7:11-12; 10:19
Isaiah 5:8
Jeremiah 48:36
Hosea 12:8
Matthew 6:19-21; 13:22;
19:16-29
Mark 4:19; 10:17-25

Luke 12:15; 18:18-25
1 Timothy 6:4-11,17-19
James 2:6-7; 5:1-5
1 John 3:17

**Rights of Property
Owners**
In Real Estate:
Genesis 21:25-30; 23:17-
18; 26:18-22; 47:22
Exodus 21:4; 22:5-6
Leviticus 25:29-33;
27:14-25
Numbers 27:1-11; 36:1-9
Deuteronomy 19:14; 27:17
1 Kings 21:15-16
2 Kings 8:1-6
Ecclesiastes 2:21
Personal
Exodus 20:17; 21:28-36;
22:9-15
Deuteronomy 5:21; 22:1-
3; 23:25
Leviticus 6:3-4; 27:9-13,
26-33
Proverbs 22:26-27
Jeremiah 32:7

Wages
Genesis 29:15-30; 30:28-
34; 31:7,41
Leviticus 19:13
Deuteronomy 24:14-15;
25:4
Jeremiah 22:13
Haggai 1:6
Malachi 3:5
Matthew 10:10; 20:1-15
Luke 3:14; 10:7
Romans 4:4; 6:23
Colossians 4:1
James 5:4

APPENDIX 2—MODERN-DAY LIBERAL WORLDVIEW CHART

	Education	Science/Medicine	Religion/Church	Government	Family	Entertainment & Media
Theology Atheism-No such thing as God	Secular Humanism from kindergarten through college	Darwinian Evolution	Secular & Cosmic Humanism (New Age Movement) is only accepted religion; heaven on earth	Since there is no God, government is the highest form of authority	Not instituted by God but created by man to be whatever brings pleasure	Sitcoms mock God and Christians & Christian morality
Philosophy Naturalism	No spiritual or supernatural world	Man has no soul. Survival of the fittest is the rule; therefore abortion, euthanasia, & embryonic stem cell research is acceptable	Humanist John Dewey, signer of the Humanist Manifesto I said there is no reason for religion because man has no soul	Since there is no God, He does not move in the affairs of men and there is no divine providence	Fathers and mothers have no spiritual responsibility to their children	Life portrayed as having no meaning
Ethics Moral Relativism	Situational ethics, values clarification courses.	Moral relativism allows doctors to ignore Hippocratic Oath & perform abortions & active euthanasia	Humanists say people are basically good & Christianity is evil and intolerant because it proclaims absolute truth	Moral relativism allows legislation for abortions, active euthanasia and other such violations of the moral law	Abortion on demand & active euthanasia	Hedonism is the pursuit of pleasure and is the highest pursuit of life
Biology Darwin's Evolution	Darwin's Evolution based on natural selection & DNA mistakes	Evolution is taught to the exclusion of creationism	Life devalued by doctors that reject man's being created in the image of God. Scientists explore other planets looking for the origin of life	U.S. Supreme Court outlaws creation being taught alongside evolution in 1987 decision	Families evolve into whatever society accepts as normal	Evolution promoted as fact and creationism as unscientific and accepted by uneducated Christians
Psychology Man Has No Soul	Death education and life boat values clarification scenarios promote that man dies and that is it	Abortion & euthanasia are acceptable because man dies and that is it	Man can solve his own problems & has no need for religion or God; Cosmic Humanists believe man can save himself	Supreme Court legalizes abortion & outlaws bans on partial birth abortion and refuses case on active euthanasia in 2005	No spiritual heritage to develop and pass on to children because there is no spiritual world	Man can solve his own problems & New Age themes promote that man can save himself while Secular Humanists promote death is the end

Appendix 2

This chart was written by Brannon S. Howse and adapted from the basic chart of Summit Ministries.

	Education	Science/Medicine	Religion/Church	Government	Family	Entertainment & Media
Sociology Non-Traditional Families	Curriculum promotes alternative lifestyle under the guise of tolerance	Artificial reproduction for same-sex couples	Hate-speech legislation threatens pastors & Christians for speaking against same-sex marriage	2004 U.S. Supreme Court declares state sodomy laws unconstitutional	Judges and legislatures battle over same-sex marriages	Same-sex marriage and same-sex couples promoted as normal and acceptable lifestyle
Law Positive Law (moral relativism applied to the law)	Courts don't allow students to pray, read the Bible, be taught creationism or invoke the name of God at graduations or pray at football games	Laws allow doctors to perform abortions, partial-birth abortions and active euthanasia in certain states	Separation of church & state lie allows for persecution of Christians and secularization of America	Supreme Court embraces concept that truth is relative, morals evolve and laws should do the same; court looks to foreign law to support decisions	Special rights for same-sex couples; parental authority undermined by laws that allow minors to have abortions without parental consent	Judges embracing legal positivism held forth as heroes while judges, legislators & citizens that believe in absolute truth are ridiculed
Politics Globalism & World Government	National Education Association promotes loyalty to the United Nations & global citizenship		UN passes tolerance declaration calling for prosecution of missionaries & Christians preaching Gospel	UN and World Court threaten American sovereignty	UN Convention on the Rights of the Child threatens parental authority; U.S. Senate has yet to ratify this	United Nations promoted as noble organization with admirable goals
Economics Socialism	Radical environmentalism bemoans capitalism & promotes redistribution of everyone's wealth but that of the liberal elite	Attempts to pass national health care continue as means to redistribute others' wealth	Humanists continue to call for churches and Christian organizations to lose tax-exempt status	Bigger government, higher taxes, more regulations on business to redistribute wealth	Tax laws punish marriage, reward co-habitation, & higher taxes force moms into workforce & kids into daycare	Materialism is promoted as god and key to happiness
History Begins by Accident Through Darwinian Evolutionary Theory	Revisionist history denies America's Godly heritage & providential origin	Advancements & discoveries by Christian doctors and scientists ignored	Founding Fathers that were pastors & the men of their church that were involved in American Revolution are ignored	Original Intent of Founding Fathers is ignored by U.S. Supreme Court in making decisions	Godly heritage, history & legacy is ignored and even discouraged as old fashioned, intolerant and out of date	Revisionist history promotes lies about Founding Fathers, our Godly heritage, the separation of church & state & contribution of Christians

215

APPENDIX 3—GLOSSARY OF WORLDVIEW-RELATED TERMS

Active euthanasia: Voluntary, active euthanasia occurs when a doctor uses medical means to take the life of patient at the request of the patient. Involuntary, active euthanasia occurs when a doctor uses medical means to take the life of a patient without the patient's permission.

Agnostic: One who believes it is impossible to know whether there is a God or not.

Apologetics: The discipline of defending, contending for, and explaining the truth and validity of Biblical Christianity.

Atheism: The belief there is no God. A Secular Humanist is an atheist.

Cosmic Humanism: Another word for the New Age Movement. Cosmic Humanists believe only in the spiritual world and hold that the natural world is essentially an illusion. Cosmic Humanists believe in reincarnation.

Deist or Deism: One who believes that God created the world but does not intervene in the affairs of mankind.

Diversity: A masking term for the promotion of homosexuality, bi-sexuality, transgender sexuality, and the transvestite life style.

Dualism: The belief that man has a mind/soul and a body, and they are distinct from each other. Christians believe the mind/soul lives forever.

(Michel) Foucault: French philosopher who is considered one of the founders of postmodern thinking. Among his ideas, Foucault believed that homosexuality is a species, not an action.

Hedonism: The belief that the goal or purpose of life is the pursuit of pleasure.

Humanist Manifestos: *Humanist Manifesto I* was written in 1933, *Humanist Manifesto II* was written in 1973, and *Humanist Manifesto 2000* was written in 2000. Each manifesto details the worldview of Secular Humanism in many disciplines of life such as law, science, economics, history, religion, family, and education.

Intolerance: When a person proclaims a belief from a morally absolute foundation or worldview. Christianity is considered intolerant because it claims that Jesus is the only way, truth, and life and that truth is only that which is consistent with the character and nature of God.

Karma: That which determines how a person evolves through the process of reincarnation. Good karma allows a person to ascend to a higher order in the reincarnation process, and bad karma causes one to descend in the reincarnation process.

Knowledge: The acquisition of truth.

Legal positivism: The application of the philosophy of moral relativism to the law. Secular Humanism and its core beliefs of moral relativism and Darwinian evolution is the new, postmodern foundation on which America's courts and law schools are built. Legal positivism says that as society and morals evolve so should the law.

Multiculturalism: Revisionist history that is anti-American and promotes the liberal, leftist view of tolerance, pluralism, moral relativism, and socialism. Multiculturalism pits one cultural or ethnic group against another and has no desire to make America one nation out of many—contrary to the American motto *e plurabis unum.*

Modern-Day Liberal: Secular Humanist.

Monism: The belief that all is one. In regard to humanity, it is the belief that the body and the mind are not separate and both stem from a naturalistic process. There is no spiritual aspect to man, and he does not have a soul. The mind, thoughts, and ideas have no ultimate meaning or purpose. The mind as well as body evolved through a random process known as Darwinian evolution.

Moral Absolutes: Ethical beliefs that are considered true for all time, places, and people.

Moral Relativism: The belief that everything is relative, and there are no absolute truths for all time, people, and places.

Nihilism: The belief that life has no meaning and that nothing can be known for sure.

Open Theism: The belief that God is not sovereign and does not know the future.

Pantheism: The belief that God is all and all is God. God is in everything, such as nature, as well as every individual.

Passive euthanasia: Voluntary, passive euthanasia occurs when a patient has left a specific request for doctors not to take extraordinary measures to keep the patient alive—such as a feeding tube or artificial respiration—but instead allows nature to take is natural course. Involuntary, passive euthanasia occurs when a patient has not left any specific requests and cannot communicate with the doctors, but doctors allow nature to take its course based on their own evaluation or at the request of a family member.

Pluralism: The belief that all religions and beliefs are equal.

Political Correctness: Related to compromise, collectivism, socialism, tolerance, and moral relativism, political correctness is a masking term for beliefs and ideas that stem from Secular Humanism, also known as modern-day liberalism.

Postmodernism: The belief that truth (and the consequent reality) is not discovered but is created by mankind. A postmodern worldview allows that two opposing truth claims can be equal—unless one of the views is based on a fixed moral standard. An "absolute" view is not seen by the postmodernist as being equal but as being unacceptable because it is "intolerant."

Presuppositional Worldview: The foundational idea upon which your worldview is based. Every person must begin with the presupposition that God is, God is not, or that His existence cannot be known, and from that presupposition, a person builds his or her worldview, which is the basis of values and actions.

Reincarnation: The belief that a person's soul passes repeatedly from one body to another at death. The process continues until the soul reaches a state of perfection when its good karma (good deeds) outweigh its bad karma (bad deeds). Accumulating good karma results in a soul being reincarnated into a desirable state. If someone accumulates bad karma, he or she will be reincarnated into a less desirable state.

Religion: *Random House Unabridged Dictionary of the English Language* defines *religion* as "a set of beliefs." *Webster's New World Dictionary* defines *religion* as "a system of belief."

Secular Humanism: The religious worldview that starts from its declaration and presupposition that there is no God. People are the highest order of creation, and there is no such thing as the spiritual world, only the natural world. A Secular Humanist believes people die, and that's it—there is nothing beyond the grave.

Socialism: The belief that the outcome of everyone's work can and should be equal. Socialism also advocates the elimination of private property and seeks to redistribute wealth. It is consistent with the humanist worldview because humanists deny the sin nature of mankind and as a result believe socialism will work if people just try hard enough to implement its principles. In reality, people are sinful from birth, battling greed, selfishness, pride, anger, bitterness, envy, laziness, and dishonesty. All of these sinful human qualities prevent a system of economics based on equal work, equal income, and shared benefits from working.

Sovereignty: An attribute of God that relates to His ultimate authority, control, and supremacy in all areas. God is not surprised or shocked. Nothing happens that God could not have prevented.

Theistic Evolution: The belief that God used Darwinian evolution to give us the life we know today.

Theistic Worldview: Says there is only one God and that there is both a spiritual world and a natural world.

Theology: One's view of God. Either He exists (theism); or He doesn't exist (atheism); or He is in everything (pantheism). Everyone has a theology.

Truth: That which corresponds to reality and fact. For example, if it is raining outside, the truth is, "it is raining outside".

Wisdom: The application of truth.

Worldview: The "lens" through which a person views the world. It is the foundation of values which, in turn, determine how a person acts and lives his or her life. Whether conscious of it or not, every person has a worldview. You are surrounded by people who have their own way of looking at things, and many of these hold views that oppose Christianity. A worldview answers such questions as where did we come from, why are we here, and what happens after we die. A worldview can be applied to life disciplines such as law, science, economics, history, religion, family, and education.

APPENDIX 4—ABOUT WORLDVIEW WEEKENDS

Christians today are bombarded with information and opinions by the media, schools, and government. No one can hope to assimilate the avalanche of data. So who could possibly understand the times in which we live? Not many! But those men and women who do become the next generation of leaders.

The Bible speaks of a small tribe in Israel that "understood the times" and knew "what Israel ought to do," and as a result, they became leaders (1 Chronicles 12:32). God expects His people to seek earnestly for the truth, rewarding with greater responsibility those who comprehend. Worldview Weekend Conferences are dedicated to teaching you how to understand our times and grasp the opportunity that will give you for leadership.

Worldview Weekend features nationally known speakers such as Dr. David Noebel of Summit Ministries, Josh McDowell, David Limbaugh, David Barton, Kirk Cameron, Kerby Anderson, Star Parker, Al Denson, Erwin Lutzer and others. U.S. Congressman Tom DeLay has been a keynote speaker at Worldview Weekend, as well as the Honorable Dick Armey when he was U.S. House Majority Leader.

All the conferences start on Friday evening and conclude on Saturday afternoon. The recommended age of attendance is age 11 to adult.

To find out more about how to attend the Worldview Weekend of your choice, go to www.worldviewweekend.com.

Notes

[1] Donald Kagan, "Nihilism rejects any objective basis for society and its morality, the very concept of objectivity, even the possibility of communication itself," Academic Questions 8, no. 2 (Spring 1995): 56.

[2] William J. Federer, *3 Secular Reasons Why America Should Be Under God* (St. Louis: Amerisearch, Inc., 2004), p. 66.

[3] John Adams, *A Defense of the Constitution of Government of the United States of America* (Philadelphia: William Young, 1797), Vol. III, p. 217, from "The Right Constitution of a Commonwealth Examined," Letter VI.

[4] David Barton, *Original Intent* (Aledo, TX: Wallbuilders Press, 1997), p.172, quoting John Quincy Adams, *Letters...to His Sons,* p. 61.

[5] Ibid., pp. 70-71.

[6] Ibid., p. 173, quoting Noah Webster, *Collection of Papers*, pp. 291-292, from his "Reply to a letter of David McClure on the subject of the Proper Course of Study in the Girard College, Philadelphia. New Haven, October 25, 1836."

[7] See *Griswold v. Connecticut*, 381 U.S. 479, 529 n.2 (1965) Stewart, J., dissenting: most criminal prohibitions coincide with the prohibitions contained in the Ten Commandments.

[8] William J. Federer, *The Ten Commandments & Their Influence on American Law* (St. Louis: Amerisearch, Inc., 2003), p. 14.

[9] Ibid.

[10] Matthew Staver, *The Ten Commandments in American Law and Government,* citing *Florida v. City of Tampa*, 48 So.2d 78, 79 (Fla. 1950); see also *Commissioners of Johnston County v. Lacy* 93 S.E. 482, 487 (N.C. 1917).

[11] Ibid., quoting United States District Court (1983), Western District of Virginia, in the case of *Crockett v. Sorenson*, 568, F.Supp. 1422, 1425-1430 (W.D. Va. 1983).

[12] Ibid., quoting *Wisconsin v. Schultz*, 582, N.W. 2d 112, 117 (Wis. App. 1998) (Quoting *Sumpter v. Indiana*, 306, N.E. 2d 95, 101 (Ind. 1974)).

[13] Federer, *The Ten Commandments & Their Influence on American Law*, p. 32.

[14] Ibid., p. 35, quoting the speech given by former Prime Minister Margaret Thatcher on February 5, 1996, in New York.

[15] John Eidsmoe, *Christianity and the Constitution*, (Grand Rapids: Baker Book House, 1987), p. 391.

[16] Ibid., p. 394.

[17] Barton, *Original Intent*, p. 228.

[18] Oliver Wendell Holmes, Jr., "The Law in Science-Science in Law." *Collected Legal Papers* (New York: Harcourt, Brace and Company, 1920), p. 225.

[19] Kerby Anderson, *Moral Dilemmas* (Nashville: Word Publishing, 1998), p. 221.

[20] Ibid., p. 220.

[21] Ibid.

[22] Joseph Story, *Commentaries*, Vol. III (1873), p. 731.

[23] David Barton, *The Foundations of American Government* (Aledo, TX: Wallbuilders Press, 1993), p. 5.

[24] Ibid., p. 41.

[25] Thomas Jefferson, *Memoir*, Vol. IV, pp. 103-104, to the Rev. Samuel Miller on January 23, 1808.

[26] Joseph Story, *Commentaries on the Constitution of the United States* (Boston: Hilliard, Gary and Company, 1833), Volume II:593, quoted in Robert L. Cord, *Separation of Church and State: Historical Fact and Current Fiction* (New York: Lambeth Press, 1982), p. 13.

[27] Jefferson, *Memoir*, Vol. IV, pp. 103-104, to Samuel Miller on January 23, 1808.

[28] Ann Coulter, "Disestablish the Cult of Liberalism," June 15, 2001.

[29] David Limbaugh, "Warring with Christianity," September 27, 2003.

[30] David Barton, *America's Godly Heritage* (Aledo, TX: Wallbuilders Press, 1993), p. 15.

[31] Ibid., p. 16.

[32] David Barton, *Original Intent*, (Aledo, TX: Wallbuilders Press, 1996), p. 17.

[33] Walz at 701-703, Douglas, J. (dissenting)

[34] Michael Drummond, *Participatory Democracy in the Making* (New York: Carnell, 1923), p. 19.

[35] Barton, *Original Intent*, p. 228.

[36] John Dewey, *The Public and Its Problems* (New York: Henry Hold and Company, 1927), p. 34.

[37] David Barton, *Original Intent*, p. 441.

[38] Thomas Jefferson, *The Writings of Thomas Jefferson*, Albert Ellery Bergh, editor (Washington D.C.: The Thomas Jefferson Memorial Association, 1904), Vol. XII, p. 392, to Governor John Tyler on May 26, 1810.

[39] D.G Lindsay, *Foundations for Creationism* (Dallas: Christ for the Nations, 1998).

[40] D.M.S. Watson, "Adaptation," *Nature*, 124:233, p. 1929.

[41] Richard Lewontin, article title: "Billions and Billions of Demons," *The New York Review*, January 9, 1997, p. 31.

[42] Dr. Walter Brown, *In the Beginning.*

[43] Robert Jastrow, *God and the Astronomers* (New York: Warner Books, 1978), p. 111.

[44] N.L. Geisler & R.M. Brooks, *When Skeptics Ask* (Wheaton: Victor Books, 1990), p. 220.

[45] Henry Margenau, "Modern Physics and the Turn to Belief in God," *The Intellectuals Speak Out About God*, ed. Roy Abraham Varghese (Dallas: Lewis and Stanley, 1984), p. 43.

[46] Charles Colson and Nancy Pearcey, *How Now Shall We Live?* (Wheaton: Tyndale House Publishing, 1999), p. 85.

[47] Gordon Rattray Taylor (former Chief Science Advisor, BBC Television), *The Great Evolution Mystery* (New York: Harper & Row, 1983), p. 48.

[48] L. Spetner, *Not by Chance* (Brooklyn, NY: The Judaica Press, Inc., 1997), pp. 131-132, 138, 143.

[49] James F. Crow (Professor of Genetics, University of Wisonsin), "Genetic Effects of Radiation," *Bulletin of the Atomic Scientists*, Vol. 14, 1958, pp. 19-20.

[50] Frank B. Salisbury (Plant Science Department, Utah State University), "Natural Selection and the Complexity of the Gene," *Nature*, Vol. 224, October 25, 1969, p. 342.

[51] S.C. Meyer, "The Methodological Equivalence of Design and Descent: Can There Be a 'Scientific Theory of Creation?'" *The Creation Hypothesis*, by S.C. Meyer (Downers Grove, IL: Intervarsity Press, 1994), p. 98.

[52] N.L. Geisler, *Baker Encyclopedia of Christian Apologetics*, Baker Reference Library (Grand Rapids: Baker Books, 1999), p. 574.

[53] William Paley, *Evidence of Christianity* (London: 1851)

[54] Tan, P.L. (1996, c1979). *Encyclopedia of 7700 Illustrations : A Treasury of Illustrations, Anecdotes, Facts and Quotations for Pastors, Teachers and Christian Workers* (Garland, TX: Bible Communications, 1999).

[55] Dr. Walter T. Brown, Jr., *In the Beginning* (Phoenix, AZ: Center For Scientific Creation, 1989), p. 2.

[56] Ibid. p. 2.

[57] Tan, P.L.

[58] Dr. Frank Harber, *Reasons for Believing: A Seekers Guide to Christianity* (New Leaf Press, Green Forest, AR, 1998), p. 29-30.

[59] Tan, P.L.

[60] D.G. Lindsay, *Harmony of Science and Scripture* (Dallas: Christ for the Nations, 1998).

[61] Ibid.

[62] *National Geographic* (September 1976), p. 355.

[63] Lindsay, *Harmony of Science and Scripture*,

[64] Harber, p. 33.

[65] Bill Gates, *The Road Ahead*, rev. ed. (New York: Penguin, 1996), p. 228.

[66] Lindsay, *Harmony of Science and Scripture*,

[67] Behe, Michael J., *Darwin's Black Box* (New York: Free Press, 1996), p. 187.

[68] Ibid., p.160.

[69] N.L. Geisler & P.K. Hoffman, *Why I Am a Christian: Leading Thinkers Explain Why They Believe* (Grand Rapids: Baker Books, 2001), p. 93.

[70] Ibid., p. 9.

[71] The First Nine Months of Life (brochure), Focus on the Family, Colorado Springs, CO, 1995.

[72] Article by David Barton at his website wallbuilders.com.

[73] From the website of Citizens Against Government Waste.

[74] Article by David Barton at his website wallbuilders.com.

[75] Ibid.

[76] John Stossel, *Myths, Lies and Downright Stupidity* (JFS Productions, Inc. and American Broadcasting Companies, Inc., 2006), p. 62.

[77] Ibid., p. 63.

[78] Article by David Barton at his website wallbuilders.com.

[79] A government study cited online at rushlimbaugh.com.

[80] Sidney Hook, *Out of Step* (New York: Harper & Row, 1987), p. 600.

[81] Kerby Anderson, "A Biblical View of Economics," posted at probe.org.

[82] *What Does the Bible Say About—: The Ultimate A to Z Resource Fully Illustrated,* Nelson's A to Z Series (Nashville: Thomas Nelson, 2001), p. 272.

[83] Rush Limbaugh, *See, I Told You So* (New York: Simon & Schuster, 1993), pp. 78-80.

[84] Ibid.

[85] David Noebel, *The Battle for Truth* (Eugene: Harvest House Publishers, 2001,) p. 276.

[86] John Dewey, *Liberalism and Social Action* (New York: G.P. Putnam's Sons, 1935), p. 88.

[87] Ibid., pp. 356-357.

[88] John Kenneth Galbraith, *Economics, Peace and Laughter* (Boston: Houghton Mifflin, 1971), p. 101.

[89] Dewey, pp. 79-80.

[90] Marvin Zimmerman, "Hooked on Freedom and Science," in *Sidney Hook: Philospher of Democracy and Humanism*, ed. Paul Kurtz (Buffalo: Prometheus Books, 1983), p. 80.

[91] Robert Scheaffer, "Socialism Is Incompatible with Humanism," *Free Inquiry*, Fall 1989, p. 19.

[92] David Noebel, *The Battle for Truth*, (Eugene: Harvest House Publishers, 2001), p. 275.

[93] Tan, P.L.

[94] Kerby Anderson, "Welfare Reform: A Look Back," posted at probe.org.

[95] Ibid.

[96] Theodore Dalrymple, *Life at the Bottom: The Worldview That Makes the Underclass* (Chicago: Ivan R. Dee, 2001), p. vii.

[97] Ibid., p.viii.

[98] Ibid., p. ix.

[99] Ibid;., p. x.

[100] Ibid., pp. xi-xii.

[101] Dr. Dennis Cuddy, *Chronology of Education with Quotable Quotes* (Highland City, FL: Pro Family Forum Inc., 1993), p. 9.

[102] Benjamin S. Bloom, *Taxonomy of Educational Objectives*, 1964, p. 54.

[103] Governor Roy Romer, while serving as Chairman of the National Governor's Association, said this before an educational meeting being covered by C-Span.

[104] Brannon Howse, *No Retreats, No Reserves, No Regrets*, (St. Paul: Stewart House Press, 2000), p. 115.

[105] *The Cincinnati Post*, May 23, 1996.

[106] *New York Times International*, March 16, 1992.

[107] This was from a conversation Brannon Howse had with Mrs. Tucker when they testified before a Senate committee in Kansas on the dangers of School to Work.

[108] Aldous Huxley, *Brave New World*

[109] In the February 4, 1998, issue of *Education Week*, Mark Tucker was quoted in an article written by Millicent Lawton

[110] Dr. D. James Kennedy, *Character and Destiny* (Grand Rapids, MI: Zondervan Publishing House, 1994), p. 135.

[111] Howse, *No Retreats, No Reserves, No Regrets*, p. 113.

[112] The California state Parent Teacher Organization paper on School-To-Work.

[113] A series of newpaper columns published by Lynn Cheney that were adapted from her testimony before the House Appropriations Subcommittee on Labor, Health and Human Services, and Education Feb. 3, 1998.

[114] Ibid.

[115] Ibid.

[116] Ibid., p. 26.

[117] *Humanist Manifesto II* by the American Humanist Association, 1973.

[118] Sidney Simon and Louis E. Raths, *Values Clarification* (New York, NY: Hart, 1978), p. 18.

[119] Richard A. Baer, Jr., "Parents, Schools, and Values Clarification," *Wall Street Journal*, April 12, 1982.

[120] *Drug Prevention Curricula*, U.S. Department of Education, 1988.

[121] W. R. Coulson, Memorandum to Federal Drug Education Panel, April 23, 1988, p. 11.

[122] Laura Rogers, "In Loco Parentis: The Brave New Family in Missouri," *Freedom Report*, February 1993, p. 15.

[123] Brannon Howse, *Reclaiming a Nation at Risk* (Alpha & Omega Press, 1996).

[124] Arthur Herman, *The Idea of Decline in Western History* (New York: The Free Press, 1997), p. 355.

[125] Ibid., pp. 356-357.

[126] Stanley J. Grenz, *A Primer on Postmodernism*, (Grand Rapids: William B. Eerdmans Publishing Company, 1996.), p. 14.

[127] John Leo, Overdosing on Non-Judgementalism, *U.S. News and World Report*, July 21, 1997, p. 14.

[128] William Spady, "Future Trends: Considerations in Developing Exit Outcomes," Sept 1987, quoted in Goals 2000 Research Manual, compiled by James R. Patrick (Moline, IL: Citizens for Academic Excellence, 1994), p. 121.

[129] Al Gore on His Life and Times, *The New Yorker*, September 2004.

[130] John Witherspoon, *The Works of the Rev. John Witherspoon* (Philadelphia: William W. Woodward, 1802), Vol. III, p. 46.

[131] Roger Rosenblat, "Essay: God Is Not on My Side. Or Yours," *Time*, Dec. 17, 2001, p. 92.

[132] Alison Hornstein, "The Question That We Should Be Asking," *Newsweek*, December 17, 2001, p. 14.

[133] Ibid.

[134] Phyllis Schlafly, *Who Controls Education Policies?* Vol. 37, No. 1, August 2003.

[135] Ibid., p. 74.

[136] David Limbaugh, "NEA: Politicizing 'Education,'" July 12, 2003.

[137] Dr. Dennis Cuddy, *NEA: Grab for Power* (Oklahoma City: Hearthstone Publishing, 1993), p. 55.

[138] Brannon Howse, *One Nation Under Man?* (Nashville: Broadman & Holman Publishers, 2005), pp. 68-69.

[139] Dr. Dennis Cuddy, *President Clinton Will Continue the New World Order* (Oklahoma City: The Southwest Radio Church, 1993), p. 26.

[140] Ibid.

[141] Ibid.

[142] Ibid.

[143] Christopher Lasch, "Hillary Clinton, Child Saver: What She Values Will Not Help the Family," *Harper's* Magazine, October 1992.

[144] Transcript from trial court in H.R.V. Alabama Dept of Human Resources. 609. So. 2d 477 (Ct. Civ. App Ala. 1992).

[145] Cuddy, *President Clinton Will Continue the New World Order*, p. 26.

[146] Ibid.

[147] Matter v. Ray, 408, N.Y.S. 2d 737 (1978).

[148] James P. Lucier, "Unconventional Rights," Report by Family Research Council.

[149] Thomas Sowell, *Inside American Education*, (New York, NY: Free Press, 1993), p. 48.

[150] Dr. Dennis Cuddy, *President Clinton Will Continue The New World Order.*

[151] Ibid., p. 26.

[152] James P. Lucier, "Unconventional Rights," *Family Policy*, Family Research Council.

[153] *Washington Times*, April 27, 1996, p. A1.

[154] Mark E. Howerter, *Washington Times*, May 6, 1996.

[155] *Pocono Record*, March 22, 1996.

[156] Phyllis Schlafly, *Education Reporter*, October 1999.

[157] Ibid.

[158] Article by John Eldredge, "A Call For Social and Political Involvement, Why Christians Should Be Involved" Focus on the Family website, 1998.

[159] *The Master's Seminary Journal*, Vol. 8, p. 222.

[160] Tedd Tripp, *Shepherding a Child's Heart* (Wapwallopen, PA: Shepherd Press, 1995), p. 6.

[161] Ibid, p. 123.

[162] W.D. Edwards, W. J. Gabel, & F.E. Hosmer, *Journal of the American Medical Association*, 1986:255:1455-1463.

[163] Ibid.

[164] Dr. Frank Harber, *Reason for Believing* (Green Forrest, AR: New Leaf Press, 1998), pp. 119-120.

[165] Tim LaHaye, *Jesus Who Is He?* (Sisters, OR: Multnomah Books, 1996), p. 265.

[166] Ibid.

[167] Tim LaHaye and David Noebel, *Mind Siege: The Battle for Truth in the New Millennium* (Nashville: Word Publishing, 2000), quoting Ian S. Markham, ed., *A World Religions Reader*, 2nd ed. (Malden, MA: Blackwell Publishers, 2000).

[168] David Noebel, *Clergy in the Classroom: The Religion of Secular Humanism* (Manitou Springs, CO: 1995), p. 77.

[169] Ibid.

[170] Erwin Lutzer, *Christ Among Other Gods* (Chicago: Moody Press, 1994), pp. 62-64.

[171] *Time*, December 7, 1987.

[172] Kevin Ryerson, *Spirit Communication: The Soul's Path* (New York: Bantam Books, 1989), p. 84.

[173] Ken Ham, Jonathan Sarfati, Carl Weiland, *The Revised & Expanded Answers Book* (Green Forrest, AR: Master Books, 1990), p. 17.

[174] Josh McDowell and Bob Hostetler, *Beyond Belief to Convictions* (Wheaton: Tyndale House, 2002), p. 54.

[175] Ibid.

[176] Ibid., p. 55.

[177] Ray Comfort, "Hell's Best Kept Secret" at www.livingwater.com

[178] George Grant, *The Family Under Siege* (Minneapolis: Bethany House Publishers, 1994), p. 44.

[179] Radio Commentary by Paul Harvey.

[180] David Barton, *America to Pray? Or Not to Pray?* (Aledo, TX: Wallbuilders Press, 1988), pp. 26-45.

[181] John W. Whitehead, *The Second American Revolution*, p. 89.

[182] Ibid.

[183] Gary DeMar, *God and Government*, Vol. 3. (Powder Springs, GA: American Vision, Inc. 2001), pp.165-166.

[184] From an article by Rick Wade posted on probe.org in which he reviews the book *The New Absolutes* by William Watkins.

[185] Ibid.

[186] Paul Copan, *True for You, But Not for Me* (Minneapolis: Bethany House Publishers, 1998), pp. 32-33, cites D.A. Carson, *The Sermon on the Mount* (Grand Rapids: Baker Books, 1978), p. 97.

[187] Bob Knight, "Talking Points on Marriage," posted at nogaymarriage.com.

[188] Stanley Kurtz, "The End of Marriage in Scandinavia: The 'Conservative Case' for Same-Sex Marriage Collapses," *The Weekly Standard*, February 2, 2004, p. 27.

[189] Theo G.M. Sandfort, Ron de Graaf, Rob V. Bijl, Paul Schnabel, "Same-Sex Sexual Behavior and Psychiatric Disorders: Findings from the Netherlands Mental Health Survey and Incidence Study (NEMESIS)," *Archives of General Psychiatry* 58 (2001), pp. 85-91.

[190] Peter Sprigg delivered these remarks on March 29, 2004, at the World Congress of Families III in Mexico City, Mexico.

[191] Ibid.

[192] Scott Shane, "Many Swedes Say 'I Don't' to Nuptials, Unions," *Baltimore Sun*, January 16, 2004, p. 1A.

[193] Timothy J. Dailey, *Comparing the Lifestyles of Homosexual Couples to Married Couples*

[194] "OLR Backgrounder: Legal Recognition of Same-Sex Partnerships," *OLR Research Report* (October 9, 2002), p. 1.

[195] Maria Xiridou, et al, "The Contribution of Steady and Casual Partnerships to the Incidence of HIV Infection among Homosexual Men in Amsterdam," *AIDS* 17 (2003), p. 1031.

[196] A.P. Bell and M.S. Weinberg, *Homosexualities: A Study of Diversity Among Men and Women* (New York: Simon and Schuster, 1978), pp. 308, 309; see also A.P. Bell, M.S. Weinberg, and S.K. Hammersmith, *Sexual Preference* (Bloomington: Indiana University Press, 1981).

[197] Paul Van de Ven et al., "A Comparative Demographic and Sexual Profile of Older Homosexually Active Men," *Journal of Sex Research* 34 (1997), p. 354.

[198] Sex Survey Results, *Genre* (October 1996), quoted in "Survey Finds 40 Percent of Gay Men Have Had More Than 40 Sex Partners," *Lambda Report*, January 1998, p. 20.

[199] Mary Mendola, *The Mendola Report* (New York: Crown, 1980), p. 53.

[200] William Aaron, *Straight* (New York: Bantam Books, 1972), p. 208.

[201] Bob Knight, "Talking Points on Marriage," posted at nogaymarriage.com.

[202] Ibid.

[203] Dr. Timothy J. Dailey, "The Slippery Slope of Same-Sex Marriage," posted at frc.org.

[204] Kerby Anderson, *Moral Dilemmas* (Nashville: Word Publishing, 1998), p. 8.

[205] Ibid., pp. 27-28.

[206] *U.S. News & World Report*

[207] Dr. Neil Chadwick in a sermon entitled "A Christian Response to Gambling."

[208] Tan, P.L.

[209] *New American Standard Bible* (LaHabra, CA: The Lockman Foundation, 1995).

[210] Ibid.

[211] Southern Baptist Convention Ethics and Religious Liberty Commission

[212] Robert Goodman, *The Luck Business*

[213] The Heartland Institute, 1993

[214] Anderson, *Moral Dilemmas*, p. 19.

[215] Ibid., p. 19.

[216] Ibid., p. 20.

[217] Ibid., p. 20.

[218] R. Finigsen, "The Report of the Dutch Committee on Euthanasia," *Issues in Law and Medicine*, July 1991, pp. 339-44.

[219] Anderson, *Moral Dilemmas*, pp. 27-28.

[220] J.S. Feinberg, P.D. Feinberg, & A. Huxley, *Ethics for a Brave New World* (Wheaton: Crossway Books, 1996).

[221] U.S. War Department Training Manual, No. 2000-25, published in 1928, the U.S. Government's definition of a democracy.

[222] Article 4, Section 4 of the U.S. Constitution.

[223] Fischer Ames, *Works of Fischer Ames* (Boston: T.B. Wait & Co., 1809), p. 24, speech on biennial elections delivered on January 15, 1788.

[224] *The Letters of Benjamin Rush*, L.H. Butterfield, editor (Princeton: Princeton University Press, 1951), Vol. I, p. 454, quoting John Joachim Zubly, Presbyterian pastor and delegate to Congress, in a letter to David Ramsay in March or April 1788.

[225] John Adams, *The Works of John Adams, Second President of the United States* (Boston: Charles C. Little and James Brown, 1851), Vol. VI, p. 484, "Discourses on Davila; A Series of Papers on Political History."

[226] Noah Webster, *The American Spelling Book: Containing an Easy Standard of Pronunciation: Being the First Part of a Grammatical Institute of the English Language, To Which is Added, an Appendix, Containing a Moral Catechism and a Federal Catechism* (Boston: Isaiah Thomas and Ebenezer T. Andrews, 1801), pp. 103-104.

[227] John Witherspoon, *Witherspoon, Works*, 1815, Vol. VII, p. 101, Lecture 12 on Civil Society.

[228] U.S. War Department, Training Manual No. 2000-25, printed November 30, 1928.

[229] Noah Webster, *History of the United States* (New Haven: Durrie & Peck, 1832), p. 6.

[230] David Barton, *Keys to Good Government* (Aledo, TX: Wallbuilders Press, 2000), p. 8.

[231] John Adams, "Thoughts on Government," quoted in John R. Howe, Jr., *The Changing Political Thought of John Adams* (Princeton: Princeton University Press, 1966),

[232] Alexander Hamilton, *The Federalist*, "Federalist #15," p. 80.

[233] William Blackstone, *Commentaries on the Laws*

[234] Alexander Hamilton, *The Papers of Alexander Hamilton*, Harold C. Syrett, editor (New York: Columbia University Press, 1961), Vol. I, p. 87, February 23, 1775, quoting William Blackstone (Philadelphia: Robert Bell, 1771), Vol. I, p. 41.

[235] Rufus King, *The Life and Correspondence of Rufus King*, Charles R. King, editor (New York: G.P. Putnam's Sons, 1900), Vol. VI, p. 276, to C. Gore on February 17, 1820.

[236] Found at barna.org.

[237] Ibid.

[238] Ibid.

[239] Barton, *Original Intent*, pp. 337-338.

[240] Benjamin Rush, *Essays, Literary, Moral and Philosophical* (Philadelphia: Thomas and Samuel F. Bradford, 1798), pp. 93-113, "A Defense of the Use of the Bible as a School Book, Addressed to the Rev. Jeremy Belknap, of Boston.

[241] Noah Webster, *History of the United States*, p. 6.

[242] Jedidiah Morse, "A Sermon, Exhibiting the Present Dangers and Consequent Duties of the Citizens of the United States of America," delivered at Charlestown, April 25, 1799, The Day of the National Fast (Boston: Samuel Etheridge, 1799), p. 11.

[243] *The Daily Advertiser*, New York, May 1, 1789, p. 2.

[244] *The Papers of James Madison, Vol. III*, Henry Gilpin, editor (Washington: Langtree and O'Sullivan, 1840), p. 1391, August 22, 1787.

[245] Barton, *Original Intent*

[246] Dr. John MacArthur, *Why Government Can't Save You: An Alternative to Political Activism*, p. 6.

[247] David Barton, "Was the American Revolution a Biblically Justified Act?"

[248] Ibid., pp. 223-224.

[249] Kenneth L. Woodward with David Gates, "How the Bible Made America: Since the Puritans and the pioneers, through wars and social conflicts, a sense of Biblical mission has united us, divided us and shaped our national destiny," *Newsweek*, 27 December 1982, p. 44.

[250] Federer, *The Ten Commandments & Their Influence on American Law*, p.19.

[251] Ibid. Federer's sources are as follows: Donald S. Lutz and Charles S. Hyneman, "The Relative Influence of European Writers on Late Eighteenth-Century American Political Thought." *American Political Science Review* 189 (1984): 189-197. (Courtesy of Dr. Wayne House of Dallas Theological Seminary.) John Eidsmoe, *Christianity and the Constitution— The Faith of Our Founding Fathers* (Grand Rapids, MI: Baker Book House, A Mott Media Book, 1987; 6th printing, 1993), pp. 51-53. *Origins of American Constitutionalism*, (1987). Stephen K. McDowell and Mark A. Beliles, *America's Providential History* (Charlottesville,

VA: Providence Press, 1988), p. 156.

[252] John Jay, *The Correspondence and Public Papers of John Jay*, 1794-1826, Henry P. Johnson, ed. (Reprinted NY: Burt Franklin, 1970), Vol. IV, p. 393.

[253] Barton, *Original Intent*, p. 214.

[254] President George Washington's *Farewell Address*.

[256] Eidsmoe, *Christianity and the Constitution*, pp. 360-361.

[257] Ibid. John Eidsmoe quoting Martin Diamond, "The Declaration and the Constitution: Liberty, Democracy, and the Founders," *The Public Interest*, No. 41, Fall 1975, pp. 39-55 at 46ff.

[258] Ibid., p. 362.

America's Original Commitment to a Biblical Worldview
David Barton

The "Bottom Strip" of the Christian Faith
Kirby Anderson

Continuing My Family's Spiritual Legacy
Steve Saint

Preparing for Your Flight Out of This World
Russell O'Quinn

The Impact of Your Worldview
Star Parker

How to Keep the Secular Humanist Worldview from Harming Your Family
Bob Lepine

How to Bring Children to Christ and Keep Them There
Ray Comfort

Soundly Saved
Kirk Cameron

Calling America Back to the Bible
Dr. Woodrow Kroll

Seeking Pleasure or Seeking After God
David Jeremiah

Countering the Lies About Jesus Christ and God
Dr. Erwin Lutzer

Understanding the Hard Sayings of Jesus
Dr. Michael Youssef

Truth or tragedy?
Sean McDowell

Judge Not, Lest You Be Judged
Josh McDowell

The Incredible Faith of Atheism
Dr. Frank Harber

The Danger and error of the Da Vinci Code
Kerby Anderson

'04 – '05 Branson Worldview Weekend Family Reunion TV Special DVD $20

2 DVD set containing hilarious comedy, variety acts, and praise and music sure to please the entire family!

Battle for the Mind 2 DVDs, (3 hrs.) Was $75 Now only $12
David Noebel, David Barton, and Ken Ham

See detailed descriptions of each DVD by visiting:
www.worldviewweekend.com

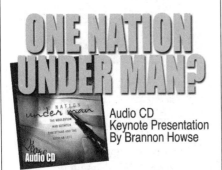

Study Notes

Study Notes

Study Notes